The Cerebellum in Emotions and Psychopathology

This groundbreaking volume examines the complex role of the cerebellum in emotional regulation and disorders that are insufficiently understood, subverting the widely held belief that the cerebellum is solely involved in balance and motor functions.

Beginning with the evolution of the cerebellum toward a structure dedicated to homeostatic regulation and socio-emotional behavior, the book examines the growing body of evidence supporting the importance of the cerebellum in emotions, cognition, and psychopathology. Going on to discuss the implications of cerebellar abnormalities, Schutter analyzes groundbreaking research and explores how cerebellar abnormalities are associated with disruption in associative learning in anxiety, the pathophysiology of depression and cognitive regulation, the synchronization of information processing in schizophrenia, the aberrant connectivity patterns in autism spectrum disorders, and explosive forms of aggressive behavior.

Collating pioneering research on the multifaceted role of the cerebellum, this book will be essential reading for students and researchers of neurology and psychopathology.

Dennis J.L.G. Schutter is an associate professor of experimental psychology at Utrecht University, the Netherlands. He is an award-winning researcher on the role of the cerebellum in motivation and emotion, and an expert in non-invasive brain stimulation.

The Cerebellum in Emotions and Psychopathology

Dennis J.L.G. Schutter

LONDON AND NEW YORK

First published 2021
by Routledge
2 Park Square, Milton Park, Abingdon, Oxon OX14 4RN

and by Routledge
52 Vanderbilt Avenue, New York, NY 10017

Routledge is an imprint of the Taylor & Francis Group, an informa business

© 2021 Dennis J.L.G. Schutter

The right of Dennis J.L.G. Schutter to be identified as author of this work has been asserted by him in accordance with sections 77 and 78 of the Copyright, Designs and Patents Act 1988.

All rights reserved. No part of this book may be reprinted or reproduced or utilised in any form or by any electronic, mechanical, or other means, now known or hereafter invented, including photocopying and recording, or in any information storage or retrieval system, without permission in writing from the publishers.

Trademark notice: Product or corporate names may be trademarks or registered trademarks, and are used only for identification and explanation without intent to infringe.

British Library Cataloguing in Publication Data
A catalogue record for this book is available from the British Library

Library of Congress Cataloging-in-Publication Data
A catalog record has been requested for this book

ISBN: 978-1-138-50278-9 (hbk)
ISBN: 978-1-138-50280-2 (pbk)
ISBN: 978-1-315-14508-2 (ebk)

Typeset in Sabon
by Taylor & Francis Books

To

My wife, Jiska, and my children Emmelie and Ruben

Contents

Preface		ix
Foreword		xii
1	Evolution and basic anatomy of the cerebellum	1
2	The cerebellum link to motivation and emotion	20
3	Disorders of fear and anxiety: a big role for the little brain?	38
4	The cerebellar basis of mood disorders	64
5	Cerebellum and affective dysmetria in schizophrenia	87
6	The socio-emotional cerebellum in autism spectrum disorder	106
7	Emotionally explosive minds: a cerebellum-oriented theory on reactive aggression	125
8	Epilogue	148
	Index	154

Preface

The cerebellum has drawn the interest of scientists for many centuries. The earliest views on cerebellar functions were speculative and devoid of solid scientific evidence. However, this speculative stance towards the cerebellum changed when Luigi Rolando (1809) was the first to show that destruction of the cerebellum causes severe disturbances in posture and voluntary movements (Schmahmann, 2016). This functional-anatomic relation was replicated in various mammals, including rabbits and monkeys. Subsequent studies established the role of the cerebellum in coordinating voluntary movements, gait, and dexterity. Another notable discovery was the existence of somatotopy in the anterior lobe of the cerebellum. Another hallmark in the history of cerebellum research was the detailed description of the cellular architecture of the cerebellar cortex, including the Purkinje cell (Schmahmann, 2016).

Suggestions in the late 19th century that the cerebellum projects to other brain areas, including cortical and subcortical areas in a topographical fashion, were later confirmed in studies that started mapping the cerebellar connections to the motor cortex (e.g., Allen & Tsukuhara, 1974). Together with the discovery that the vermis and the lateral cerebellar hemispheres play a critical role in the neural circuit of movement, the cerebellum became known as a motor-dedicated brain region. Alongside the empirical work that, for example, established cerebellar feedforward and feedback loops in the coordination of movements, several studies also reported on the existence of functional connections between the cerebellum and limbic structures, including the amygdala, hippocampus, and septum (e.g., Heath & Harper, 1974). These findings were among the first hints that the cerebellum may be more than a motor-dedicated brain region, and may play a role in motivation and emotion, and psychopathology.

With the cerebellum comprising more than half of the total number of nerve cells that make up the brain and showing the largest volumetric expansion in the history of human brain evolution, it is surprising that our scientific knowledge of the cerebellum in the 21st century is still, for the most part, limited to the motor domain.

Among scientists, there is still considerable controversy about the role of the cerebellum in non-motor related functions. However, growing empirical evidence unmistakably shows that the cerebellum can no longer be neglected in functional neuroanatomical studies dedicated to cognition and emotion. The schism between motor versus non-motor functions that is so often applied by the scientific community and popular media may to a certain degree be arbitrary, serving primarily heuristic purposes. Even though it is true that the brain comprises functionally specialized circuits, the neural networks dedicated to motor, cognitive, and emotive processes are deeply intertwined. This is, for example, illustrated by neuropsychological studies showing that lesions to the cerebellum can cause impairments in all three domains.

It has been proposed that the cerebellum compares and integrates internal and external signals to safeguard internal homeostasis. In other words, the cerebellum contributes to maintain a relatively stable internal bodily state that persists despite changes in the world outside. Disruptions in homeostasis, either caused by physical or psychological stressors, will activate the motivation and emotion dedicated brain circuits. The accompanying physiological and emotional responses contribute to the initiation of an 'action-plan' designed to effectively deal with the stress and reinstate internal homeostasis. The ability of an organism to deal with stressors is critical for physical health and psychological well-being, while failure of successful homeostatic regulation will incontestably lead to disorders of the body and the mind.

The main goal of this book is to introduce the cerebellum to psychology and psychiatry and related disciplines, and demonstrate its importance for when it comes to understanding the biological basis of motivation and emotion (Schutter, 2013). Furthermore, I hope to show that the time is ripe to extend our contemporary cortico-limbic centered brain models and theories in order to achieve a more comprehensive understanding of how our brains contribute to normal and pathological forms of human behavior.

The first chapter summarizes the evolutionary trajectory and gross neuroanatomy of the cerebellum together with its connections throughout the central nervous system. This chapter provides the structural backbone for cerebellar contributions to motivation and emotion and the cerebellum's role in internal homeostatic functioning.

In the second chapter, the neuroanatomical correlates of motivation, emotion, and regulation are discussed, and neuroscientific evidence favoring involvement of the cerebellum is presented.

The third chapter explores the role of the cerebellum in fear and anxiety. The well-documented role of the cerebellum in associative and skill learning is extended to the domain of fear conditioning.

Participation of the cerebellum in the pathophysiology of depressive disorders with an emphasis on the cerebello-hypothalamic pathway and chronic disruption of internal homeostasis is covered in the fourth chapter.

The fifth chapter addresses the emotional disturbances observed in persons suffering from schizophrenia and how these disturbances can be understood from a cerebellum-oriented view.

Chapter six covers the implication of cerebellum dysfunction in impaired socio-emotional functioning in autism spectrum disorder associated with the experience of emotions and theory of mind.

Impaired cerebellar inhibition of the subcortical circuits linked to anger and fight-flight responses to explain aggression and impulsivity-related disorders is discussed in chapter 7.

This introductory book is a modest yet sincere attempt to provide the reader with a scientific overview of empirical work and theories on a highly under-studied brain structure and often ignored in the context of non-motor related functions. In line with the modern academic tradition of interdisciplinary research, this book brings together evidence from psychology, neurology, psychiatry, biology, and neurosciences to showcase the cerebellum and its contributions to the neuroanatomic basis of motivation, emotion, and psychopathology. It's the little things can ultimately make the big difference.

Dennis J.L.G. Schutter
Spring 2020

References

Allen GI, Tsukuhara N (1974). Cerebrocerebellar communication systems. *Physiol. Rev.* 54, 957–1008.

Heath RG, Harper JW (1974). Ascending projections of the cerebellar fastigial nucleus to the hippocampus, amygdala, and other temporal lobe sites: Evoked potential and histological studies in monkeys and cats. *Exp. Neurol* 45, 2682–2687.

Schmahmann JD (2016). A brief history of the cerebellum. In: DL Gruol, N Koibuchi, M Manto, M Molinari, JD Schmahmann, Y Shen (Eds), *Essentials of cerebellum and cerebellar disorders*. Switzerland: Springer International Publishing, pp 5–19.

Schutter DJ (2013). Human cerebellum in motivation and emotion. In: M Manto, DL Gruol, JD Schmahmann, N Koibuchi, F Rossi (Eds), *Handbook of the cerebellum and cerebellar disorders*. Dordrecht: Springer Science Business Media, pp. 1771–1783.

Foreword

The cerebellum has always fascinated the scientific community. With its highly geometrical cytostructure and the most numerous neuronal populations, this part of the brain has become a major interest in understanding how the human brain achieves tasks of daily life, from an apparently simple movement of a finger to a complex cognitive operation. Research groups and clinicians have moved jointly towards a critical question that will impact the understanding and therapies of brain disorders in this century: Is the cerebellar circuitry a pure motor computer or does it play a genuine role in cognitive and affective processes?

Dennis Schutter's book arrives just in time in this journey. Divided into seven chapters, the book starts with the evolution of the cerebellum, then in successive chapters explains in a very lucid way how cerebellar circuitry is involved in motivation, emotion, fear, anxiety, and mood. The book explains the cerebellum's contributions in schizophrenia and autism. The importance of the cerebellum in bodily homeostatic functions is also underlined. Anatomical paths are explained throughout the book, incorporating data from recent neuroimaging techniques such as DTI, recent investigational tools such as neurostimulation, and advanced modelling tools.

Despite its scientific accuracy, the book remains very easy to grasp and will give readers advanced knowledge in the field. Indeed, Dennis Schutter takes the reader by the hand to explain the scientific advances of these last four decades and to highlight the conceptualization of cerebellar functions in the framework of complex mental or emotional tasks of our human life. The author guides readers in deciphering the code of affective regulation and the mechanisms of cognitive regulation.

This book will provide an inspiration to promote social and affective research from a physiological and pathophysiological standpoint. Disorders of fear and anxiety in response to stress, obsessive compulsive disorders, post-traumatic stress syndrome, or social phobia all contain an anticipatory component, which, from the evolutionary perspective, is an elemental process.

The Cerebellum in Emotions and Psychopathology is a master-piece to integrate behavioral activities in internal models. The book elegantly explains how the cerebellum participates in such processes. This book is highly recommended for students and trainees, as well as neuroscientists in general.

Prof. Mario Manto, MD, PhD
CHU-Charleroi, Charleroi, Belgium
University of Mons, Mons, Belgium

Chapter 1

Evolution and basic anatomy of the cerebellum

The cerebellum in evolution

Fossil records of the cranial capacity of our ancestors suggest that an initial slow increase in brain volumes early in hominin brain evolution was followed by a period of more rapid expansion over the last 2 million years (Reyes & Sherwood, 2015). Comparative anatomical studies indicate that the increase of human brain size was likely associated with the extension of the frontal, temporal and parietal association areas (Finlay & Darlington, 1995). Furthermore, it has been proposed that the expansion of the association areas was paralleled by a substantial increase in long-range white matter connectivity between these neo-cortical regions (Verendeev & Sherwoord, 2017). The ability of hominins to express behavioral flexibility in unpredictable environments, incorporate contextual information into adaptive decision making, and learn from experience across situations has been directly linked to the growth of the neo-cortical areas and its connections (Lefebvre, 2004). Especially, the large volumetric increase in gray as well as white matter of the prefrontal cortex is designated as being among the hallmarks of cortical brain evolution and behavioral repertoire of the human species as compared to non-human primates (Balsters et al., 2010). However, this view has been criticized as 'cortico-centric myopia' for neglecting the co-evolution of other interconnected subcortical brain regions (Parvizi, 2009). This view proposes that evolutionary changes in brain constitution and our mental capacities should be understood in terms of alterations in functional systems that involve interconnected regions. According to a line of comparative studies, the cerebral cortex supposedly evolved from two sub-cortical (limbic) brain structures: the amygdala and hippocampus (Sanides, 1964). This framework of mammalian brain evolution proposes that each structure contributed to two trajectories of cortical development (Giacco, 2006). The ventral system arguably originates from the amygdala and is involved in evaluating and assigning meaning (saliency) to stimuli, giving rise to motivational tendencies. This stream includes orbitofrontal and ventrolateral prefrontal cortex, insula and temporal lobe areas. The dorsal stream supposedly stems from the hippocampus and is specialized in representing the environment

2 Evolution and basic anatomy

in space and time. The dorsal stream can be further subdivided into the dorsolateral and medial frontal cortex areas, supplementary motor area, and parietal lobe areas. These regions are involved in orchestrating goal-directed actions.

Based on the assumed functional differentiations between the ventral and dorsal cortical streams and their subcortical sources, the latter is more specialized in processing sensory-perceptual and cognitive regulation, whereas the former is dedicated to the processing of visceral and affective signals. The development of the cerebral cortex thus has its roots in the more ancient subcortical parts of the brain. This suggests that the cortical expansion represents a functional specialization of the older neural circuits, which in turn offers a neural foundation for extended mental abilities and a wide range of behavioral expressions. As we will see throughout this book, the structural neuro-anatomical architecture implies that our higher cortico-centered cognitive faculties are nested in the primordial limbic circuitries dedicated to motivation and emotion. Throughout evolution, the emergence of functional specialized brain circuits allowed animals to adapt to changing environmental demands and increase the likelihood of survival of the species.

It has been proposed that our brain consists of three phylogenetically distinct circuits (Maclean, 1990). According to the triune brain framework, the evolutionary oldest system is comprised of the brainstem-striatal complex that harbors the regulation of our vital bodily functions and primary forms of behavior (e.g., fight or flight) associated with survival and procreation. Subsequent (limbic) regions, including the thalamo-cingulate connections, are arguably evolved from the brainstem-striatal complex and associated with increasingly more complex patterns of (socio-emotional) behavior. These regions have been collectively termed the limbic system. (Note: the term limbic lobe has been subject to much discussion in academia.) This system is more developed in mammals as compared to reptiles and birds. Finally, the cerebral cortex and its connections with limbic and striatal regions is the seat of our higher mental (cognitive) capacities that endow humans with the ability to consciously reflect on emotions, intentions and actions, and learn and regulate behavior.

Most neuro-evolutionary accounts of higher mental functions in humans ascribe a large role to the frontal cortex and its reciprocal connections to the subcortical regions. Even though there is no scientific reason to doubt its correctness, it turns out to be part of the whole (hi)story.

As we will see in the second part of this chapter, several taxonomies have been described that provide standards for a functional and structural de-compartmentalization of the cerebellum. Referring to the afferent connectivity-based tripartite classification, a similar phylogenetic trajectory is applicable to the cerebellum. The cerebellum has evolved out of the vestibular nuclei and began as a small outgrowth of the brainstem. These first rudiments of a cerebellum appeared in pre-vertebrate jawless fish (e.g., lampreys) over 500 million years ago (mya). Cartilaginous fishes that lived 400 mya show a well-developed cerebellum that already exhibits the basic organizational properties found in the modern human cerebellum. The cerebellum, which is Latin for 'little brain,' owes its name to its resemblance to the big brain (cerebrum). Like the cerebrum, the cerebellum consists of two hemispheres with white matter fibers that project to and from the cerebellar cortex and subcortical (deep) nuclei.

In concordance with the topographic connectivity maps of the cerebellum that appear to parallel the phylogenetic discourse of the triune brain concept, the vestibulocerebellum is the most ancient part of the cerebellum and is known as the archicerebellum. Its afferent and efferent connections are exclusively with the lower regions of the central nervous system (i.e., brainstem and spinal cord). The paleocerebellum, the evolutionary nickname for the spinocerebellum, shows a wide range of connections to subcortical brain regions, of which many involve the limbic system. Documented observations of strong visceral and emotional responses to intracranial electric stimulation of the vermis in animals (Zanchetti & Zoccolini, 1954), as well as correlations between increased neural activity in the fastigial nucleus of the deep cerebellar nuclei (DCN) during fear and anger in humans (Heath et al., 1974) not only concur with the available neuroanatomical findings, but clearly demonstrate the need to seriously consider the cerebellum part of the ancestral affective circuits of the human brain (Anand et al., 1959). The medial part of the cerebellum is aptly called the 'limbic' cerebellum (Schmahmann, 2000).

The posterolateral hemispheres of the cerebellum or neocerebellum have developed relatively recently in human brain evolution. The cerebellar cortex projects to the dentate nucleus of the DCN, which in turn connects to the thalamo-cortical system. The seminal work by Peter Strick and colleagues has provided us with detailed anatomical maps of the dentate nucleus. Approximately 30 percent of the output channels in the dentate projects to the primary motor cortex, suggesting that the majority of output channels project to non-motor related cortical areas (Strick et al., 2009). For example, the output channels to the prefrontal cortex are found to cluster in the ventral regions of the dentate, whereas the output channels to the motor cortex are located more dorsally. Thus, connections to association areas of the cerebral cortex make the neocerebellum particularly apt to participate in neural processes associated with non-motor-related functions. In addition, the lateral part of the dentate is evolved more recently than the medial part and coincided with the expansion of the cerebellar hemispheres and the temporal and frontal cerebral cortical regions (Dow, 1942). These observations added to the notion that the cerebellum and cerebral cortex evolved in concert. Further evidence for the reciprocal evolution of the cerebellum and cerebral cortex has been provided using endocranial analyses (Weaver, 2005). Even though this kind of analyses faces several difficulties, such as finding reliable markings on the inside of the cranium, the cerebellum provides an exception, as it occupies the well delineated posterior cranial fossa (Weaver, 2005).

Modelling based on endocasts suggests that the evolution of the cerebellum and cerebral cortex of the human species is characterized by three phylogenetic stages (Weaver, 2005).

4 Evolution and basic anatomy

During the Pliocene and Early Pleistocene (~5.3 million–781,000 years ago), encephalization (i.e., increase brain–body ratio) was associated with volumetric expansion of the cerebral cortex and humans demonstrated technical advancements in foraging. It was not until the Middle to Late Pleistocene (~780,000–126,000 years ago) that extensive encephalization occurred that mainly involved enlargement of the cerebral cortex. The human species started to display increasing complex behavior that arguably involved substantial neocortical volumes. The Late Pleistocene (126,000–11,700 years ago) witnessed an increase in cerebellar capacity that may have further contributed to the socio-emotive and cognitive capacities of the human species (Weaver, 2005).

Researchers recently discovered that, among protein coding genes, there is no reason to assume that selection of genes is restricted or biased towards the development of the cerebral cortex exclusively (Harrison & Montgomery, 2017). In other words, protein-coding genes involved in the development of the cerebellum stand an equal chance of being selected as genes associated with cerebral cortical development. In fact, preliminary evidence indicates that protein-coding genes involved in cerebellum development may explain the accelerated rate of cerebellar volumes during the Late Pleistocene era (Harrison & Montgomery, 2017).

Moreover, a study that examined evolutionary rate changes along the branches of phylogenetic trees showed that the brains of humans and other apes in fact developed larger cerebella relative to neocortical volumes in comparison to other primates (Barton & Venditti, 2014). This can be taken as evidence to support the idea that the cerebellum is involved in complex functions that are thought to be mainly rooted in the neocortex.

While the neocortical expansion was dominated by relative larger increases in white (connections) to gray (neurons) matter (neurons), the opposite was happening to the cerebellum (Herculano-Houzel, 2010). As white matter evolved less rapidly in the cerebellum, the number of neurons in the cerebellum started to exceed the number of neurons in the neocortex by a 4:1 ratio (Herculano-Houzel, 2010). As such, the role of the cerebellum in molding the cerebello-cortical pathways in the evolutionary discourse may have been more important than previously thought (Whiting & Barton, 2003). Furthermore, the cortico-cerebellar system appears to be largely conserved throughout human evolution primary, favoring the view of the re-scaling of existing assemblies and its connections rather than the formation of new structures (Balsters et al., 2010).

As we will see in the second part of this chapter, the cerebellum has widespread topographical mappings unto other parts of the brain that seem to reflect the different neurophylogenic stages. Also, the cerebello-cortical connections are not random, but organized in a series of modular loops that show an isomorphic-like architecture (Ramnani, 2006). In agreement with Maclean's evolutionary framework of functional brain organization, the cerebello-cortical loops between the posterior cerebellar hemispheres and the heteromodal cortical association areas provide the most recent anatomical argument for cerebellar involvement in non-motor functions and higher order mental functions.

Neuroanatomy of the cerebellum

The cerebellum is a major feature of the hindbrain and is located under the posterior temporal and occipital lobules in what is termed the posterior fossa of the cranium (Figure 1.1). Figure 1.2 shows a sagittal section of an obducted human cerebellum on the left panel and an anatomic magnetic resonance (MR) image of the cerebellum from three different orientations. The branchlike appearance of the white matter is called the arbor vitae which means tree of life.

The cerebellum differentiates as early as seven weeks after conception (Manto, 2002). The ventricular zone in the roof of the fourth ventricle is responsible for producing nerve cells that ultimately form the efferent (output) parts of the cerebellum. In addition, the superior part of the hindbrain (rhombic lip) proliferates to form the structural foundation for the cerebellum. In week 27 of embryogenic development, cells will migrate to the outer layer of the cerebellum and will produce granular cells. These cells will eventually migrate to form an internal granular layer that deals with afferent (input) cerebellar signals. Even though the cerebellum clearly shows distinct anatomical features on the macroscopic level after 24 weeks of fetal development, the cerebellum does not reach its structural completion until several months after birth (Manto, 2002).

While the cerebellum occupies more than 10 percent of the total brain volume, hence the term 'little,' more than half of total neurons that constitute the human brain are localized in the little brain (Azevedo et al., 2009). For

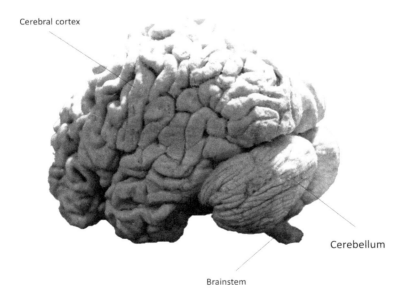

Figure 1.1. Human brain specimen

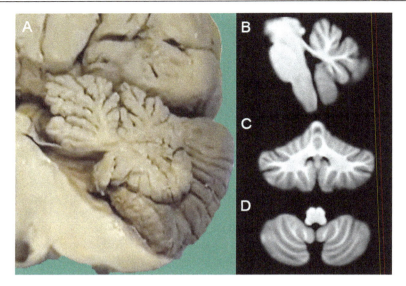

Figure 1.2. Cross section of human cerebellum specimen (A). Sagittal (B), coronal (C), and axial MRI slice of the cerebellum (D).

example: a simple calculation shows that the neuron density of the cerebellum is almost 10 times higher than that of the cerebral cortex.

Microscopic anatomy

One of the remarkable features of the cerebellar cortex is its uniform morphological structure. The cortex of the cerebellum consists of three distinct layers (Figure 1.3).

The outermost molecular layer contains inhibitory gamma-aminobutyric acid (GABA) driven basket and stellate nerve cells (feedforward inhibition). Basket cells descend to the middle layer that is comprised of Purkinje cells where their axon terminals surround the soma of the Purkinje cells. Stellate interneurons are smaller than basket cells and synapse on the dendrites of the Purkinje cells. Purkinje cells are named after the Czech discoverer Jan Evangelista Purkyně (1787–1869) and arranged as a monolayer. Purkinje cells are large inhibitory neurons and are exclusively found in the cerebellum. Purkinje cells are characterized by their extensive and complex dendritic branches. With its estimated total number of 15×10^6, Purkinje cells are the sole output channels of the cerebellar cortex. Just under the Purkinje cell layer, Lugaro cells can be found. Each of these inhibitory interneurons projects to approximately 5–15 Purkinje cells and, in turn, receives inhibitory input from Purkinje axons forming a closed loop (Lainé et al., 1998).

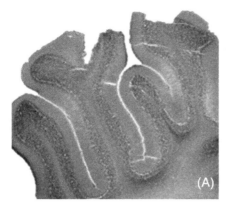
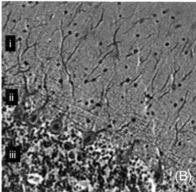

Figure 1.3. The homogenous cellular organization of the cerebellum (A: 40x magnified). The (i) molecular, (ii) Purkinje, (iii) granular cell layer of the cerebellar cortex (B: 400x magnified). Source: https://fankhauserblog.wordpress.com/1992/12/31/histology-of-the-cerebrum-and-cerebellum/

The third inner-layer is called the granular layer and comprises small granule cells and inhibitory interneurons. Granule cells have an oval shape and provide excitatory input to the Purkinje cells. The long axons of each of the $10^9 \times 10^9$ granule cells extend into the molecular layer where the axon bifurcates, making up parallel fibers that contact the dendritic spines of the Purkinje cells. Parallel fibers are among the thinnest of all vertebrate axons (Wyatt et al., 2005), and each fiber has on average 200,000 contact points. The unipolar brush cells are intermediate sized glutamatergic interneurons that are found in the granular layer. The brush cells receive excitatory input from mossy fibers and excite granular cells to augment signals from the vestibular system.

Another class of interneurons found in the granular cell layer are the Golgi cells. Golgi cells are large GABAergic inhibitory nerve cells whose dendrites ascend to the molecular layer where they receive excitatory input from the parallel fibers (Colin et al., 2002). Golgi cells receive inhibitory signals from Purkinje cells as well as from basket and stellate cells (feedback inhibition). The axons of Golgi cells terminate on the dendrites of granular cells, enabling them to regulate spontaneous activity in Purkinje cells by inhibiting parallel fiber activity. Golgi cells also exert their inhibitory influence via glomeruli. The glomerulus is a mass of fibers consisting of axon terminals of Golgi cells and post-synaptic dendrites of granule cells that synapse on mossy fibers.

Mossy fibers together with climbing fibers form the input channels to the cerebellum. Mossy fibers are heavily myelinated axons that originate from numerous extra-cerebellar regions including the vestibular system and cerebral cortex. In addition to being part of the glomerulus, mossy fibers synapse directly on granule cells and are excitatory (glutamatergic) of nature. Climbing fibers are myelinated axons that originate from inferior olive neurons in the

8 Evolution and basic anatomy

medulla oblongata that, like mossy fibers, project to the contralateral cerebellar hemisphere. A climbing fiber can innervate several Purkinje cells through thousands of synaptic glutamatergic connections. Each Purkinje cell receives input from only one climbing fiber. The strong, but slow excitatory drive of climbing fibers drive the 1 Hz burst of action potentials (i.e., complex spikes) generated by the Purkinje cells.

The third type of cerebellar afferents are made up of aminergic (i.e., serotonergic and nor-adrenergic) fibers that originate from the raphe nuclei and locus coeruleus in the brainstem, respectively. These fibers have inhibitory contact points with the molecular and granular cell layer. Figure 1.4 depicts a schematic representation of the cerebellar cortical circuit.

Macroscopic anatomy

The cerebellar cortex together with the deep nuclei and white matter tracts constitute the basic form of the cerebellum. The mammalian cerebellum consists of two hemispheres, each containing three lobes that are separated by deep fissures: (1) the flocculonodular lobe, (2) the anterior lobe and (3) the posterior lobe.

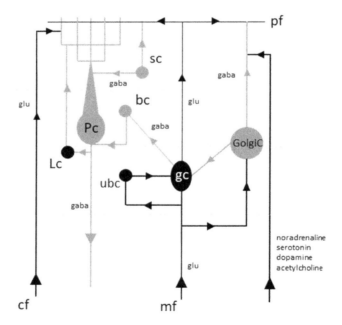

Figure 1.4. Microcircuitry of the cerebellum
Abbreviations: bc: basket cell, cf: climbing fiber, GABA: gamma-aminobutyric acid, gc: granule cell, glu: glutamate, GolgiC: Golgi cell, Lc: Lugaro cell, mf: mossy fiber, Pc: Purkinje cell, pf: parallel fiber, sc: stellate cell, ubc: unipolar brush cell.

The flocculonodular lobe is located on the antero-inferior surface of cerebellum and consists of two flocculi that are connected to the nodulus. The anterior and posterior lobe can be further subdivided in a medial, intermediate and lateral part. The medial part is called the vermis (Latin for 'worm') and is a longitudinal band of cortex that runs from the front to the back of the cerebellum (O'Hearn & Molliver, 2001). The lateral cerebellar hemispheres and vermis are separated by a narrow intermediate cortical zone, termed the paravermis. The lobes can be further subdivided into so-called lobules or leaves (folia) (Figure 1.4).

In addition, the seminal work by Dutch anatomist Jan Voogd showed that the cerebellar cortex is organized in longitudinal stripes (parasagittal zones) that run in an anterior-posterior direction and can extend one or more lobules (Voogd & Glickstein, 1998). As depicted in Figure 1.5, these white-matter compartments have been proposed to constitute the functional units of the cerebellum.

An alternative taxonomy is based on the topographical mappings the incoming (afferent) mossy fibers which sections the cerebellum into three parts: vestibulocerebellum, spinocerebellum and cerebrocerebellum. The vestibulocerebellum comprises the flocculonodular lobe and the lingula part of the vermis.

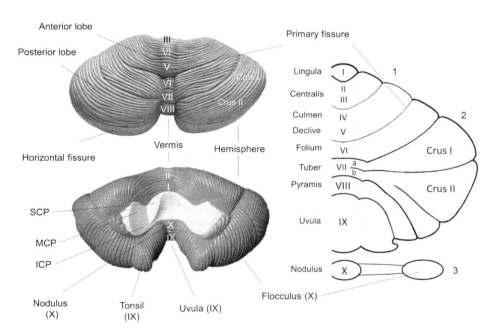

Figure 1.5. Topography of the mammalian cerebellum
Abbreviations: ICP: inferior cerebellum peduncle (restiform body), MCP: medial cerebellar peduncle (brachium pontis), SCP: superior cerebellar peduncle (brachium conjunctivum).

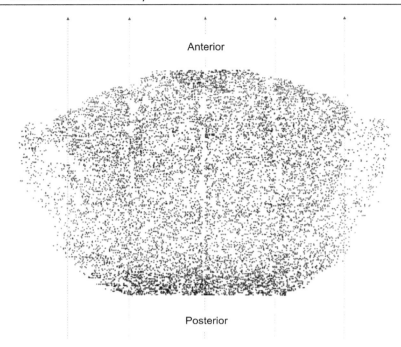

Figure 1.6. The cerebellar parasagittal zones

The vestibulocerebellum is reciprocally connected to the vestibular nuclei and inferior olive and regulates reflex eye movements, gait and balance. The anterior lobe, the vermis and paravermis receive massive spinal afferents that together form the spinocerebellum which is thought to be mainly involved in muscle tone and movement control. The spinocerebellum constitutes the second part, and its afferents carry proprioceptive (somatosensory) input from the dorsal columns of the spinal cord and trigeminal nerve. Furthermore, analogous to the cerebral cortex, although less detailed, the spinocerebellum contains somatosensory maps associated with the position of the body in space (Figure 1.7). In particular, the vermis receives input signals from the trunk and proximal portions of the limbs, while the paravermis gets input from the distal portions of the limbs.

Based on somatosensory input, the spinocerebellum can predict the future position (end-point) of a body part during movement execution. In addition, the spinocerebellum receives input from the vestibular nuclei, inferior olive and reticular formation.

Finally, the cerebrocerebellum consists of the two lateral hemispheres and occupies most of the posterior lobe. The cerebrocerebellum receives its main input from the cerebral cortex via the pontine nuclei of the brain stem and returns projections to the cerebral cortex by relaying signals through the

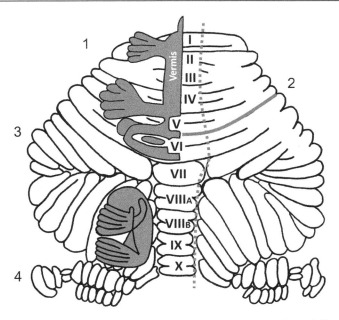

Figure 1.7. Somatosensory information enters the cerebellum via ipsilateral fibers. 1: anterior lobe, 2: primary fissure, 3: posterior lobe, 4: flocculonodular lobe

thalamus. Motor planning, initiation of movement, learning and motor memory are part of its functional repertoire.

Deep cerebellar nuclei

Whereas the cerebellar cortex receives input from the vestibular system, inferior olive and pontine nuclei, output signals of the cerebellar cortex are propagated from the Purkinje cells via four pairs of deep cerebellar nuclei to the rest of the brain (Figure 1.8).

The fastigial nucleus is located in the most medial part and connects bilaterally to the vestibular nuclei and reticular formation. The fastigial nucleus receives its main input from the vermis. The globose and emboliform nucleus are located lateral from the fastigial nucleus and receive afferent signals from the paravermis and anterior lobe and are collectively called the interposed nuclei. The latter name stems from its location between the fastigial and dentate nucleus. The highly convoluted dentate nucleus is the largest of the four nuclei and has a saw tooth-like appearance and gets input from the lateral cerebellar hemispheres. As mentioned earlier, the dentate can be functionally segregated in a dorsal and ventral structure, wherein the dorsal part is dedicated to motor function and the ventral part is more involved in non-motor functions (Strick et al., 2009).

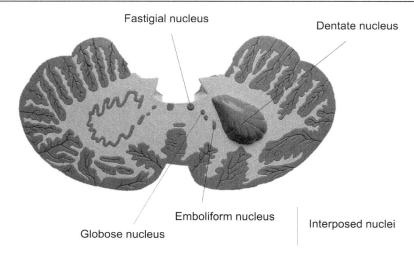

Figure 1.8. Transversal view of the deep cerebellar nuclei (DCN)

Cerebellar peduncles

Three bundles of white matter pathways make up the communication channels between the cerebellum and the central nervous system (Figure 1.9).

The restiform body is the inferior cerebellar peduncle and carries both afferent (input) and afferent (output) signals that connect the vestibulo- and spinocerebellum with the brainstem and spinal cord. The brachium pontis or the middle cerebellar peduncle is the largest of the three fiber tracts that receives projections from the contralateral pontine nuclei and relays the afferent signals to the cerebrocerebellum. The brachium conjunctivum constitutes the superior cerebellar peduncle and is a large white matter fiber bundle that arises from the dentate nucleus. Most of these efferent projections terminate in the red nucleus and the thalamus. The red nucleus is localized in the anterior part of the midbrain, and together with substantia nigra form the core of the extrapyramidal tract dedicated to involuntary movements, such as reflexes, locomotion and postural control. The thalamus is a structure located in the forebrain between the midbrain and the cerebral cortex and serves as a relay station for signal transfer from and to the cerebral cortex.

Cerebello-thalamo-cortical projections

The output of DCN is directed to motor and non-motor related thalamic nuclei. The ventrolateral nucleus of the thalamus receives input from the interposed nuclei and dorsal dentate nucleus which projects to the motor cortex (Stoodley & Schmahmann, 2010). The ventral part of the dentate nucleus projects to the mediodorsal and ventral thalamic nuclei, which in turn are

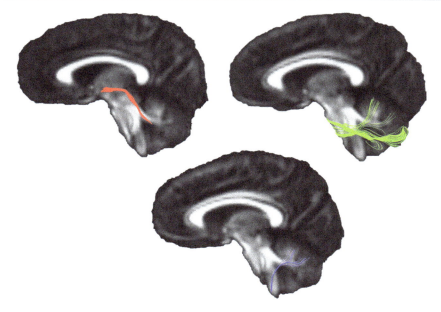

Figure 1.9. Sagittal diffusion weighted image of human brain illustrating reconstructed fibers that are part of the inferior (blue), middle (green) and superior cerebellar peduncles (red)

connected to the prefrontal cortex. This discovery was made using retrograde trans-synaptic transport of herpes simplex virus which showed that neurons in the dentate nucleus project via the thalamus to the prefrontal cortex. The finding provided for the first time an anatomical substrate for cerebellar contributions to higher order (mental) functions in primates (Middleton & Strick, 1994, 2001). In a subsequent study that used retrograde trans-synaptic transport using a rabies virus, it was demonstrated that the Purkinje cells in Crus II of the cerebellar cortex provide input to the dorsolateral prefrontal cortex (Kelly & Strick, 2003). Additional trans-synaptic tracer studies have shown that the parietal cortex is also connected to the dentate nucleus in monkeys (Clower et al., 2001) and sends signals back to the cerebellum via the pons (Glickstein et al., 1994). More recently, neuroimaging studies started to statistically correlate resting state activity between subregions of the cerebellum and cerebral cortex to provide a proxy for functional cerebello-cortical connectivity in humans (Evarts et al., 1969). Evidence was found that the cerebellum can be divided into at least two zones: the primary sensorimotor and supramodal zone. The primary sensorimotor zone consists of lobules V, VI and VIII and shows functional connections with the domain-specific motor, somatosensory, visual and auditory cortical regions. The supramodal zone, which is made up of lobules VII, Crus I and II, is coupled to activity in the prefrontal and parietal cortex

(O'Reilly et al., 2009). The specificity of these zones may indicate distinct functional cerebello-cortical units that together with the thalamus and pons form closed loops.

Developments in the field of tractography now provide ways to visualize the white matter connections of the human brain in vivo that can provide a structural neuroanatomical basis for functional connectivity. Diffusion tensor imaging (DTI) is an MRI-based neuroimaging technique that can reconstruct whiter matter pathways based on the diffusion of water molecules alongside the axons. Using DTI, the well-known cerebellar anatomical pathways have been reconstructed, and further evidence has been provided for cerebellar connections to the parietal cortex (Keser et al., 2015). In addition, cerebellar white matter connections to the vision (occipital) and language (temporal)-dedicated cortical areas have been observed, and fit with the idea that the cerebellum is involved in both motor and non-motor related processes that likely span the entire cerebral cortex.

Cerebello-subcortex connections

While the posterior cerebellar hemispheres show intricate connections with the cerebral cortex, the evolutionary more ancient parts of the cerebellum are more strongly linked to areas in the subcortex that include areas in the brainstem, midbrain and limbic lobe.

The reticular formation is an assembly of interconnected cell bodies distributed across the brainstem that is densely connected to the cerebellum. A considerable amount of cerebellar afferent projections originates from serotonergic raphe nuclei and noradrenergic locus coeruleus (Newman & Ginsberg, 1992).

Furthermore, anatomical observations in animals have demonstrated that myelinated axonal fibers from the fastigial nucleus terminate in the catecholamine system, which includes the locus coeruleus and dopaminergic ventral tegmental area (VTA). Evidence indicates that lesioning in the vermis and paravermis causes long-term changes in noradrenaline and dopamine levels (Snider et al., 1976). Efferent connections of the cerebellum to the reticular reformed are established via the deep cerebellar nuclei. The reticular formation plays a critical role in arousal, attention and consciousness. More specifically, the reticular formation is involved in cardiac and vasomotor control, balance and posture, and conveys nociceptive (pain) signals from the lower extremities of the body to the cerebral cortex.

The cerebellar connections to the red nucleus (cerebello-rubral tract) of the midbrain and offers an anatomical basis for involvement of the cerebellum in the processing of sensorimotor information and coding of unexpected events (Habas et al., 2010). Diffusion tractography in humans has demonstrated the presence of fibers between the periaqueductal gray (PAG) to the cerebellum (Sillery et al., 2005). The PAG is located in the midbrain around the cerebral aqueduct of the ventricular system and known for its role in pain modulation. The release of opioid compounds into the spinal cord and sending ascending signals to the thalamo-cortical regions are proposed mechanisms by which the PAG contributes to pain relief (Adams, 1976; Sillery et al., 2005). Findings of cerebellar activation to peripheral nociceptive stimulation further substantiate the anatomical and functional link between the cerebellum and PAG (Svensson et al., 1997; Linnman et al., 2012).

The cerebello–limbic connection and emotions

The term limbic (Latin for 'border') lobe was originally introduced by French physician Paul Broca (1824–1880) and presents a collection of brain structures that lies in between the cerebral cortex and brainstem of all mammalian species. The limbic lobe was initially thought to be primary involved in smell due to its connections with the bulbus olfactorius at the base of the frontal lobe, but in 1937, James Papez published a speculative paper in which he proposed that a set of interconnected limbic regions that collectively constitutes a neural circuit involved in motivation and emotion (see also Chapter 2). Papez conjectured that the thalamo–hypothalamic route generates motivational (action) tendencies and emotions, whereas the thalamo–cortical–cingulate pathway is dedicated to the conscious experience and regulation of feelings and actions. Structural and functional neuroimaging studies have largely confirmed the basic assumptions of Papez and identified additional subcortical limbic elements that included the amygdala. Electric stimulation of the cerebellar vermis and fastigial nucleus of animals has shown to produce physiological effects in several limbic regions, including electric responses in the hippocampus and amygdala (Whiteside & Snider, 1953; Heath & Harper, 1974). Also, the existence of monosynaptic reciprocal axonal connections between the deep cerebellar nuclei and hypothalamus (Haines et al., 1984) yield anatomical evidence for a functional role of the cerebellum in the limbic circuitry and the modulation of the autonomic nervous system in mammals (Snider & Maiti, 1976). Finally, the connection between the cerebellum and cingulate cortex found in the animal brain has been verified in the human brain using diffusion tensor tractography (Kamali et al., 2010). It is therefore not surprising that the term 'limbic cerebellum' was introduced to illustrate the tight connection of the vestibulo- and spinocerebellum with the limbic system (Schmahmann, 2000).

The connections between the cerebellum and the basal ganglia are presumed to be solely established via the cerebral cortex. However, findings in animals have challenged this presumption by identifying subcortical pathways that connect the cerebellum with the basal ganglia. A recent DTI study confirmed the existence of a direct route between the cerebellum and basal ganglia in humans (Milardi et al., 2016). More specifically, connections were observed between the cerebellar cortex and subthalamic nucleus, as well as a

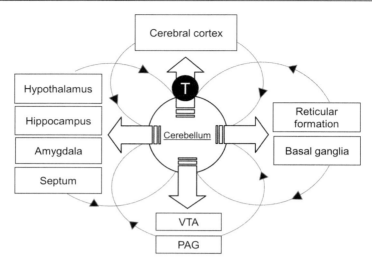

Figure 1.10. The cerebellum and its structural and functional connections
Abbreviations: DCN: deep cerebellar nuclei, T: thalamus.

direct route linking the dentate nucleus of the DCN with the globus pallidus and substantia nigra. The basal ganglia are a subcortical group of gray matter structures that is involved in behavioral control and movement. In addition to the pallidum, substantia nigra, the basal ganglia consist of the striatum (i.e., putamen and caudate nucleus) and subthalamic nucleus. These heavily dopaminergic driven regions are connected to the anterior regions of the cerebral cortex and limbic system, and play a role in motivation and emotion associated with positive (e.g., euphoria) and negative states (e.g., disgust). Neurodegenerative disorders of movement, including Huntington's and Parkinson's diseases, that involve dysfunctions of the basal ganglia can cause emotional disturbances, including deficient emotion recognition and expression, apathy and major depressive disorder. Figure 1.10 shows an overview of structural and functional cerebellar connections to other brain areas that provide a neuroanatomical schematic for involvement in emotion and emotion-related disorders.

Conclusion

This chapter introduced the evolution and basic anatomy of the cerebellum and its connections. The cellular architecture is highly homogenous and uniform, and constitutes the micro-circuitry of the cerebellum that allows for dealing with neural signals of different origin. This idea is strengthened by the existing input (afferent) and output (efferent) connections of the cerebellum to the rest of the brain. Modern neuroimaging techniques have confirmed that the cerebellar neuroanatomical pathways in lower mammals also exist in humans. In addition, sophisticated white matter tractography studies have identified new cerebellar contact points that underscore the importance of the cerebellum in the operational architectonics of the brain. The widely held dogma that the contributions of the cerebellum are limited to motor-related functions is no longer viable—an idea that in fact dates back to as early as the first part of the 19th century when clinicians were already documenting cognitive and emotional disturbances in patients suffering from lesions to the cerebellum (Schmahmann, 1997).

References

Adams JE (1976). Naloxone reversal of analgesia produced by brain stimulation in the human. *Pain* 2, 161–166.

Anand BK, Malhotra CL, Singh B, Dua S (1959). Cerebellar projections to limbic system. *J. Neurophysiol.* 22, 451–457.

Azevedo FAC, Carvalho LRB, Grinberg LT, Farfel JM, Ferretti REL, Leite REP, Filho WJ, Lent R, Herculano-Houzel S (2009). Equal numbers of neuronal and nonneuronal cells make the human brain an isometrically scaled-up primate brain. *J. Comp. Neurol.* 513, 532–541.

Balsters JH, Cussans E, Diedrichsen J, Phillips KA, Preuss TM, Rilling JK, Ramnani N (2010). Evolution of the cerebellar cortex: the selective expansion of prefrontal-projecting cerebellar lobules. *NeuroImage* 49, 2045–2052.

Barton RA, Venditti C (2014). Rapid evolution of the cerebellum in humans and other great apes. *Curr. Biol.* 24, 2440–2444.

Clower DM, West RA, Lynch JC, Strick PL (2001). The inferior parietal lobule is the target of output from the superior colliculus, hippocampus, and cerebellum. *J. Neurosci.* 21, 6283–6291.

Colin F, Ris L, Godaux E (2002). Neuroanatomy of the cerebellum. In: Manto M, Pandolfo M (eds), *The cerebellum and its disorders*. Cambridge: University Press, pp. 6–29.

Dow RS (1942). The evolution and anatomy of the cerebellum. *Biol. Rev.* 17, 179–220.

Evarts EV, Thach WT (1969). Motor mechanisms of the CNS: cerebrocerebellar interrelations. *Annu. Rev. Physiol.* 31, 451–498.

Finlay BL, Darlington RB (1995). Linked regularities in the development and evolution of mammalian brains. *Science* 268, 1578–1584.

Giaccio RG (2006). The dual origin hypothesis: an evolutionary brain-behavior framework for analyzing psychiatric disorders. *Neurosci. Biobehav. Rev.* 30, 526–550.

Glickstein M, Gerrits N, Kralj-Hans I, Mercier B, Stein J, Voogd J (1994). Visual pontocerebellar projections in the macaque. *J. Comp. Neurol.* 349, 51–72.

Habas C, Guillevin R, Abanou A (2010). In vivo structural and functional imaging of the human rubral and inferior olivary nuclei: A mini-review. *Cerebellum* 9, 167–173.

Haines DE, Dietrichs E, Sowa TE (1984). Hypothalamo-cerebellar and cerebello-hypothalamic pathways: a review and hypothesis concerning cerebellar circuits which may influence autonomic centers affective behavior. *Brain Behav. Evol.* 24, 198–220.

Harrison PW, Montgomery SH (2017). Genetics of cerebellar and neocortical expansion in anthropoid primates: A comparative approach. *Brain Behav. Evol.* 89, 274–285.

Heath RG, Cox AW, Lustick LS (1974). Brain activity during emotional states. *Am. J. Psychiatry* 131, 858–862.

Heath RG, Harper JW (1974). Ascending projections of the cerebellar fastigial nucleus to the hippocampus, amygdala, and other temporal lobe sites: evoked potential and histological studies in monkeys and cats. *Exp. Neurol.* 45, 2682–2687.

Herculano-Houzel S. (2010). Coordinated scaling of cortical and cerebellar numbers of neurons. *Front Neuroanat*, 4, 12.

Kamali A, Kramer LA, Frye RE, Butler IJ, Hasan KM (2010). Diffusion tensor tractography of the human brain cortico-ponto-cerebellar pathways: a quantitative preliminary study. *J. Magn. Reson. Imaging* 32, 809–817.

Kelly RM, Strick PL (2003). Cerebellar loops with motor cortex and prefrontal cortex of a nonhuman primate. *J. Neurosci.* 23, 8432–8444.

Keser Z, Hasan KM, Mwangi BI, Kamali A, Ucisik-Keser FE, Riascos RF, Yozbatiran N, Francisco GE, Narayana PA (2015). Diffusion tensor imaging of the human cerebellar pathways and their interplay with cerebral macrostructure. *Front. Neuroanat.* 9, 41.

Lainé J, Axelrad H (1998). Lugaro cells target basket and stellate cells in the cerebellar cortex. *Neuroreport* 9, 2399–2403.

Lefebvre L (2004). Brains, innovations and evolution in birds and mammals. *Brain Behav. Evol.* 63, 223–246.

Linnman C, Beucke JC, Jensen KB, Gollub RL, Kong J (2012). Sex similarities and differences in pain-related periaqueductal gray connectivity. *Pain* 153, 444–454.

Maclean PD (1990). *The triune brain in evolution: Role in paleocerebral functions.* New York: Plenum.

Manto M, Pandolfo M (2002). *The cerebellum and its disorders.* Cambridge: University Press.

Middleton FA, Strick PL (1994). Anatomical evidence for cerebellar and basal ganglia involvement in higher cognitive function. *Science* 266, 458–461.

Middleton FA, Strick PL (2001). Cerebellar projections to the prefrontal cortex of the primate. *J. Neurosci.* 21, 700–712.

Milardi D, Arrigo A, Anastasi G, Cacciola A, Marino S, Mormina E, Calamuneri A, Bruschetta D, Cutroneo G, Trimarchi F, Quartarone A (2016). Extensive direct subcortical cerebellum-basal ganglia connections in human brain as revealed by constrained spherical deconvolution tractography. *Front. Neuroanat.* 10, 29.

Newman DB, Ginsberg CY (1992). Brainstem reticular nuclei that project to the cerebellum in rats: A retrograde tracer study. *Brain Behav. Evol.* 39, 24–68.

O'Hearn E, Molliver ME (2001). Organizational principles and microcircuitry of the cerebellum. *Int. Rev. Psychiatry* 13, 232–246.

O'Reilly JX, Beckmann CF, Tomassini V, Ramnani N, Johansen-Berg H (2009). Distinct and overlapping functional zones in the cerebellum defined by resting state functional connectivity. *Cereb. Cortex* 20, 953–965.

Pandya DN, Seltzer B, Barbas H (1988) Input–output organization of the primate cerebral cortex. In: Steklis H, Erwin J (eds) *Comparative primate biology.* Volume 4. Neurosciences. New York: Alan R. Liss, pp 39–80.

Parvizi J (2009). Corticocentric myopia: old bias in new cognitive sciences. *Trends Cogn. Sci.* 13, 354–359.

Ramnani N (2006). The primate cortico-cerebellar system: anatomy and function. *Nat. Rev. Neurosci.* 7, 511–522.

Reyes LD, Sherwood CC (2015). Neuroscience and human brain evolution. In: Bruner E (ed) *Human paleoneurology*. Switzerland: Springer, pp 11–37.

Sanides F (1964). The cyto-myeloarchitecture of the human frontal lobe and its relation to phylogenetic differentiation of the cerebral cortex. *J. Hirnforsch.* 6, 269–282.

Schmahmann JD (1997). Rediscovery of an early concept. *Int. Rev. Neurobiol.* 41, 3–27.

Schmahmann JD (2000). The role of the cerebellum in affect and psychosis. *J. Neuroling.* 13, 189–214.

Sillery E, Bittar RG, Robson MD, Behrens TE, Stein J, Aziz TZ, Johansen-Berg H (2005). Connectivity of the human periventricular-periaqueductal gray region. *J. Neurosurg.* 103, 1030–1034.

Snider RS, Maiti A (1976). Cerebellar contributions to the Papez circuit. *J. Neurosci. Res.* 2, 133–146.

Snider RS, Maiti A, Snider SR (1976). Cerebellar connections to catecholamine systems: anatomical and biochemical studies. *Trans. Am. Neurol. Assoc.* 101, 295–297.

Stoodley CJ, Schmahmann JD (2010). Evidence for topographic organization in the cerebellum of motor control versus cognitive and affective processing. *Cortex* 46, 831–844.

Strick PL, Dum RP, Fiez JA (2009). Cerebellum and nonmotor function. *Annu. Rev. Neurosci.* 32, 413–434.

Svensson P, Minoshima S, Beydoun A, Morrow TJ, Casey KL (1997). Cerebral processing of acute skin and muscle pain in humans. *J. Neurophysiol.* 78, 450–460.

Verendeev A, Sherwood CC (2017). Human brain evolution. *Curr. Opin. Behav. Sci.* 16, 41–45.

Voogd J, Glickstein M (1998). The anatomy of the cerebellum. *Trends Neurosci.* 21, 370–375.

Weaver AH (2005). Reciprocal evolution of the cerebellum and neocortex in fossil humans. *Proc. Natl. Acad. Sci. U.S.A.* 102, 3576–3580.

Whiteside DG, Snider RS (1953). Relation of cerebellum to upper brain stem. *J. Neurophysiol.* 16, 397–413.

Whiting BA, Barton RA (2003). The evolution of the cortico-cerebellar complex in primates: anatomical connections predict patterns of correlated evolution. *J. Hum. Evol.* 44, 3–10.

Wyatt KD, Tanapat P, Wang SS (2005). Speed limits in the cerebellum: constraints from myelinated and unmyelinated parallel fibers. *Eur. J. Neurosci.* 21, 2285–2290.

Zanchetti A, Zoccolini A (1954). Autonomic hypothalamic outbursts elicited by cerebellar stimulation. *J. Neurophysiol.* 17, 475–483.

Chapter 2

The cerebellum link to motivation and emotion

The term emotion comes from the Latin 'emovère' and means 'moving energy' or 'drive.' On the conceptual level, emotions can be defined as action-oriented expressions of motivational tendencies. These expressions involve a complex mixture of physiological changes, experiential feelings, and behavioral responses that occur in response to internal bodily and/or external environmental events. As such, emotions can be conceptualized as forms of kinetic energy that are transformed from potential energy (i.e., motivational tendencies) due to forces (i.e., internal or external events) that perturb a (biological) system. In the American Psychological Association's *APA Dictionary of Psychology* (https://dictionary.apa.org/emotion), an emotion is defined as a complex reaction pattern involving experiential, behavioral, and physiological elements, by which an individual attempts to deal with a personally significant matter or event. The quality of the emotion is determined by the specific significance of the event/context. For example, if the significance involves threat, fear is likely to be generated; if the significance involves frustration, anger is likely to be generated.

Emotions generally involve feelings but differ by having an overt or implicit engagement with the world. Dutch psychologist and emotion researcher Nico Frijda (1927–2015) considered bodily symptoms/arousal, motor expression, and subjective experience as essential parts of an emotion. In particular, he proposed that action tendencies and preparation for action (e.g., fight-flight) are prominent when defining an emotion (Frijda, 1986). American psychologist Paul Ekman (b. 1934), a pioneer in the study of human emotions and facial expressions, discovered six universal and discrete emotions in mankind: anger, disgust, fear, happiness, sadness, and surprise (Ekman et al., 1972). Ekman and colleagues' observations agreed with the biological-oriented evolutionary approach of Charles Darwin (1809–1882) who proposed that emotions were universal adaptive traits of the human species shaped by natural selection (Darwin, 1872). Evidence that emotions are in fact innate and hard-wired, and do not exclusively result from social learning, was provided by studies on the mammalian brain. These studies showed that electric stimulation of subcortical neurocircuits could selectively evoke a wide range of emotional responses in young animals that had never been exposed to social learning situations (Panksepp, 1998; Panksepp & Biven, 2012).

Although the relevance and importance of emotions in human existence are undisputed, it was not until the end of 19th century that scientists began to develop an interest in studying the anatomy of human emotions.

Early conceptualizations of emotion were firmly rooted in physiological processes and advocated the view that emotions emerge in response to detecting physiological (bodily) changes to a relevant event. This idea is better known as the James–Lange theory of emotion (Lange & James, 1922). Thus, emotional states are manifestations of context-related changes in the sympathetic and parasympathetic branches of our autonomic nervous system that do not involve cognitive processes. In contrast, cortico-centered 'read-out' theories postulate that emotions are a product of our higher mental faculties (Dalgleish, 2004). Our cognitive apparatus analyzes and interprets the somatic state in its current context and 'decides' which emotion we are experiencing.

For example, encountering a threatening situation (stressor) will elicit central and bodily reactions that prepare the organism for action to mitigate the stressor. When these complex responses reach our consciousness, the cognitive system will read out this body-context information, which gives rise to the experience of fear. One of the implications of cognition-inspired models is that the emotional experience is restricted to organisms that have a complex brain and a particularly well-developed cerebral cortex. Few scientists will disagree that the evolution of the neocortex has endowed the mammalian species to the conscious experience of emotions and regulates these emotions to promote physical and psychological well-being.

Behavioral neurosciences have provided reliable evidence that basic emotions stem from dedicated primordial subcortical brain circuits that can be found across the entire mammalian species. According to Jaak Panksepp's (1943–2017) nomenclature of emotion (Panksepp, 2011), basic emotions can be defined along several criteria: (1) has an innate stereotypical behavioral (instinctual) action pattern; (2) is elicited by unconditioned stimuli (i.e., no prior learning is involved); (3) has physiological (visceral) changes/arousal that outlast stimulus duration; (4) has arousal gates and guides sensory information processing; and (5) contributes to learning and shaping cognitive functions.

Within the neuro-evolutionary triune brain heuristic, as discussed in Chapter 1, the criteria that define an emotion constitute three generic levels of processing analogous to the three evolutionary layers of the brain (Damasio & Carvalho, 2013; Panksepp, 2011).

The *PRIMARY* process level of emotions controls the 'intentions to actions' and reflects innate instinctual (reflexive) and unconditioned behaviors. The primary-processes are closely linked to bodily homeostatic functions (e.g., maintenance of nutritional supplies, fluid balance, thermoregulation) and stereotypical approach-avoidance behavioral responses (e.g., freeze, fight-flight). The *SECONDARY* process level of emotions refers to reward- and

22 The cerebellum link to motivation

punishment-related learning, including classic and operant conditioning, and is closely linked to the limbic system. The *TERTIARY* process level of emotions involves higher order cognitive functions associated with the experience of complex feelings and encompasses the (anterior) cerebral cortex. This introspective condition enables conscious reflection and emotion regulation to facilitate 'intentions to act' (Panksepp, 2011). In other words, the subcortical antecedents associated with the *PRIMARY* and *SECONDARY* process levels contribute to conscious emotional states, but it is only on the *TERTIARY* process level in the higher cortical faculties of the brain where subjective feelings materialize to guide cognitive and situation appropriate actions (Damasio & Carvalho, 2013).

In fleshing out the neuro-anatomical details of the dedicated circuits involved in the three process levels, American anatomist James Papez (1883–1958) was among the first to present a (speculative) model on emotion processing in the human brain (Papez, 1937). He proposed that sensory information relevant to the individual arrives at the thalamus and is then channeled to the hypothalamus and cerebral cortex. He termed the route to the hypothalamus the subcortical stream of feeling and the route to the cerebral cortex the cortical stream of thinking.

According to the Papez's circuit model, the hypothalamus is responsible for the initiation of bodily responses (*PRIMARY* process level) and connects to the anterior thalamus and cingulate cortex. In the cingulate cortex, signals from the hypothalamus and sensory cortical areas are integrated, giving rise to the subjective experience of emotions (*SECONDARY* process level). The efferent connections from the cingulate cortex to the hippocampus and hypothalamus provide a basis for top-down regulation of bodily and subjective emotional responses (*TERTIARY* process level).

Interestingly, Papez's circuit has received a credible amount of support from experimental brain research in animals and humans (LeDoux, 1996). In contemporary neuroscientific theories of emotion, the amygdala has taken over the central role of the hypothalamus in Papez's emotion circuit. The amygdala is a collection of nuclei with an almond-shaped appearance situated in the medial temporal lobes. The role of the amygdala in emotion is complex and, next to being a pre-attentive valence detector of sensory input, governs other brain areas that control the peripheral nervous system (e.g., hypothalamus and locus coeruleus) and reflex-like (fight-flight-freeze) actions (e.g., periaqueductal gray). In addition, the amygdala plays a leading role in associative learning and is particularly known for its contributions to fear conditioning (Ressler & Maren, 2019).

The hierarchal conceptualization of brain functions is thus presumed to coordinate physiological needs in close interaction with the environment. It is proposed that the neural circuits at the various levels of brain organization are perception-action integrative devices specifically designed for life-sustaining purposes (LeDoux, 2012). The gradual increase in human brain complexity allows for the expression of different affective phenotypes, ranging from thirst

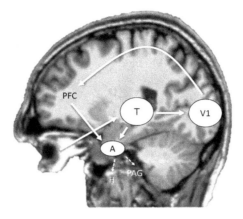

Figure 2.1. Simplified dual-pathway model of fast (implicit) thalamo-amygdala and slow thalamo-V1 (explicit) processing route of emotion-relevant visual information
Abbreviations: A: amygdala, T: thalamus, PFC: prefrontal cortex, V1: visual cortex.

to the subjective experience of intense anxiety in anticipation of a possible future negative life event. In fact, as we will see later, the complexity of the brain comes and our (affective) consciousness makes us vulnerable to psychopathological conditions. Such conditions can be viewed as life-sustaining adaptive responses gone awry (Nesse, 2000).

The homeostatic conceptualization of emotions challenges the idea that basic emotions, as proposed by Ekman, can be localized in isolated brain circuits, since emotions evolve around shared and overlapping (generic) circuits, including those involved in perception, attention allocation, cognitive control, and execution of action (PACE).

Interestingly, extensive neurobiological research in animals by Panksepp points toward the existence of an affective taxonomy in the mammalian brain consisting of seven basic emotional systems: seeking (desire system), rage (anger system), grief (separation-distress system), fear (anxiety system), lust (sexual system), care (nurture system), and play (physical social engagement system) (Panksepp, 2012). However, inferencing affective states in animals are exclusively based on equating the physiological, bodily, and (overt) behavioral expressions with the human condition. Therefore, one should be cautious in not incorrectly attributing humanlike traits to animals (i.e., the anthropomorphic fallacy). Nevertheless, closer inspection of the neural correlates of the seven emotional systems shows substantial overlap between interconnected subcortical brain structures that include the amygdala, hypothalamus, and periaquedctal gray PAG (Panksepp, 2011).

As such, the neural infrastructure of emotions is not likely to be organized in a series of discrete modalities, but more like shared circuits supporting different physiological, cognitive, and affective aspects related to an emotional state.

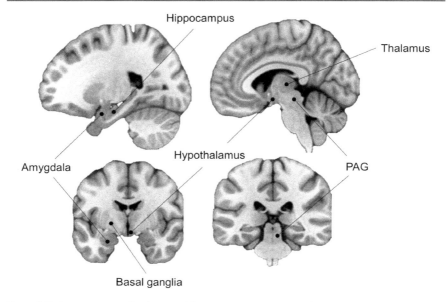

Figure 2.2. Interconnected subcortical brain regions important for motivation and emotion

Revising contemporary brain architectures of emotion: the cerebellum case

Evidence from functional neuroimaging

The introduction of positron emission tomography (PET) and functional magnetic resonance imaging (fMRI) in human experimental research caused a scientific revolution in psychology and related disciplines committed to studying human behavior. The ability to measure changes in metabolism and blood flow as a proxy of brain activity in conjunction with behavior provided seemingly endless opportunities to study the functional neuroanatomical basis of human behavior. These technological advancements have undoubtedly paved the way to the wide acceptance by scientists of studying emotions and feelings as a legitimate field of research. It was not long before functional neuroimaging studies started to reveal complex brain activation patterns in response to emotional stimuli of various sorts.

The consistent activation of subcortical and cortical loci to a large extent confirmed the idea that emotion generation and emotional learning have a firm basis in the limbic (subcortical) areas, while the conscious emotional experience and regulation (top-down control) of emotions are housed in the cerebral cortical areas of the brain. Despite the high spatial resolution of fMRI, neuroimaging studies have not yet provided convincing evidence for localizing the specialized neural circuits for each of the basic emotions.

Irrespective of whether these circuits exist or not, already during the 1980s, studies using PET found notable changes in cerebellar blood flow during emotional states. For example, a PET study investigating the neural correlates of extreme anxiety demonstrated that significant blood flow increases in several cortical and subcortical areas, including the cerebellum, during a pharmacological challenge test (Reiman et al., 1989). Following the infusion of sodium-lactate, a panic attack was evoked in patients with panic disorders. Among the activated brain regions that included the bilateral poles of the temporal cortex, insular cortex, putamen, and superior colliculus, significant activation of the cerebellar vermis was observed. Despite the activation of the vermis, the nature of this activity and its role in the experience of panic remained unaccounted for. Also, early evidence demonstrating activity of the lateral areas of the cerebellum during the perception of emotional facial expressions in healthy volunteers was not deemed functionally relevant (George et al., 1993).

In another PET study with healthy volunteers, film-generated emotions activated the sensory cortices, hypothalamus, amygdala, hippocampus, and cerebellum (Reiman et al., 1997). The fact the activated regions closely matched the hypothetical anatomical circuit substrate proposed by Papez may have been one of the reasons why the cerebellum was not discussed. In a follow-up investigation of the anatomical organization of emotions, neural responses to movie clips evoked happiness, sadness, and disgust (Lane et al., 1997). The differences in valence (positive-negative) and associated action tendencies (approach-avoidance) permit the study of emotions based on common categorical features (Lane et al., 1998). In addition to shared regional activity between all three emotions, the preliminary results also showed emotion-specific regional activity in the brain. Notably, it was observed that sadness increased signals in the vermis and lateral cerebellum, and recall-induced disgust activated the lateral cerebellum.

The series of PET experiments by Antonio Damasio et al. (2000) is among the notable exceptions. In this study, healthy volunteers were instructed to recall and re-experience personal life events of anger, fear, happiness, and sadness. Results showed regional activation of somatosensory cortices, cingulate cortex, insula, hypothalamus, and brainstem nuclei supporting the proposed link between emotion and areas associated with the homeostatic body regulation. In addition, Damasio's group observed distinct activation patterns in midline cerebellar structures. Albeit cerebellum activation had already been demonstrated in prior PET studies, the authors were among the first to formulate a theory of cerebellar activation in emotion. The brainstem (pontine) nuclei receive input from cerebral cortical and subcortical (limbic) regions and transfer these signals to the medial parts of the cerebellum (i.e., vermis). The vermis constitutes the evolutionarily older structure of the cerebellum and may be involved in the coordination of emotional responses, and in the learned adjustment of responses in social settings (Damasio et al., 2000). In sum, these findings provide a neural framework showing that the processes of feeling emotions are rooted in dynamic neural maps that represent changes of internal states as a function of external input.

The introduction of fMRI with its higher anatomical precision and no need for intravenous injections of isotopes quickly substituted PET scanning in cognitive, social, and affective neuroscientific research. Despite this important technological development, many studies kept neglecting cerebellum activation in emotion and cognition up to the point that neural responses in the cerebellum are not even collected during data acquisition. This gives rise to an interesting phenomenon that can be viewed as the inverse of the file-drawer problem. The file-drawer problem, known as the confirmation bias in psychology, describes the issue of studies that are not published because of their negative (null) findings. This publication bias thus questions the reliability of findings reported in the literature from a meta-scientific perspective. In the case of the cerebellum, the opposite phenomenon seems to occur. It should be noted that this file drawer of positive findings or disconfirmation bias in psychological terms may also occur in scientific contexts in which unexpected findings are not published because they undermine 'established' theories.

Results of one of the first meta-analyses involving PET (n = 3) and 1.5T fMRI (n = 6) studies revealed that the processing of emotional stimuli was associated with left-sided activation of lobule VIIA and Crus I, and right-sided activation of lobule VI (Stoodley & Schmahmann, 2009). A search in the BrainMap library using the key words [PET] and [fMRI], and [emotion] using Sleuth software, returned 544 published human brain imaging studies matching the search criteria. Peak coordinates of the significantly activated brain regions reported in the papers were entered in the GingerALE format (Eickhoff et al., 2009, 2012; Turkeltaub et al., 2012) to plot the distribution neural activation pattern during emotion-related tasks. This software application treats foci of activation as spatial probability distributions centered on the specific coordinate and models a Gaussian probability distribution around the coordinate to account for spatial uncertainty in neuroimaging data (www.brainmap.org). Results show significant activation of not only the usual suspects, including the amygdala, insula, cingulate cortex, precuneus, and midbrain, but also the cerebellum (Figure 2.3).

In support of the earlier meta-analysis, these findings further show that the cerebellum is a structure that is consistently activated during emotions. Clearly, the studies are highly heterogeneous in terms of methodology and with the question of how emotions were assessed across the experiments. Consequently, the activation patterns shown in Figure 2.3 only provide a global indication of brain areas that are involved in processing emotional content. On the other hand, the common activation pattern found in the many different studies does point towards the cerebellum as an intricate part of the neural architecture of emotion.

Next, the critical question is what those activation patterns represent, both functionally and mechanistically, when it comes to unravelling the myriad of processes that constitute emotions and feelings. Research that studies the functional topography of emotion processes in the cerebellum is still limited. Based on the proposal that the neural pathways involve connections between the cerebellum

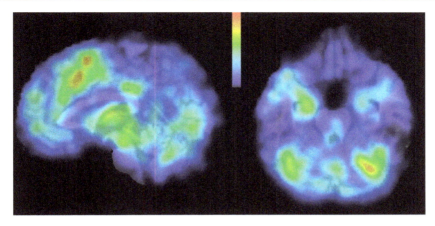

Figure 2.3. Sagittal image illustrating the activation of brain regions associated with emotion processing

and cortico-limbic circuits, one can assume that distinct sub-regions of the cerebellum might subserve the processing of different primary emotions (Baumann & Mattingley, 2012). This hypothesis was tested using fMRI in 30 healthy volunteers who were instructed to categorize happiness, anger, disgust, fear, and sadness. Emotions were elicited by presenting participants with images from the standardized International Affective Picture System (Lang et al., 1999).

Results showed distinct patterns of activity located in cerebellar midline and the posterior lobes of the cerebellum for the five emotions. Shared activation of the emotions was seen in parts of the vermis that support the close association between emotion and autonomic activity. The emotions fear and anger showed separate but also overlapping activation of the vermis and paravermis of the right cerebellar hemisphere. In addition, distinct activation of Crus I was observed for anger, while activity for fear was also found in Crus II, both in the right cerebellar hemisphere. Disgust showed a more left lateralized activity in paravermal lobule VI as well as bilateral activity patterns of vermal lobules V, VI, VIII, and IX. Sadness and happiness yielded unique midline activity, but also elicited partially overlapping activity in the vermis.

Even though the complex findings in this study provide some evidence for a topographical mapping of the five basic emotions, results unequivocally demonstrate involvement of the midline vermal and paravermal regions in the experience of emotions. These functional data reported here concur with the PET findings by Damasio et al. (2000) and the neuroanatomical pathways described in Chapter 1 issuing the close link between the cerebellar vermis and limbic system. In sum, functional neuroimaging studies have confirmed the role of the cerebellum in emotion processing. In agreement with both structural and functional neuro-anatomical data, the vermis plays a direct and distinct role in emotion processing.

While studies have been successful in isolating different parts of the cerebellum during emotion processing, what about their time course? To address this question, magnetoencephalography (MEG) was used in a study that examined the spatiotemporal characteristics of gamma band (> 30 Hz) activity in the cerebellum of healthy volunteers while they were viewing emotional scenes (Styliadis et al., 2015). MEG is able to record and localize magnetic fields produced by electric currents occurring in the brain, using very sensitive magnetometers, called superconducting quantum unit interference devices (SQUIDs). The recording and accurate localization of signals originating from deep structures, such as the cerebellum, with a MEG is challenging. Furthermore, neural activity in the gamma band range is susceptible to electromyogenic artifacts from cranial and ocular muscles.

However, with the introduction of novel ways to overcome these issues, there is now increasing evidence that MEG can pick up neural signals in the cerebellum. In line with other non-MEG studies, results demonstrated local activation of the cerebellum during emotion processing in the vermis and the left cerebellar hemisphere. Analysis of the temporal features of the signals showed that the declive of the vermis and Crus II were first activated in response to arousal around 160 ms following scene onset and lasted until 860 ms in Crus II. Activation of lobule VI between 420 and 530 ms was associated with valence processing followed by an arousal-valence interaction in lobule V and Crus I between 570 and 640 ms. Finally, an effect of arousal was again observed in the vermis, but had now shifted more posteriorly to the pyramidal region of the vermis. The early arousal-related activation of the vermis can be understood by afferent input from subcortical regions including the reticular formation, PAG, and amygdala that forward signals associated with fast and implicit evaluation of potentially relevant information.

The subsequent recruitment of cerebellar lobule VI then compares the level of arousal and the emotional content (valence) to establish the significance of the situation. Next, lobule V and Crus I integrate the outcome of the latter comparative analysis with the current goals and needs, and contribute to an internal predictive model. In collaboration with the cerebral cortex, the cerebellum will be able to rapidly evaluate action outcome and, if necessary, signal higher order cortical areas to adjust behavior. In terms of defining emotions as disruptions of bodily homeostasis, the cerebellum monitors and guides behavior aimed at restoring internal balance.

The cerebellum has a sentinel-like function (servo-controller) that has access to both interoceptive and exteroceptive processing streams. The cerebellum is able to integrate the different processing time-scales of the fast but shallow processing of the thalamo-amygdala-PAG route and the slow but refined processing of the amygdala-thalamo-cortical pathway. Activation of the posterior vermis may represent modulatory output signals to the limbic circuit associated with homeostatic regulation. These connections allow the cerebellum to integrate different information processing streams in parallel. The involvement of the cerebellar lobules can be explained by emotional appraisal, as they contribute to assigning affective meaning to the emotional stimuli and prepare the body for action. The fact that the cerebellum is involved in timing indicates that it is capable of handling information processes at different time scales and secures coherent processing in the neural networks implicated in organizing goal-directed behavior.

Reports from the clinic: Schmahmann's syndrome

In 1998, Jeremy Schmahmann and Janet Sherman from Harvard Medical School published a seminal study in the journal *Brain* that reported on a series of neurological examinations of 20 patients with damage confined to the cerebellum (Schmahmann & Sherman, 1998). Damage resulted from stroke (n = 13), midline resection (n = 1), postinfectious cerebellitis (n = 3), and cerebellar cortical atrophy (n = 3). Each patient underwent a comprehensive medical evaluation, neurological examination, and bedside mental state testing. Patients were examined neurologically between 1 week and 6 years from the onset of the illness.

The primary study aim was to determine whether there is a predictable pattern of clinically relevant non-motor related behavioral changes in these patients. Clinically relevant behavioral changes were observed in patients with lesions involving the posterior lobe of the cerebellum and the vermis. In addition to disturbance in executive functioning (i.e., planning, set shifting, working memory, and verbal fluency) and spatial cognition, significant changes in personality were observed, including flattening or blunting of affect and disinhibited or inappropriate behavior. This constellation of deficits was interpreted as a disruption of cerebellar modulation of the neural circuits that included prefrontal, parietal, and temporal regions of the cerebral cortex, as well as the subcortical (limbic) brain areas (Schmahmann & Sherman, 1998). The signs and symptoms associated with cerebellar damage lead to a new clinical entity called the 'cerebellar cognitive affective syndrome' (CCAS).

Since this key publication in 1998, many reports have appeared in the medical literature describing defects of cognitive and affective processes following cerebellar disease (Manto & Marien, 2015). Additional reports in cerebellar patients confirmed the four distinct clusters of signs and symptoms of CCAS: (1) impaired executive functioning, (2) defects in visuospatial cognition, (3) language deficits, and (4) behavioral-affective/personality changes.

During the 7th International Symposium of the Society for Research on the Cerebellum and Ataxias (SRCA) that took place in Brussels, Belgium (May 2015), CCAS was recognized as the third syndrome in clinical ataxiology, following the cerebellar motor syndrome characterized by ataxic dysarthria (speech), limb ataxia, and postural/gait deficits, and the vestibule-cerebellar syndrome, which encompasses vertigo, dizziness, imbalance, and oculomotor defects. Finally, the cerebellar cognitive affective syndrome, referred to as

Schmahmann's syndrome, captures the non-motor related cerebellar functions. As depicted in Figure 2.4, the syndromes display a fair amount of location specificity with respect to the affected area.

Damage to the anterior (sensorimotor) sector (lobules I–IV, IX) results in signs and symptoms of CMS. VCS is associated with lesions to the dorsal oculomotor vermis (lobules V–VIII) and flocculonodular lobe (lobules IX and X). Schmahmann's syndrome is more likely to occur after injury to the (para)vermian regions (lobules VII–VIII, IX) and posterior cerebellar hemispheres (Crus I and II).

Neuropsychological research in 57 patients with a hereditary or other neurodegenerative ataxia or acquired injury to the cerebellum demonstrated that complex cerebrocerebellar degeneration as well as isolated cerebellar disease or injury can cause impairments in the identification of emotional states of others (Hoche et al., 2016). The identification of emotional states is closely associated with empathy and theory of mind involving several basic operations: (1) extracting emotionally salient information from the environment, (2) generating a physiological and subjective emotional experience, and (3) regulation of this emotional experience.

The revised Reading the Mind in the Eyes test (Baron-Cohen et al., 2001), that correlates inversely with social cognitive skills, showed that cerebellar

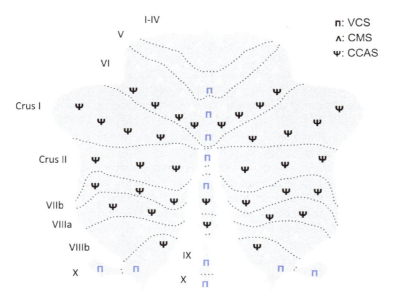

Figure 2.4. Schematic overview of the areas involved in the cerebellar motor syndrome (Λ), Schmahmann's syndrome (Ψ), and the vestibulo-cerebellar syndrome (Π). The syndromes display relatively separable contours in terms of symptom-lesion mapping (adapted from Marien & Manto, 2015)

patients had difficulties in identifying the emotional facial expressions from the eyes. Even though cerebellar pathology in the patients examined in this study was diffuse, both diffuse cerebrocerebellar degeneration as well as more isolated cerebellar disease or injury were enough to cause impairments in emotion attribution (Hoche et al., 2016).

However, the recent results seem to partially contradict other studies that have not found cerebellar-related deficits in identifying happy facial expressions (Adamaszek et al., 2014). In the latter studies, the whole face was shown, providing patients with additional physiognomic composites (e.g., drawing the angle of the mouth in a superior-posterior direction) of a prototypical happy facial expression (Hoche et al., 2016). Upon closer inspection, the cerebellar damage of the 15 patients examined by Adamaszek et al. (2014) is biased towards the left cerebellar hemisphere. In addition to demonstrating impaired selection and matching of facial emotions in patients with ischemic cerebellar lesions as compared to controls, the authors found impairments for the emotion fear (Adamaszek et al., 2014).

On a side note, even though it is much too early to assume lateralized involvement of the cerebellar hemispheres in the processing of different emotions, the crossed cerebello-cortical lateralization theory of motivation and emotion predict this selective disruption of fear-related processing in cerebellar patients. This theory is an expansion of the prefrontal lateralization model of motivated direction, wherein the left prefrontal cortex is involved in the regulation of approach (fight) related behavior and anger, and the right prefrontal cortex is associated with avoidance (flight) related behavior and fear (Schutter & Harmon-Jones, 2013).

Given the joint evolution and the existing anatomical contralateral wiring between the cerebellum and prefrontal cortex, it is theorized that the left cerebellum contributes to right PFC processes related to fear and avoidance, while the right cerebellum contributes to the left PFC processes related to anger and approach. An earlier case report described two cerebellar patients with right-sided lesions who showed rigidity of thought, impulsivity, lack of criticism, and inappropriate behavior. In another patient with left-sided cerebellar lesion apathy, emotional blunting, social isolation, anergia, and general cognitive slowing was observed (Siuda et al., 2014). These (active) behavioral symptoms linked to right cerebellar lesions can hypothetically be tied to the approach-related behavior in the left frontal cortex, whereas the behavioral symptoms shown for the patient with left cerebellar damage may be linked to the avoidance-related motivational system in the right frontal cortex. Since the output of the cerebellar cortex to the frontal cortex is inhibitory, it is tempting to interpret these findings in terms of crossed-cerebellar diaschisis, wherein loss of inhibitory cerebellar input causes a heightened state of activity in distal connected cortical regions (Vella & Mascalchi, 2018).

Even though cerebellar patients typically show a rather diffuse pattern of damaged regions, neuropsychological evidence does point towards the direction

32 The cerebellum link to motivation

that lesions to the vermis and paravermis cause difficulties in the autonomic-affective domain, while lesions to the more posterior lateral parts produce more problems in the cognitive domain. Indeed, clinical reports show that lesions involving the limbic cerebellum (vermis and fastigial nucleus) can result in hyperactivity, impulsiveness, disinhibition, anxiety, depressive symptoms, stereotypical behaviors, lack of empathy, aggression, and irritability (Schmahmann et al., 2007). The authors categorized the constellation of symptoms in three conceptual neurological factors related to (1) exaggeration (overshoot, hypermetria), (2) diminution (hypotonia, or hypometria), and (3) fluctuations between state 1 and 2 in response to signals originating from the internal and/or external environment (Schmahmann et al., 2007).

The idea that cerebellar lesions can lead to non-motor related behavioral changes is complemented by cerebellar contributions to social cognition. Social cognition is about the mental aspects related to generating understanding and regulating behavior in social contexts. Meta-analytic results of task-based fMRI studies showed that cerebellar activity reflects distinct somatosensory mirroring, emotion attribution, and mentalizing ('mind reading') functionality, and that these cerebellar activation patterns are connected to the corresponding cerebral cortical regions including the tempo-parietal junction (Van Overwalle et al., 2015).

Cerebellum stimulation

In addition to neuropsychological studies, targeting nerve tissue with probes that generate magnetic fields or electric current either directly inserted in the brain or transcranially provides a means to transiently perturb local activity. In sharp contrast to magnetic or electric stimulation of the cerebral cortex, stimulation of the deep subcortical nuclei can evoke intense emotional states (Panksepp, 1998). Interestingly, a similar parallel can be drawn with the cerebellum. Electric stimulation of the posterior hemispheres typically does not elicit strong emotional responses, while stimulation of the midline structures, like the vermis and fastigial nucleus, can elicit strong physiological and behavioral responses in both animals and humans (Heath et al., 1978, 1980). High frequency (100 Hz) electric stimulation of the vermis of cats, including the deeper underlying folia of the vermis and the fastigial nuclei, elicits neural responses in the septal area and medial amygdala, while spike activity was inhibited in the hippocampus and lateral cells of the amygdala. The changes in responsivity of the various subcortical regions have been linked to stimulation of parts of the brain's pleasure/reward system and inhibition of the brain's aversive/punishment system (Heath et al., 1980).

Interestingly, electric stimulation of the posterolateral cerebellar cortex and the dentate nucleus in emotionally disturbed patients failed to produce any notable psychological effects, indicative for the cerebellar anatomic specificity of the cerebral cortical and subcortical (limbic) connections. Furthermore, these findings concur with the neuropsychological studies described earlier that relate cognitive impairments to lesions of the lateral parts of the cerebellum, while emotional disturbances more often occur following damage to the medial parts of the cerebellum (Schmahmann & Sherman, 1998).

A much less invasive way of targeting the human cerebellum is by using transcranial magnetic stimulation (TMS). TMS is based on Faraday's law of electromagnetic induction, which states that near conductive material (e.g., nerve cells) a magnetic pulse is transformed into an electric current (Schutter et al., 2004). Applied over the scalp, the electromagnetic induction can result in the depolarization of underlying nerve cells that are tangentially oriented to the magnetic field (Bohning, 2000). Disruptive TMS applied to the cerebellum increases self-reports of negative mood as a result of impaired emotion regulation (Schutter et al., 2009a).

In contrast, facilitatory TMS applied to the cerebellum is able to increase attentional biases for happy facial expressions (Schutter, 2009). Observations of anterior scalp-recorded theta (4–7 Hz) oscillations following excitation of the human cerebellum with single-pulse TMS can be interpreted as electrophysiological evidence for the ability of cerebellar TMS to tap into Papez's emotional brain circuit (Schutter & van Honk, 2006). Arguably, anterior scalp-recorded theta activity stems from the cingulate cortex (Cavanagh et al., 2012), which is a paralimbic cortical region and part of the circuit of Papez. The cortico-ponto-cerebellar connections allow for signal transfer from the cingulate cortex to the medial parts of Crus I and II (Stoodley & Schmahmann, 2010). Furthermore, the cingulate cortex is not only a region involved in motivation, drive, and emotion, but also serves as a functional bridge between limbic structures and the frontal cortex for linking affective experience with higher cognitive processes. Results showing that electric stimulation of the deep cerebellar nuclei elicits distinct theta oscillations in the prelimbic subdivisions of the prefrontal cortex in awake, behaving rats further support the link between the cerebellum and emotion-dedicated brain regions (Watson et al., 2014).

In another study involving healthy volunteers, TMS was applied to interfere with cerebellar activity to further examine the role of the cerebellum in explicit and implicit emotional face processing (Ferrari et al., 2018). In line with the authors' expectations, evidence was found that interfering with cerebellar activity impairs task instructed (explicit) categorization of facial emotional expressions and hindered incidental processing (implicit) of the gender identity of the emotional, but not neutral faces. Even though human studies deploying TMS do not yet provide insights into the exact underlying cerebellar mechanisms, they do further signify the importance of the cerebellum in neural processes related to emotional and social relevant information of the intact brain.

A general cerebellar-oriented theoretical outline of emotion

Cerebellar activity in the context of emotional processes is still considered by many scientists as either an anomaly or reflecting some generic activity pattern associated with the motor system. The fact that the mammalian cerebellum partakes in many non-motor processes puts forward the possibility that the cerebellum represents an important node in the complex emotion circuits. Multiple independent lines of evidence illustrate the close connections of the cerebellum with both the limbic circuit, being the core of emotion generation, and the higher cortical areas that are more closely connected to the conscious experience and regulation of emotions.

Along the tripartite process conceptualization of affect as suggested by Panksepp (2011), the *PRIMARY*-process emotions that consist of visceral and homeostatic (interoceptive) signaling, flight-fight action systems, and (somato) sensory-triggered positive-negative emotional states may be organized along the vermal-fastigio-midbrain-limbic system axis. The *SECONDARY*-process emotions arising from classical and instrumental/operant conditioning are supported by the vermal-fastigio-basal ganglia axis. Finally, the *TERTIARY* affects associated with rumination, emotion regulation, and executive functions are connected to the lateral cerebello-dentato-thalamo-cortical axis (Figure 2.5).

Obviously, this organization is pragmatic and does not do full justice to the complex infrastructure of the brain, but it nonetheless may provide a theoretical basis and direction of how we could begin to understand how the cerebellum is implicated in emotion.

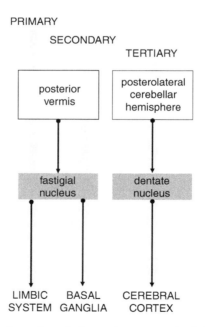

Figure 2.5. Conceptualization of cerebellar pathways organized along three axes corresponding to the *PRIMARY, SECONDARY,* and *TERTIARY* process emotions

In sum, the question whether the cerebellum is part of the neural circuitry dedicated to emotion seems no longer trivial, and it is time to take the next step and go beyond the cortico-limbic centered architectures of emotion and emotion-related disorders. In the next chapters, empirical evidence and theoretical accounts will be discussed to illustrate that emotions not only play a prominent role in psychopathological conditions but can at least in part be understood in terms of cerebellar dysfunctions.

References

Adamaszek M, D'Agatam F, Kirkby KC, Trenner MU, Sehm B, Steele CJ, Berneiser J, Strecker K (2014). Impairment of emotional facial expression and prosody discrimination due to ischemic cerebellar lesions. *Cerebellum* 13, 338–345.

Baron-Cohen S, Wheelwright S, Hill J, Raste Y, Plumb I (2001). The 'Reading the mind in the eyes' test revised version: A study with normal adults, and adults with Asperger syndrome or high-functioning autism. *J. Child Psychol. Psychiatry* 42, 241–251.

Baumann O, Chan E, Mattingley JB (2012). Distinct neural networks underlie encoding of categorical versus coordinate spatial relations during active navigation. *NeuroImage* 60, 1630–1637.

Bohning DE (2000). *Introduction and overview of TMS physics*. In MS George and RH Belmaker (eds.), *Transcranial magnetic stimulation in neuropsychiatry*. Washington: American Psychiatric Press, pp. 3–44.

Cavanagh JF, Zambrano-Vazquez L, Allen JJ (2012). Theta lingua franca: A common mid-frontal substrate for action monitoring processes. *Psychophysiology* 49, 220–238.

Dalgleish T (2004). The emotional brain. *Nature Reviews Neuroscience* 5, 583–589.

Damasio A, Carvalho GB (2013). The nature of feelings: Evolutionary and neurobiological origins. *Nat. Rev. Neurosci.* 14, 143–152.

Damasio AR, Grabowski TJ, Bechara A, Damasio H, Ponto LL, Parvizi J, Hichwa RD (2000). Subcortical and cortical brain activity during the feeling of self-generated emotions. *Nat. Neurosci.* 3, 1049–1056.

Darwin C (1872). *The expression of the emotions in man and animals*. London: John Murray.

Eickhoff SB, Bzdok D, Laird AR, Kurth F, Fox PT (2012). Activation likelihood estimation revisited. *NeuroImage* 59, 2349–2361.

Eickhoff SB, Laird AR, Grefkes C, Wang LE, Zilles K, Fox PT (2009). Coordinate-based activation likelihood estimation meta-analysis of neuroimaging data: A random-effects approach based on empirical estimates of spatial uncertainty. *Hum. Brain Mapp.* 30, 2907–2926.

Ekman P, Friesen W, Ellsworth P (1972). *Emotion in the human face: Guidelines for research and an integration of findings*. New York: Pergamon Press.

Ferrari C, Cattaneo Z, Oldrati V, Casiraghi L, Castelli F, D'Angelo E, Vecchi T (2018). TMS over the cerebellum interferes with short-term memory of visual sequences. *Sci. Rep.* 8, 6722.

Frijda NH (1986). *The emotions*. London: Cambridge University Press.

George MS, Ketter TA, Gill DS, Haxby JV, Ungerleider LG, Herscovitch P, Post RM (1993). Brain regions involved in recognizing facial emotion or identity: An oxygen-15 PET study. *J Neuropsychiatry Clin. Neurosci.*, 384–394.

Heath RG, Dempesy CW, Fontana CJ, Myers WA (1978). Cerebellar stimulation: Effects on septal region, hippocampus, and amygdala of cats and rats. *Biol. Psychiatry* 13, 501–529.

Heath RG, Llewellyn RC, Rouchell AM (1980). The cerebellar pacemaker for intractable behavioral disorders and epilepsy: Follow-up report. *Biol. Psychiatry* 15, 243–256.

Hoche F, Guell X, Sherman JC, Vangel MG, Schmahmann JD (2016). Cerebellar contribution to social cognition. *Cerebellum* 15, 732–743.

Lane RD, Reiman EM, Ahern GL, Schwartz GE, Davidson RJ (1997). Neuroanatomical correlates of happiness, sadness, and disgust. *Am. J. Psychiatry* 154, 926–933.

Lane RD, Reiman EM, Axelrod B, Yun LS, Holmes A, Schwartz GE (1998). Neural correlates of levels of emotional awareness: Evidence of an interaction between emotion and attention in the anterior cingulate cortex. *J. Cogn. Neurosci.* 10, 525–535.

Lang PJ, Bradley MM, Cuthbert BN (1999). *International affective picture system (IAPS): Technical manual and affective ratings*. Gainesville: Center for Research in Psychophysiology.

Lange C G, James W (1922). *The emotions*. Baltimore, MD: Williams & Wilkins Co.

LeDoux J (1996). *Synaptic self: How our brains become what we are*. London: Penguin Books.

LeDoux J (2012). Rethinking the emotional brain. *Neuron* 73, 653–676.

Manto M, Mariën P (2015). Schmahmann's syndrome: Identification of the third cornerstone of clinical ataxiology. *Cerebellum Ataxias* 2, 2.

Nesse RM (2000). Is depression an adaptation? *Arch. Gen. Psychiatry* 57, 14–20.

Panksepp J (1998). *Affective neuroscience: The foundations of human and animal emotions*. New York: Oxford University Press.

Panksepp J (2011). The basic emotional circuits of mammalian brains: Do animals have affective lives? *Neurosci. Biobehav. Rev.* 35, 1791–1804.

Panksepp J, Biven L (2012). *The archeology of mind: Neuroevolutionary origins of human emotions*. New York: W.W. Norton.

Papez JW (1937). A proposed mechanism of emotion. *Arch. Neurol. Psychiatry* 38, 725–743.

Reiman EM, Lane RD, Ahern GL, Schwartz GE, Davidson RJ, Friston KJ et al. (1997). Neuroanatomical correlates of externally and internally generated human emotion. *Am. J. Psychiatry* 154, 918–925.

Reiman EM, Raichle ME, Robins E, Mintun MA, Fusselman MJ, Fox PT et al. (1989). Neuroanatomical correlates of a lactate-induced anxiety attack. *Arch. Gen. Psychiatry* 46, 493–500.

Ressler RL, Maren S (2019). Synaptic encoding of fear memories in the amygdala. *Curr. Opin. Neurobiol.* 54, 54–59.

Schmahmann JD, Sherman JC (1998). The cerebellar cognitive affective syndrome. *Brain* 121, 561–579.

Schmahmann JD, Weilburg JB, Sherman JC (2007). The neuropsychiatry of the cerebellum- insights from the clinic. *Cerebellum* 6, 254–267.

Schutter DJ, Enter D, Hoppenbrouwers SS (2009). High-frequency repetitive transcranial magnetic stimulation to the cerebellum and implicit processing of happy facial expressions. *J. Psychiatry Neurosci.* 34, 60–65.

Schutter DJ, van Honk J (2006). An electrophysiological link between the cerebellum, cognition and emotion: Frontal theta EEG activity to single-pulse cerebellar TMS. *Neuroimage* 33, 1227–1231.

Schutter DJ, van Honk J (2009). The cerebellum in emotion regulation: A repetitive transcranial magnetic stimulation study. *Cerebellum* 8, 28–34.

Schutter DJ, van Honk J, Panksepp J (2004). Introducing transcranial magnetic stimulation (TMS) and its property of causal inference in investigating brain-function relationships. *Synthese* 141, 155–173.

Schutter DJ, Harmon-Jones E (2013). The corpus callosum: A commissural road to anger and aggression. *Neurosci. Biobehav. Rev.* 37, 2481–2488.

Siuda K, Chrobak AA, Starowicz-Filip A, Tereszko A, Dudek D (2014). Emotional disorders in patients with cerebellar damage- case studies. *Psychiatr. Pol.* 48, 289–297.

Stoodley CJ, Schmahmann JD (2009). Functional topography in the human cerebellum: A meta-analysis of neuroimaging studies. *Neuroimage* 44, 489–501.

Stoodley CJ, Schmahmann JD (2010). Evidence for topographic organization in the cerebellum of motor control versus cognitive and affective processing. *Cortex* 46, 831–844.

Styliadis C, Ioannides AA, Bamidis PD, Papadelis C (2015). Distinct cerebellar lobules process arousal, valence and their interaction in parallel following a temporal hierarchy. *NeuroImage* 110, 149–161.

Turkeltaub PE, Eickhoff SB, Laird AR, Fox M, Wiener M, Fox P (2012). Minimizing within-experiment and within-group effects in activation likelihood estimation meta-analyses. *Hum. Brain Mapp.* 33, 1–13.

Van Overwalle F, D'aes T, Mariën P (2015). Social cognition and the cerebellum: A meta-analytic connectivity analysis. *Hum. Brain Mapp.* 36, 5137–5154.

Vella A, Mascalchi M (2018). Nuclear medicine of the cerebellum. *Handb. Clin. Neurol.* 154, 251–266.

Watson TC, Becker N, Apps R, Jones MW (2014). Back to front: Cerebellar connections and interactions with the prefrontal cortex. *Front. Syst. Neurosci.* 8, 4.

Chapter 3

Disorders of fear and anxiety
A big role for the little brain?

Anxiety is a healthy emotional reaction to situations that threat the psychological and/or physiological well-being of a person. Anxiety is coupled to rapid activation of the central and peripheral nervous system. It allocates attention toward to the perceived danger and prepares the body for actions that can be physical, such as approach- and or avoidance behavior, or mental, like cognitive reappraisal. Anxiety is characterized by subjective feelings of tension, uncertainty, and rumination associated with elevation in blood pressure and muscle tone, sweating, and the release of the stress-hormone cortisol. This constellation of events is driven by the evolutionary ancient neural circuits that act as a relevance detector. These circuits are an intricate part of mammalian heritage of the human brain's survival system (LeDoux, 2012). Even though the emotions anxiety and fear have much in common and are sometimes even used interchangeably, they are not identical. Typically, anxiety is associated with hypothetical events in the future that are anticipated on the basis of previous experience. In other words, anxiety is the anticipation of fear. In some instances, anxiety can generalize and becomes 'objectless' leading to excessive, uncontrollable, and irrational worry.

Anxiety is proposed to involve cerebral cortical structures as one needs the capacity to construct and hold a conscious representation of the anticipated threat. Our ability to mentally time travel allows us to make precautions and tailor our behavior in such a way that we can successfully prevent the threat from becoming a physical reality.

Fear and anxiety are considered adaptive as long as the psychological and physiological reactions are proportional to the situation that elicits the emotion. It goes without saying that tachycardia, a sharp rise in blood pressure, and cortisol release by the adrenal cortex in conjunction with experiencing intense feelings of fear when encountering a black mamba in the jungle is a healthy natural response because it gets your body into survival mode. However, such a stressful reaction, which is metabolically speaking very costly, seems less apt when you see a black mamba on television while sitting on a comfortable couch at home. Next to the stress response itself, an important aspect is the time it takes for the organism to regain its internal (bodily) homeostasis. In other words, when the threat is no longer present or turns out to be harmless, the stress response should subside as a result of activation of cortical inhibitory mechanisms and the parasympathetic nervous system.

A large body of research on the neuroanatomical basis of threat processing has highlighted the roles of two main afferent routes involving the amygdala (LeDoux, 1996). The first is the (fast) thalamo–amygdala route that can process crude sensory aspects of incoming stimuli and transfer this information to the amygdala, permitting fast physiological and bodily responses that, among many subcortical regions, also include activation of the hypothalamus and periaqueductal gray (PAG). The second route is the (slow) thalamo-cortico-amygdala pathway that allows for a more complex analysis of the sensory stimulus and enables more accurate threat evaluation and modification of the initial (fast) response. Thus, the slower route gives the possibility for cognitive control and coping strategies. Figure 3.1 depicts the proposed dual pathways in the mammalian brain (see also Chapter 1).

One of the implications of this circuit is that, when it comes to threat detection, the brain is hardwired to generate many false positives in order to avoid any misses that could be fatal. Even though this mode is positively biased towards generating stress (threat) responses that turn out to be harmless (i.e., false alarms), adopting this 'better safe-than-sorry' mode has an evolutionary advantage and makes fear and anxiety adaptive emotions. Importantly, the role

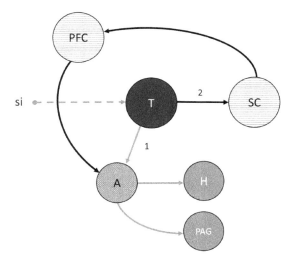

Figure 3.1. The thalamo-amygdala (1) route for processing of potential threat signals that can evoke fast physiological responses related to activation of the fight-flight circuit and the thalamo-cortical route (2) that allows for more detailed analyses of the threat.
A: amygdala, H: hypothalamus, PAG: periaquaductal gray, PFC: prefrontal cortex, SC: sensory cortex, si: sensory input.

40 Disorders of fear and anxiety

of the thalamo-cortical pathway is either to downregulate the stress responses in cases of a false alarm or to recruit cognitive resources to deal with the threat.

In addition to the initial detection of a potential threat, the proximity of the threat determines the physiological and emotional response. Functional neuroimaging research has shown that when a threat is near, in this case a virtual predator in a computer game that is able to inflict actual pain (i.e., electric shocks), this will activate the brain's subcortical survival network (Mobbs et al., 2007). The central parts of the amygdala and PAG are parts of this network that are implicated in fight-flight and panic. In contrast, when the threat is more distal, this will elicit activity in the basolateral amygdala and prefrontal cortex, which is associated with feelings of fear and the initiation of coping ('escape') strategies. In humans, the physical threat can be extended to the psychological domain, such as the experience of distress when anticipating the emotional pain of being separated from someone close to you sometime in the near future.

Another notable finding in this study was the cerebellar activation during threat exposure and experience of anxiety. These results concur with the results of an activational likelihood estimation analysis involving nearly a hundred experiments that investigated threat, fear and anxiety. These experiments (n = 99) were identified with the Sleuth software (BrainMap, Texas) using key words 'fMRI' and 'fear' or 'anxiety' and meta-analyzed with GingerALE software (BrainMap, Texas) using a cluster level family-wise error rate of 0.01 (p < 0.05). Results showed that next to activation of the amygdala, the insula, midbrain, and cortical areas showed significant bilateral and midline activation of the cerebellum. The surface flatmap shown in Figure 3.2 gives an impression of activation in the anterior lobe, as well as in the posterior lobe and vermal regions under conditions of fear and anxiety.

Interestingly, research in rats has shown that the anterior parts of the cerebellar vermis (lobules V and VI) are implicated in learned fear and that increased activity is part of the neural substrate of fear memory (Sacchetti et al., 2004). The observed findings in humans may reflect an analogous process in which cerebellar activation contributes to the formation of memory traces associated with threat. This interpretation is in line with the role of the cerebellum in SECONDARY process emotion mentioned in the previous chapter. In particular, abnormalities in threat anticipation based on fear-related conditioning and memorization, including the inability to make proper associations between safe and non-safe (threat) situations, is generally considered to be one of the dysfunctional mechanisms that contributes to anxiety disorders.

Disorder of anxiety

Abnormalities in these routes are suggested to play a role in excessive stress responsivity and reduced capacity to regulate stress responses to the extent that

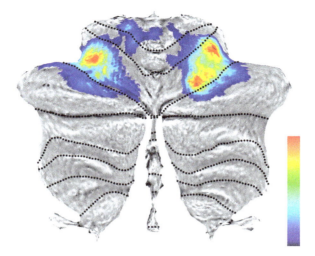

Figure 3.2. Bilateral activity in human cerebellar lobule VI during fear and anxiety-related processing

the associated emotions fear and anxiety lose their adaptive function. People become hypervigilant to their surroundings, start to worry excessively and even experience helplessness. These feelings and thoughts can become so dominant that a person is no longer able to function properly in daily life and suffers from an anxiety disorder. In addition to the psychological agony, the chronic experience of stress directly affects the immune system and makes a person more vulnerable to infections and may negatively affect brain functions. For example, chronic elevations of the stress-related catabolic hormone cortisol can cause hippocampal atrophy and memory impairments, and worsen clinical symptoms of anxiety.

Obsessive compulsive disorder

Obsessive compulsive disorder (OCD) is an anxiety disorder that is characterized by recurrent and persistent thoughts, urges, or impulses that are experienced, at some time during the disturbance, as intrusive and unwanted, and that in most individuals cause marked anxiety or distress. In addition, the person tries to ignore or suppress these thoughts, urges, or impulses by performing an action (i.e., compulsion). Compulsions are expressed by repetitive behaviors (e.g., checking and hand washing) and mental acts (e.g., praying and counting) that the person feels compelled to perform in response to the obsession (DSM-5). The compulsions are primarily aimed at relieving stress or anxiety or to prevent a particularly feared event or situation from occurring. The

42 Disorders of fear and anxiety

behaviors are not context-appropriate in the sense that they are connected in a realistic way to the goal the behavior serves. The obsessions and compulsions are time consuming and cause significant impairments in daily-life activities.

Brain research has identified abnormalities in the lateral orbitofrontal cortico-striatal circuit and its connections to cingulate gyrus and the amygdala (Barahona-Corrêa et al., 2015).

Compulsions stem from an imbalance between an overactive orbitofrontal cortex (OFC) and anterior cingulate cortex paralleled by an hypoactive dorsolateral PFC. According to this brain model, hyperactivity of the OFC and ACC elicits negative emotional feelings that give rise to error signals associated with a conflict between one's experienced and ideal self-image (egodystonic) (Westenberg et al., 2007). These error signals are resistant to top-down feedback information from higher order mental faculties including the dorsolateral prefrontal cortex (DLPFC). This causes rumination and stereotypical forms of repetitive behavior to reduce uncertainty, and is linked to the cortico-striatal-thalamo-cortical (CSTC) circuit (Van den Heuvel et al., 2016).

The CSTC circuit has extensive connectivity to numerous cortical and subcortical regions. The dysregulation of this circuit in OCD is associated with impaired executive performance, heightened error monitoring, and emotion dysregulation (Hou et al., 2014). The intrusive feelings of anxiety associated with obsessions are linked to hyperactivity of the amygdala and connected regions, including the hypothalamus and midbrain regions. Higher-than-normal dopaminergic tone in the mesolimbic areas, in conjunction with lower levels of serotonergic activity in the OFC and DLPFC, provide a neurochemical basis for the experience of distress as well as impairments in cortical regulation.

The structural and functional link of the cerebellum to the CSTC circuit and the cortico-limbic system point towards the involvement of the little brain in OCD, an assumption that has recently been confirmed by several meta-analyses. In one of these meta-analyses of 25 studies, increased gray matter volume in the striatum and reduced gray matter volumes in the prefrontal cortex were found in young and adult OCD patients (Hu et al., 2017). In addition, increased left cerebellar gray matter volumes were observed in adults. Even though a medication effect could not be excluded, the authors speculated that the dorsal parts of the cerebellar cortex that are connected to the motor cortex might be associated with the regulation of habit-like compulsive behaviors.

On the other hand, the ventral parts of the cerebellum and its connections to the prefrontal cortex have been proposed to be more closely tied to the obsessions (Hu et al., 2017). This speculation concurs with a previous multicenter VBM mega-analysis that found larger cerebellar gray matter volumes in both the dorsal and ventral parts of the left cerebellum (de Wit et al., 2014). Furthermore, a whole-brain data-driven graph theoretical analysis of resting state fMRI in 44 OCD and 43 matched controls showed that in OCD patients the basal ganglia and cerebellum were more strongly connected to one another as compared to healthy control subjects (Vaghi et al., 2017). In line with previous research, the striatal-cerebellar connectivity in OCD is implicated in habits, emotion regulation, and cognitive flexibility. The cerebellar volume changes and its connections may thus be directly related to emotional and cognitive dysfunctions and OCD symptomatology (de Wit et al., 2014).

Post-traumatic stress syndrome

Cerebellar abnormalities have also been demonstrated in individuals who suffer from post-traumatic stress syndrome (PTSS) after being exposed to intense levels of stress.

As illustrated by the previously mentioned study with the virtual predator, proximate and/or unavoidable threat will activate the fight-flight survival system to prevent physical and psychological damage. While this is part of a healthy adaptive response, extreme stress may cause hypersensitivity of the survival system. The survival system can be triggered by seemingly harmless stimuli causing extreme anxiety and even panic. Neuroimaging data suggest a relation between increased regional cerebellar activity of the cerebellum and PTSS. One the first studies examined brain blood flow in PTSS trauma survivors using PET scanning to demonstrate elevated blood flow in the cerebellum of PTSS patients as compared to controls (Bonne et al., 2003). In addition, cerebellar and extrastriate regional cerebral blood flow were positively associated with depressive symptoms and PTSS severity (Bonne et al., 2003).

Another neuroimaging study used tensor-based morphometry to examine the association between brain volumes and functional connectivity in unmedicated individuals with PTSS (Holmes et al., 2018). Analyses revealed smaller cerebellar volume in individuals with PTSS as compared to healthy control participants, and a negative association was seen between PTSS symptom severity and connectivity in the cerebellar volume and gray matter volume of the dorsolateral prefrontal cortex. These results further contribute to the involvement of the cerebellum in PTSS and suggest a role for the cerebellum in stress regulation.

To further investigate changes in brain activity associated with symptom improvement, 19 acute PTSS and nine non-PTSS volunteers who all experienced a psychological traumatic event underwent clinical assessment and were scanned during the viewing of trauma-related and neutral pictures (Ke et al., 2016). A subgroup of 17 patients was followed up to two years after the traumatic event and completed a second clinical evaluation and fMRI scan. Results showed that acute PTSS patients exhibited greater activation in the vermis and posterior cingulate cortex and significantly less activation in the parietal and prefrontal cortex compared to controls in the traumatic versus neutral viewing condition. At follow-up, reductions of activation of the posterior cingulate cortex and cerebellum during traumatic picture viewing in the PTSS group was predictive for symptom improvement (Ke et al., 2016). These findings further strengthen the link between the cerebellum and PTSS symptoms and add to the

44 Disorders of fear and anxiety

evidence that the vermis contributes to the emotional (regulatory) disturbances observed during and after extreme levels of stress.

Further support for the latter assumption comes from a study that examined the effects of psychological therapy on changes in cerebellar functional connectivity and autonomic regulation in volunteers who experienced traumatic-related stress symptoms associated with a cancer-related event (Monti et al., 2018). Treatment success lowered emotional and autonomic reactivity to traumatic stimuli and increased resting state cerebello-limbic connectivity (Figure 3.3).

The negative impact of traumatic experience on the cerebellum has been further highlighted by a study that found reduced cerebellar gray matter volumes in maltreated adolescents with PTSS symptoms as compared to maltreated adolescents without symptoms and non-maltreated volunteers (De Bellis & Kuchibhatla, 2015). Furthermore, reductions in cerebral cortical volumes were also observed in the maltreated group with PTSS symptoms, which indicates that morphological differences in these brain regions may result from a shared trauma-related mechanism and/or reflect an innate vulnerability to develop PTSS symptoms to traumatic experiences (De Bellis & Kuchibhatla, 2015).

These results extend earlier findings in which smaller cerebellar volumes were observed in a group of psychotropic-naïve maltreated children and adolescents with a diagnosis of PTSS (De Bellis & Kuchibhatla, 2006). Interestingly, the

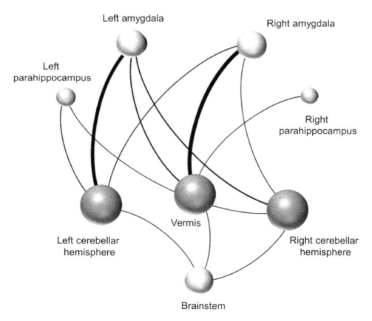

Figure 3.3. Strengthening of resting state connectivity of cerebello-limbic network after positive treatment effects

volumetric effect of the cerebellum remained significant after controlling for total cerebral cortical volume and suggests that the reduction observed in the former study may be more pronounced for the cerebellum as compared to the cerebral cortex. Furthermore, the effect was neither influenced by socio-demographic factors nor IQ, ruling out a number of important confounders that can explain the effect on cerebellar volumes.

Activation of the hypothalamic-pituitary-adrenal (HPA) stress axis and the subsequent release of the steroid hormone cortisol during stress may provide one explanation of the relation between PTSS symptoms and smaller cerebellar volumes. The primate cerebellum contains high concentrations of corticoid binding sites (Sánchez et al., 2000).

Analogous to the hippocampal volume reductions, which are at least in part caused by the catabolic properties of cortisol, a similar endocrinological mechanism could perhaps play a role in smaller cerebellar volumes (Schutter, 2012). However, results of a meta-analysis and meta-regression of studies comparing concentrations of salivary cortisol, which reflects the unbound free fraction that can freely enter the brain, showed that salivary cortisol samples collected in the morning were lower in patients with PTSD than in controls (Pan et al., 2018). Diminished salivary cortisol release after developing PTSS symptoms may evolve as a compensatory anti-glucocorticoid feedback mechanism in response to hyperactivity of the HPA-axis during trauma experience (Morris et al., 2012). Furthermore, the influence of diurnal fluctuations of cortisol levels over the course of day has not yet been investigated in humans. Lower than normal cortisol provides little to no information about circadian rhythms nor on HPA axis hypersensitivity to stressors.

In sum, even though there is currently no evidence for a role for cortisol levels in cerebellar volumes and PTSS, a negative influence of high psychological stress levels on cerebellar volumes is well documented. Finally, as stress-related genetic and early environmental factors add to variation in stress reactivity and subcortical brain volumes (Pagliaccio et al., 2014), the degree to which the relation between cerebellar volume and PTSS can be understood in terms of a neural predisposition to develop clinical symptoms to traumatic experience or cerebellar volume reductions as a consequence of traumatic experience, or both, remains an open question. In addition to volumetric deviations, analyses of resting state functional connectivity patterns in PTSS show heightened signal correlations of the anterior lobe (lobule I-V) to the fusiform gyrus (visual processing), insula (interoceptive awareness), and hippocampus (memory and learning), whereas reductions in signal correlation were observed between Crus I and the prefrontal cortex (executive functioning) (Rabellino et al., 2018).

It has been proposed that the cerebellum contributes to hypervigilance and compromised stress regulation by overpredicting aversive stimuli (Allen et al., 2019). Enhanced acquisition and resistance to extinction during fear conditioning, especially during uncertain circumstances, can be explained by internal prediction errors of the cerebellum leading to hypervigilant states, chronic levels

46 Disorders of fear and anxiety

of stress, and anxiety. The structural and functional abnormalities cause cerebellar overprediction of threat and compromise one's ability to distinguish between safe and threatening situations. As a consequence, seemingly insignificant events can trigger a full-blown traumatic episode in individuals suffering from PTSS.

General anxiety disorder (GAD)

GAD is characterized by persistent and excessive worry about a number of different things. People with GAD may anticipate disaster and may be overly concerned about money, health, family, work, or other issues, and find it very difficult to control their worry. Symptoms of GAD include irritability, difficulty in concentrating, headaches, insomnia, fatigue, and restlessness.

A meta-analysis on structural (n = 35) and functional MRI studies (n = 74) in GAD and controls found reduced volumes in the hippocampus, anterior cingulate cortex (ACC), and the amygdala. The dorsolateral prefrontal cortex and ACC showed reduced functional connectivity with the amygdala (Kolesar et al., 2019). The pattern of findings hints towards reduced information transfer between the cortical-oriented central executive network and the limbic-centered saliency network. In terms of functions, this result can be interpreted along the lines of reduced top-down inhibitory control and cognitive flexibility.

Information less available to the anterior vermis (lobule IV–V), due to reduced functional coupling with the amygdala may indicate impairments in context-appropriate experience and awareness of emotions. The increased functional connectivity of the posterior cerebellum with the amygdala may be associated with dominant self-referential processes linked to worry and rumination at the expense of coordinating executive control processes. Higher levels of functional connectivity may thus represent dysfunctional afferent (input) and efferent (output) cerebellar signalling in individuals suffering from GAD.

Additional evidence for the involvement of the cerebellum in rigid and perseverative thoughts (cf. OCD) was found in an fMRI study that examined self-reported worry during a low demand visuo-motor tracking task in GAD (Makovac et al., 2019). Compared to healthy controls, persons with GAD showed reduced activation of anterior lobules I–IV of the cerebellar vermis during episodes of off-task thoughts associated with rumination and worry (Makovac et al., 2019). This result, together with the reduced functional coupling with the amygdala, could perhaps explain the presence of anxiety-related somatosensory symptoms such as vertigo, dizziness, trembling, and postural instability.

Related to these physical reactions is having a panic attack, which is characterized by a sudden episode of extreme anxiety, associated with severe somatic reactions when there is no real threat. Thoughts that often come to the person's mind during a panic attack are losing control, having a heart attack or even dying. While panic attacks at first appear not to have an identifiable cause, persons may, in an attempt to understand the nature of the attacks, start to attribute the excessive fear with certain situations and/or conditions. As a result, people can develop specific phobias associated with objects, for example, spiders (arachnophobia), or situations, such as large open spaces (agoraphobia) or people (social phobia).

Individuals who had a panic attack can become obsessed with monitoring their own internal bodily states. Paradoxically, fearing a panic attack may actually increase the likelihood of another episode. Cholecystokinin tetrapeptide (CCK-4) is found in high amounts in brain areas involved in emotional and cognitive processes and reliably produces somatic, sensorial, and cognitive signs of panic attacks in a dose-dependent manner both in panic patients and healthy subjects. Increased activity in the cerebellum has been observed after a CCK-4 induced panic attack in healthy volunteers (Eser et al., 2009). In particular, activation of the vermis, together with the insula, anterior cingulate cortex, and brain stem, is a robust finding across studies that administered CCK-4 to induce transient states of anxiety (Benkelfat et al., 1995; Schunck et al., 2006).

Animal studies indicate that panic-like behavior following stimulation of the PAG is accompanied by deactivation of the deep cerebellar nuclei (Moers-Hornikx et al., 2011). Deactivation of the deep cerebellar nuclei (DCN) points toward abnormal inhibitory signaling of the Purkinje cells (PC). Since the PCs make up a significant portion of the cerebellar cortex, the observed increases in activation following CCK-4 administration in humans may point towards an increase PC inhibition of the deep cerebellar nuclei. Perhaps reductions of DCN activity following too strong excitatory input from climbing fibers originating in the inferior olive and from parallel fibers of the granular cells to PCs cause misfiring of the fight, flight, and freezing responses located in the midbrain and brainstem. Finally, as we will discover in the next section of this chapter, the PC-DCN connection is directly implicated in fear conditioning (Apps & Strata, 2015).

What all the different anxiety states seem to have in common is a dissociation between intero- and exteroceptive signals. Interoception refers to the perception of our internal bodily state; exteroception refers to sensations that result from input signals located outside the body. Organisms rely on both intero- and exteroceptive signals in order to promote short-term survival and long-term homeostasis (Critchley & Harrison, 2013). The optimization of internal and external processing to adequately respond to environmental demands (e.g., the emotion fear in response to facing a predator that initiates a flight response) involves the cerebellum for integrating motor, bodily, emotional, and sensory information (D'Angelo & Casali, 2013). It is therefore not surprising that cerebellar dysfunctions contribute to fear- and anxiety-related disorders. Issues in the formation of internal models and predictive coding, as briefly addressed in the PTSS section, cause impairments in one's ability to resolve ambiguous contextual information and provide a breeding ground for the development of GAD.

Social phobia

The leading feature of social phobia or social anxiety disorder is intense anxiety or fear of being judged, negatively evaluated, or rejected in a social or performance situation. People with social anxiety disorder may worry about acting or appearing visibly anxious (e.g., blushing, stumbling over words) or being viewed as stupid, awkward, or boring. As a result, they often avoid social or performance situations, and when a situation cannot be avoided, they experience significant anxiety and distress. Many people with social anxiety disorder also experience strong physical symptoms, such as a rapid heart rate, nausea, and sweating, and may experience full-blown attacks when confronting a feared situation. Although they recognize that their fear is excessive and unreasonable, people with social anxiety disorder often feel powerless against their anxiety.

Individuals with social phobia worry excessively and experience high levels of anxiety in anticipation to social interactions. To study anticipatory anxiety in social phobia, researchers often use the Trier social stress test (TSST). The TSST is an experimentally controlled procedure that elicits acute stress in participants who are instructed to prepare a presentation in front of an unresponsive interview panel (social evaluation) and have to complete a surprise mental arithmetic test. This test effectively combines two critical aspects of social phobia: social evaluation and unpredictability.

The first neuroimaging study using the TSST in healthy volunteers found that anticipatory anxiety is associated with activation of the anterior cingulate, insula, amygdala, hippocampus, thalamus, prefrontal cortex, and cerebellum (Reiman et al., 1989). A control experiment a few years later showed that activity at the temporal locations (i.e., amygdala and hippocampus) may have been produced by artificial extracranial signals caused by teeth-clenching (>Drevets et al., 1992), a phenomenon, which in itself could be a motor-related feature of high stress and anxiety. The neural (intracranial) correlates of teeth-clenching include the primary motor cortex, insula, thalamus, and cerebellum (Lin, 2018), activity in most the other regions found in the study by Reiman et al. (1989) can be explained by teeth-clenching.

A PET study that examined regional cerebral blood flow in participants with social phobia as a function of anticipation of public speaking found enhanced cerebral blood flow in the right prefrontal cortex, left inferior temporal cortex, and left amygdaloid-hippocampal region when participants, both patients and controls, experienced anticipatory anxiety. In addition, reductions in blood flow were observed in the left temporal pole and bilateral cerebellar Crus I (Tilfors et al., 2002). In contrast to the earlier study in healthy volunteers, the lateralized effects and reductions in regional blood flow during anticipatory anxiety are less likely to be confounded by motor-related variables such as teeth-clenching. Furthermore, the posterior lobules Crus I (Figure 3.4) are non-motor related functional regions of the cerebellum connected to the parietal and frontal cortical areas and involved in attention and working memory. Less activity may indicate problems in executive functioning and less cognitive resources to cope with the situation resulting from limbic-driven anxiety, worry, and rumination.

The data indicate that, in addition to the role of the amygdaloid-hippocampal area and the prefrontal cortex, the cerebellum is part of this functional network underlying anticipatory anxiety in normal and psychopathological conditions.

Further research on the large-scale brain networks involved in social anxiety disorder was performed in an fMRI study where brain activity was examined in patients with social phobia who were confronted with social situations (Nakao et al., 2011). A series of photographs of social scenes such as going to a restaurant or conference were displayed on a video screen and participants were instructed to imagine themselves in this situation. As expected, self-reported anxiety levels were significantly higher in patients than in controls. Although patients with social phobia demonstrated brain activation patterns similar to that of healthy controls, the patient group showed relatively decreased activation of the left deep cerebellar dentate nucleus, which receives direct input from Crus I, left precuneus, and bilateral posterior cingulate cortex. Each of these regions is part of the brain's default mode network (DMN) that is responsible for self-awareness, a condition during which the individual is focused more internally rather than on the external world. Although the data only highlight differences between volunteers with and without social phobia during social situations, reduced cerebellar output to the thalamo-cortical circuit may perhaps indicate altered cerebellar activity in the context of social mental imagery.

Patients with social phobia often report feelings of uneasiness and nervousness arising from thoughts about how other people perceive and evaluate them. To examine differences in neural activity between patients and controls, brain activity was assessed in volunteers who were informed that an active video camera would register any potential body movements or facial expressions (Giménez et al., 2012). A video system added to the fMRI set-up allowed for interactive visual contact between the patient and the experimenters

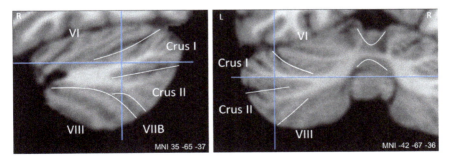

Figure 3.4. Right-sided (left sagittal image) and left-sided (right coronal image) reduction of activity in Crus I during anticipatory anxiety

immediately prior to acquisition. The control group showed activation of the frontal cortical areas, insula and left cerebellar lobule VI, while the social phobic group showed additional activation of the thalamus, right cerebellar lobule VI, and vermal lobule VIII (pyramis). Furthermore, functional connectivity analysis showed that signal correlation between the thalamus and cerebellum was significantly lower in the patient group (Giménez et al., 2012). The latter finding indicates reduced cerebellar output signalling to the thalamo-cortical networks, while the increased cerebellar activity may reflect increased arousal and processes involved in threat appraisal as well as action preparation (Styliadis et al., 2015; Talati et al., 2013).

Structural aberrations that underlie the functional abnormalities in social phobia hint at increased gray matter volumes in the left cerebellar hemisphere (Talati et al., 2013). The relation between MRI based structural and functional results in terms of identifying the mechanism(s) that can teach us something about the neurobiological basis of a disorder. For example, more gray matter does not per se imply a better developed structure and increased activity does not necessarily mean better functionality.

In social phobia, the combination of increased gray matter volume and reduced activation could be explained by deviations in apoptosis. Apoptosis is part of a natural occurring fine tuning process during brain development in which 'unused' neurons are eradicated. This leaves open the possibility that increased cerebellar gray matter volumes in adulthood result from abnormal neurodevelopmental processes that may have function-related consequences (e.g., lower activity). This is conceptually similar to high levels of activity being dysfunctional in the sense that the activity falls outside the 'normal' activity range. While there is no scientific evidence that backs up these scenarios in social phobia or any other mental disorder, when considering the nature of the observation in terms of understanding psychopathology, more is not necessarily always better.

Finally, a study has found that patients with social phobia exhibit increased resting state perfusion in the right posterior cerebellum (Crus I) and decreased perfusion in the left lobule IV of the vermis (Warwick et al., 2008). On a ruthless speculative account, this right posterior activity could reflect continuous compensatory activity to abnormalities in extracerebellar brain regions dedicated to emotion regulation and behavioral control. The concomitant reduction in the left medial part of the anterior cerebellum may be indicative for lower somatosensory activity.

Fear conditioning

Among the many processes involved in behavioral adaptation and homeostatic functions, the ability to make stimulus-response associations and learning are important aspects involved in the formation of internal models. Internal models can be conceptualized as a representation of the external environment that describes an experienced-based associative network that enables the organism to act in the external world based on causal stimulus-response linkages.

Classical conditioning is a form of associative learning in which organisms can link stimuli and responses.

Classical conditioning was discovered by the Russian physiologist Ivan Pavlov (1849–1936) who showed that a neutral object (e.g., bell) can elicit an innate response (i.e., salivating) when it is paired with a biologically potent stimulus (e.g., food) that already produces the innate (reflexive) response. The process involves the transformation of an initial neutral stimulus to a meaningful one. The biological potent stimulus is called the unconditioned stimulus, and the innate reflexive response is termed the unconditioned response (UR). After repeated pairings of the neutral stimulus with the unconditioned stimulus that elicits the UR, the organism will start to show a conditioned response (CR) to the neutral stimulus only when the conditioned stimulus is presented. The neutral stimulus has turned into a conditioned stimulus (CS). Importantly, the CR is usually like the UR, but unlike the UR, the CR is acquired through experience.

For classical conditioning to be successful, the following two requirements must be met. The first is contiguity and refers to the notion that the CS should be presented approximately half of a second prior to the US. The second requirement is contingency and states that the CS should be accompanied by the US in most cases. That is, if the CS is followed by the US in 80 instead of 50 percent of the cases, classical conditioning is more likely to occur. In other words, the CS needs to be a reliable predictor for the US to occur.

Cellular basis of cerebellar conditioning

The cerebellum is a circuit that is built on top of the brain stem circuits, which contain the innate reflexive unconditioned responses (Gerwig et al., 2007). Based on extensive eye-blink conditioning research in rabbits, a neurologically-inspired model has been developed to explain the cerebellar mechanism underlying eye-blink conditioning. Mossy fibers from the pontine nuclei in the brain stem send signals of the neutral stimulus (e.g., auditory tone) to the cerebellar cortex and DCN, while the climbing fibers stemming from the inferior olive are responsible for transmitting the US (e.g., air-puff to the eye) information to the cerebellum (Linden, 2003).

It has been proposed that the convergence of signals through mossy and climbing fibers causes excitability changes at the parallel fiber-Purkinje cells synapses of the cerebellar cortex. At the same time, the connections of the mossy and climbing fibers to the DCN indicate the involvement of the DCN in learning new associations. The net result is an increase of activity in the interposed nuclei that facilitates the formation of a connection between the neutral stimulus (i.e., auditory tone) and the UR (i.e., eye-blink reflex). The observation that lesions to the interposed nuclei abolishes the CR following the CS after success classical conditioning underline the importance of this deep cerebellar region, not only in the acquisition but also in the retention of the association (Thompson, 2005). Figure 3.5 shows a schematic of the cerebellar circuit in classical conditioning.

Even though most researchers agree that both the cerebellar cortex and interposed nuclei are involved in classical conditioning, their functional contributions remain a topic of investigation. According to the memory trace explanation of classic conditioning, the repeated pairings at the pf-Pc level result in the downregulation of synaptic efficacy/long-term depression (LTD) and a subsequent reduction of Pc-related inhibition of the DCN. LTD is brought about by activity of the excitatory synapses between parallel fibers and Purkinje cells that immediately precedes activation of the climbing fibers. The memory trace is then arguably formed through increased excitability of the interposed nuclei that enables strengthening of the mossy-fiber-interposed nuclei connection (Thompson, 2005).

The role of the cerebellar cortex in the timing of CR has been established by lesion studies that found CRs to occur too early following damage of the anterior lobe (lobules I–V). The timing of the CR is expressed in the discharge patterns of the Purkinje cells, and the correct time for eliciting the CR is with a pause in the steady stream of spike activity of the Purkinje cells (Jaeger et al., 2013) interposed nuclei and sets off the CR. Damage to Purkinje cells may

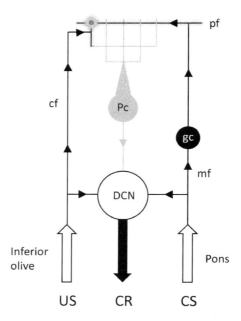

Figure 3.5. A simplified cerebellar circuit of classical conditioning

therefore cause permanent issue in the timing of the CR. It has been proposed that the cerebellar cortex stores the timing information, whereas the interposed nuclei are the sites where the memory of the learned association is stored. The latter is evidenced by studies that showed long-term memories of a learned association are 'erased' when the interposed nuclei are lesioned (Jaeger et al., 2013).

The dependent variable used in contextual or cued fear conditioning is a freezing response or other anxiety-related reaction, like heart rate slowing, that occurs in rats following pairing of an unconditioned (aversive) stimulus (US), such as foot shock or air puff, with a conditioned stimulus (CS). Contextual fear conditioning involves placing an animal or human in a novel environment, providing an aversive stimulus, and then removing the subject from this environment. When the animal or human is then reintroduced to the same environment, if they remember the association between this environment and the aversive stimulus, rats will demonstrate freezing behavior while humans will show an anxiety-related response, like heart rate slowing, Cued fear conditioning works along similar lines but involves the pairing of an acoustic stimulus with an aversive stimulus.

The nature of associative learning is assumed to consist of a modification of synaptic strength associated with long-term potentiation (LTP) or long-term depression (LTD) of excitatory or inhibitory synapses (Strata, 2015). Whereas the classic studies by David Marr (1969) and James Albus (1971) showed that associative learning involves LTD in the parallel fiber to Purkinje cell synapses during the simultaneous activation of climbing fibers, these in vitro studies indicated that LTP can be induced in the pf-Pc synapse by solely stimulating the parallel fibers (pf) (Strata, 2015).

A series of investigations examined the cerebellar mechanisms of acoustic (cued) and context fear conditioning paradigm in rats (Strata, 2015). At 10 minutes and 24 hours following successful conditioning, LTP of the parallel fiber to Purkinje synapses was observed in cerebellar slices of lobule V and VI. The synapses made by the climbing fibers did not show changes in synaptic strength. Indeed, the observed LTP arguably results from of a joint action of separate parallel fiber channels activated by the conditioned and the unconditioned stimuli (Sacchetti et al., 2004). The architecture of the cerebellar cortex consists of excitatory-inhibitory connections of the parallel fibers directly on Purkinje cells and indirectly via inhibitory interneurons in the molecular layer. So, the contribution and timing of LTP in the excitatory and inhibitory connections to the Purkinje cells are important for understanding the cerebellar mechanics of fear learning (Strata, 2015).

Animal studies have discovered that excitatory LTP provides effective signal detection while the inhibitory LTP ensures that the coincidence detection remains unchanged. This results in a high signal-to-noise ratio and 'stable' neural representation of the fear association (Strata, 2015). LTD as established by Marr and Albus can achieve a similar role in associative learning through inhibitory LTD of the pf-Pc synapse and excitatory LTD at the pf-interneuron synapse or a combination of LTP and LTD at the different synapses. LTP and LTD operate both in a synergistic and homeostatic fashion to control information locally (e.g., pf-Pc synapse) and transynaptically (e.g., Pc-interposed nuclei) in the cerebellar circuit (Mapelli et al., 2015).

It goes without saying that the cerebellum does not operate in isolation. Blocking signals from the basolateral amygdala, for example, prevents the initiation of cerebellar plasticity associated with fear conditioning. In turn, the vermis and fastigial nucleus provides input to basolateral amygdala and hippocampus. The cerebellum, together with the medial cerebellar connections to the brain regions governing autonomic processes, including the hypothalamus, PAG, and ventral tegmental area, are part of neural fear learning circuit. In particular, the cerebellum is proposed to support the acquisition and guiding of adequate physiological, emotional, and motoric responses across different relevant situations. As we saw in the previous paragraph, fear conditioning involves LTD and LTP-like processes in parallel fibers to Purkinje cells that have been found to take in lobules V–VI of the vermis (Sacchetti et al., 2004). Synaptic plasticity in these vermal areas is assumed to be involved in associative emotional memory formation (Gao et al., 2012), and lesions to these lobules cause disruptions in the acquisition and retention of fear learning and memories in animals.

Regional mapping studies

Despite most studies being performed in rabbits, there is good evidence that the results are transferable to other mammalian species. Cerebellar lesion studies have demonstrated that in humans the cerebellum plays an important role in the acquisition of classically conditioned eye-blink responses (CR). In one of the more recent studies, a group of young adults with chronic surgical lesions resulting from resection of benign tumors in the cerebellum was compared to a group of matched control subjects on a standard classical eye-blink conditioning test (Ernst et al., 2016). Structural 3T MRI scans were acquired and lesion-symptom mapping was performed on the cerebellar subjects. In agreement with previous work, CR acquisition was significantly impaired in cerebellar subjects. Results showed that reductions in CR acquisition were associated with lesions in lobule VI and Crus I. Subjects with lesions outside these critical areas demonstrated normal CR acquisition. Notably, the neuroimaging studies discussed earlier demonstrated a specific role for lobule VI and Crus I in processes associated with arousal and (pre-attentive) emotional appraisal that may well form the basis of conditioning and learning.

As noted earlier, classical conditioning is the process by which an initial neutral stimulus becomes predictive for an upcoming salient event. This event could either be positive like food, or negative such as a noxious air puff to the eye. Research has shown that classical conditioning is particularly facilitated when the upcoming event is related to threat (Öhman, 1986). This phenomenon is called 'biological preparedness' and illustrates the innate harm avoidance tendency, a cardinal feature of our mammalian evolutionary heritage representing the successful development of defense systems to deal with dangers (Öhman & Mineka, 2001). The emotion fear takes a central position within these survival dedicated fight-flight systems (LeDoux, 2012).

The relation between fear and stimulus-response contingencies was eloquently articulated by Swedish psychologist Arne Öhman:

> ...a predator may announce its presence by faint sounds or odors. By using the contingency between such cues and the potentially deadly consequence, the central motive state of fear could be conditioned to the cue, which would promote further flexibility in the relationships between stimulus and response. Viewed from the evolutionary perspective, fear is central to mammalian evolution. As a product of natural selection, it is shaped and constrained by evolutionary contingencies (Öhman & Mineka, 2001, p. 483).

The search for the functional neuro-anatomical basis of fear conditioning has revealed a central role for the amygdala. Albeit the widespread idea that the amygdala is the brain's fear module is not accurate, the almond shaped collection of nuclei located in the medial temporal cortex is nonetheless directly implicated in associative conditioning.

Evidence for amygdala activity during fear conditioning in humans was first provided in a PET study with healthy volunteers (Morris et al., 1999). Healthy volunteers were presented with pictures of two angry and two neutral facial expressions. One of the angry faces was paired with a one second aversive (100 dB) white noise burst and served as a CS+ (i.e., threat). The second angry face was not paired with an aversive stimulus and served as a CS- (i.e., safe). Following the acquisition phase, participants viewed pairs of faces. In one condition ('unseen'), the 30 ms presentation of the angry face was immediately followed a 45 ms presentation of a neutral face to mask the angry face. In the second ('seen') condition, a 30 ms presentation of the neutral face preceded the 45 ms presentation of the angry face. As expected, the contrast in brain activity between CS+ and CS- revealed significant increased amygdala activity to the CS + in both the 'unseen' and 'seen' conditions (Morris et al., 1999). This finding demonstrates a relation between fear conditioning and the amygdala as part of the brain's survival system. In addition, activity was also observed in the right cerebellum, which covaried with amygdala activity during both 'unseen.'

Transcranial direct current stimulation (tDCS) is a non-invasive technique that can be used to study the human cerebellar cortex by applying weak electric currents (Oldrati & Schutter, 2018). To establish a direct relation between the right posterior cerebellum and conditioning right-sided cerebellar, tDCS was administered during a standard delay eye-blink conditioning paradigm with a tone as

56 Disorders of fear and anxiety

conditioned stimulus (CS) and an air puff as unconditioned stimulus to the right eye (US) in 30 healthy volunteers (Zuchowski et al., 2014). Anodal tDCS significantly facilitated CR acquisition, while cathodal stimulation impaired CR acquisition as compared to sham (control) stimulation.

It has been suggested that anodal and cathodal tDCS directly modulates the baseline simple spike firing frequency of Purkinje cells through subthreshold depolarization and hyperpolarization, respectively. It should, however, be mentioned that these polarity dependent effects represent a highly simplified interpretation, and the precise mechanisms of action of cerebellar tDCS are currently not known. Electric field modelling studies on realistic anatomical head models show that lobules VI–VIII including Crus I and II of the posterior lobes can be targeted with tDCS (Grimaldi et al., 2016). As can be seen from Figure 3.6, estimation of the electric field distribution of the tDCS applied by Zuchowki et al. (2014) revealed a maximum field strength in right Crus II.

Contributions of Crus II has been noted in an fMRI study where visual conditioned stimuli (CS(+)) were paired with painful stimuli as the unconditioned stimuli (US), while other visual stimuli (CS(-)) were presented without US during aversive fear conditioning (Kattoor et al., 2014). These results add to the idea that the posterolateral hemispheres, including Crus I and lobule IV, contribute to associative learning processes involving aversive stimuli.

To establish the common functional cerebellar activation patterns of fear learning in humans, a meta-analysis was performed on 21 fMRI studies that reported activation of the cerebellum during fear conditioning (Lange et al., 2015). Results revealed six cerebellar clusters in fear conditioning consisting of

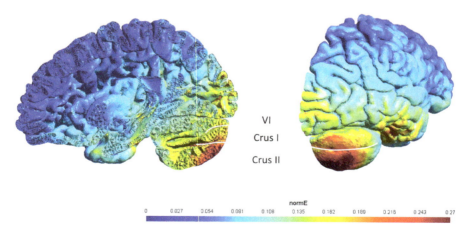

Figure 3.6. Electrical field intensities for dual electrode montage targeting the right cerebellar hemisphere using SimNIBS computational modelling software (Opitz et al., 2015). The target electrode (5x7 cm) was centered 3 cm lateral to the inion in a vertical position, and the return electrode (5 x7 cm) was placed on the ipsilateral buccinator muscle

the culmen (vermian lobule III), bilateral lobule IV–V, left lobule VI, and bilateral lobule IX (cerebellar tonsils). Lobule VI is linked to the learning rates and may play a role in the integration of valence, prediction and timing/coincidence of sensory, and motor signals processed in lobules IV–V.

The efferent connections of the anterior vermis, including the culmen, to the limbic system support the monitoring and regulation of fear conditioning-related autonomic activity, memory formation, and behavioral responses. On the generic level, the cerebellum is important for predictive control and temporal processing of emotional (relevant) information processing streams involved in associative learning from simply linking cause with effect to the formation of abstract hypothetical ('what if') scenarios. While the process of fear learning serves as a model for the development and maintenance of anxiety disorders, 'unlearning' associations is another aspect that is critical for understanding anxiety disorders. Interestingly, the meta-analysis identified lobule IX as a cerebellar region relevant for fear-related processing, which has been found to be important for extinction learning and reinstatement (Kattoor et al., 2014).

Extinction

But what about 'unlearning' formed associations? The extinction refers to the disappearance of the CR (e.g., eye-blink) when the CS (e.g., auditory tone) is no longer followed by a US (e.g., air puff). In other words, the CS stops being a predictive signal, and since the signal is not informative anymore, the organism will cease to produce a CR. It is important to note, that extinction is not the same as simply deleting bits of information or erasing a memory trace. When the CS-US pairing is re-introduced, the organism in fact needs fewer trials to reinstate the CR again. The inferior olive is considered among the key areas involved in extinction. In the rabbit brain, the CR goes accompanied by activity of the interposed nuclei. The interposed nuclei send inhibitory signals to the inferior olive. The reduction of inferior olive excitability, in turn, dampens climbing fiber (cf) activity. It is the silencing of the cf-pathway that is necessary for extinction to occur and, at the same time, indicates that both the cerebellar cortex and interposed nuclei are involved. Interestingly, lesioning the cerebellar cortex after acquisition not only interferes with timing, as mentioned earlier, but will also prevent extinction. The cerebellar processes underlying extinction in fear conditioning are proposed to play a significant role in understanding the neurobiological basis of stress-related disorders and their treatments.

Closely related to extinction is habituation or desensitization, which is a form of non-associative learning in which an unconditioned response (e.g., fear) to a stimulus decreases after repeated or prolonged exposure to this stimulus. This is the case for stimuli that neither have rewarding nor punishing consequences. A difference between habituation and extinction is that habituation occurs in the presence of the stimulus, while extinction happens in the absence of the stimulus. So essentially, an organism learns both on the implicit

58 Disorders of fear and anxiety

(reflexive) as well as explicit (conscious) level to differentiate between relevant and irrelevant information based on cause and effect. This difference explains why greater resistance to extinction following acquisition occurs where responses are only reinforced at certain intervals or ratio of time, instead of reinforcing the behavior every single time (i.e., partial reinforcement).

According to extinction theory, anxiety-related disorders are learned and can thus be unlearned as well. So, disconfirmation of anticipatory outcomes and learning that stimulus exposure does not have any negative consequences are important aspects of successful therapy. In principle, it should therefore also be possible to 'rewire' the association and couple the conditioned stimulus to a positive (reward) consequence. However, since the survival of an organism critically depends on being responsive to (potential) threat-related stimuli, it is important to note that extinction is not the same as forgetting by erasing the association. This means that while physiological and behavioral reactivity can be downregulated, there is always a heightened probability that this sleeper association is reinstated when the stimulus is reinforced again. This form of synaptic hyperplasticity complicates the treatment of anxiety disorders.

Finally, it should also be noted that while fear and anxiety are often used interchangeably, fear is a reaction to a specific, observable (proximate) danger, while anxiety is kind of an abstraction of fear that transcends to a diffuse, objectless, future-oriented (distal) threat. Neuroanatomically, fear finds its origin at the subcortical level, while anxiety also involves active contributions of the cognitive systems located in the cerebral cortex, the latter being responsible for rumination and worrying (Shin & Liberzon, 2010).

The idea that the formation of associations and non-associations based on interoceptive and exteroceptive information to generate an internal model concurs with the traditional role of the cerebellum in prediction and minimizing uncertainty. As such, the ability to differentiate between meaningful and meaningless information adds to the experience of perceived control (Ernst et al., 2019). Neuroimaging research has shown that extinction (i.e., when the CS is no longer presented with the US) involves activation of the vermis and posterior lobules, including Crus I, Crus II, IV, VI, VIIb, and IX (Kattoor et al., 2014). Interestingly, reinstating the CS-US association revealed activation in Crus I, Crus II, IV, V, and IX. The findings suggest that the cerebellum moderates the strength of learning and memorizing associations. Cerebellar signals related to the visual CS from signals related to the subsequent US (i.e., electric shock) in healthy volunteers revealed activation of cerebellar lobules Crus I and VI associated with CS+ (visual signal -> shock) compared to the CS (visual signal -> no shock) (Ernst et al., 2019). Activation of Crus I and VI disappeared during extinction when US omission became expected and provides evidence that these regions are involved in the encoding and/or processing of prediction errors, that is detecting a discrepancy between anticipated (feedforward) and actual (feedback) outcome (Ernst et al., 2019).

These findings also concur with the hypothesis that the cerebellar cortex is part of an online trace-link system (cf. Murre et al., 1996) that links and facilitates the

Disorders of fear and anxiety 59

storage of an association (trace) in the deep cerebellar interposed nuclei during extinction. The re-activation of previous learned associations following extinction may thus involve upregulation of these sleeper associations stored in the deep cerebellar nuclei following renewed cerebellar cortical input. The importance of the deep cerebellar nuclei in extinction-related processes is further evidenced by previous research showing that inactivation of the anterior part of the interposed nuclei in rabbits with the GABA-agonist muscimol prevents weakening of classically conditioned nictitating membrane responses (Ramnani et al., 1996).

In a more recent experiment, inactivation of the interposed nuclei during extinction was shown not to necessarily prevent extinction of conditioned eye-blink responses. In contrast to the former study, this study used an unpaired extinction procedure that consisted both of a series of unpaired presentations of a tone (CS) (pseudo)randomly interspersed with single presentations of a reduced intensity electric shock (US) (Burhaus et al., 2019). According to the researchers, the presence of the US throughout the unpaired extinction procedure may have bypassed the interposed nuclei and recruited other cerebellar of extra-cerebellar components (Burhaus et al., 2019). This explanation makes sense if one views the response weakening in this procedure as representing habituation rather than extinction-related processes. If extinction taps into the higher emotional and cognitive systems of the brain, then, in addition to the interposed nuclei, the dentate nucleus with its projections to the cerebral cortex will turn out to play a significant role in extinction as well.

These results point towards a distributed plasticity view of cerebellar learning. This idea has its origins in previous animal studies that discovered different sites for specific aversive classical and non-specific fear conditioning (Timmann et al., 1998). These double-dissociation studies showed that lesioning parts of the medial cerebellum prevents long-term startle reflex habituation and heart rate conditioning, but leaves eye-blink conditioning intact, while damage to the lateral parts of the cerebellum impair eye-blink conditioning, but has no noticeable effect on heart rate conditioning (Timmann et al., 1998). These observations suggest that depending on the sensory modality and type of learning, different cerebellar regions and cellular mechanisms are at work during acquisition and extinction of associations.

Conclusion

At least part of the mechanisms underlying pathological forms of anxiety involves impairments in fear learning and extinction. A meta-analysis of 44 studies showed increased fear responses to conditioned safety cues (CS-) in patients (n = 963) versus controls (n = 1,222) (Duits et al., 2015). Deficits in one's ability to differentiate between safe (CS-) and threat cues (CS+) stands in the way of forming internal prediction models to guide situation-appropriate behavior. As a result, the individual enters a continuous hypervigilant state in which everything becomes potentially dangerous. Furthermore, anxiety patients showed delayed and even incomplete fear extinction (Duits et al., 2015). In addition to proposed abnormalities of the fronto-

60 Disorders of fear and anxiety

amygdala circuit (Chauret et al., 2019), these behavioral results can be framed within a cerebellar theory of associative learning involving impairments on the cerebellar cortical level during acquisition and deficits of the deep cerebellar nuclei during extinction. On the systems' level, abnormal cerebellar activation patterns and disturbances in the functional coupling of the cerebellum to and from the amygdala, hippocampus, and prefrontal cortex may further destabilize the brain, and the adaptive value of fear and anxiety eventually goes awry.

References

Albus JS (1971). A theory of cerebellar function. *Math Biosci.* 10, 25–61.

Allen MT, Handy JD, Miller DP, Servatius RJ (2019). Avoidance learning and classical eyeblink conditioning as model systems to explore a learning diathesis model of PTSD. *Neurosci. Biobehav. Rev.* 100, 370–386.

Apps R, Strata P (2015). Neuronal circuits for fear and anxiety- The missing link. *Nat. Rev. Neurosci.* 16, 642–645.

Barahona-Corrêa JB, Camacho M, Castro-Rodrigues P, Costa R, Oliveira-Maia AJ (2015). From thought to action: How the interplay between neuroscience and phenomenology changed our understanding of obsessive-compulsive disorder. *Front. Psychol.* 6, 1798.

Benkelfat C, Bradwejn J, Meyer E, Ellenbogen M, Milot S, GjeddeA, Evans A (1995). Functional neuroanatomy of CCK4-inducedanxiety in normal healthy volunteers. *Am. J. Psychiatry* 152, 1180–1184.

Bonne O, Gilboa A, Louzoun Y, Brandes D, Yona I, Lester H, Barkai G, Freedman N, Chisin R, Shalev AY (2003). Resting regional cerebral perfusion in recent posttraumatic stress disorder. *Biol. Psychiatry* 54, 1077–1086.

Burhans LB, Schreurs BG (2019). Inactivation of the interpositus nucleus during unpaired extinction does not prevent extinction of conditioned eyeblink responses or conditioning-specific reflex modification. *Behav. Neurosci.* 133, 398–413.

Chauret M, Suffren S, Pine DS, Nassim M, Saint-Amour D, Maheu FS (2019). Fear conditioning and extinction in anxious youth, offspring at-risk for anxiety and healthy comparisons: An fMRI study. *Biol. Psychol.* 148, 107744.

Critchley HD, Harrison NA (2013). Visceral influences on brain and behavior. *Neuron* 77, 624–638.

D'Angelo E, Casali, S (2013). Seeking a unified framework for cerebellar function and dysfunction: From circuit operations to cognition. *Front. Neural Circuits* 6, 116.

De Bellis MD, Hooper SR, Chen SD, et al. (2015). Posterior structural brain volumes differ in maltreated youth with and without chronic posttraumatic stress disorder. *Dev. Psychopathol.* 27, 1555–1576.

De Bellis MD, Kuchibhatla M (2006). Cerebellar volumes in pediatric maltreatment-related posttraumatic stress disorder. *Biol. Psychiatry* 60, 697–703.

De Wit SJ, Alonso P, Schweren L, et al. (2014). Multicenter voxel-based morphometry mega-analysis of structural brain scans in obsessive-compulsive disorder. *Am. J. Psychiatry* 171, 340–349.

Drevets WC, Videen TQ, MacLeod AK, Haller JW, Raichle ME (1992). PET images of blood flow changes during anxiety: Correction. *Science* 256, 1696.

Duits P, Cath DC, Lissek S, et al. (2015). Updated meta-analysis of classical fear conditioning in the anxiety disorders. *Depress. Anxiety* 32, 239–253.

Ernst TM, Beyer L, Mueller OM, Göricke S, Ladd ME, Gerwig M, Timmann D (2016). Pronounced reduction of acquisition of conditioned eyeblink responses in young adults with focal cerebellar lesions impedes conclusions on the role of the cerebellum in extinction and savings. *Neuropsychologia* 85, 287–300.

Ernst TM, Brol AE, Gratz M, et al. (2019). The cerebellum is involved in processing of predictions and prediction errors in a fear conditioning paradigm. *Elife* 8, e46831.

Eser D, Leicht G, Lutz J, Wenninger S, Kirsch V, Schüle C, Karch S, Baghai T, Pogarell O, Born C, Rupprecht R, Mulert C (2009). Functional neuroanatomy of CCK-4-induced panic attacks in healthy volunteers. *Hum. Brain Mapp.* 30, 511–522.

Gao Z, van Beugen BJ, De Zeeuw CI (2012). Distributed synergistic plasticity and cerebellar learning. *Nat. Rev. Neurosci.* 13, 619–635.

Gerwig M, Kolb FP, Timmann D (2007). The involvement of the human cerebellum in eyeblink conditioning. *Cerebellum* 6, 38–57.

Giménez M, Pujol J, Ortiz H, Soriano-Mas C, López-Solà M, Farré M, Deus J, Merlo-Pich E, Martín-Santos R. Giménez M, et al. (2012). Altered brain functional connectivity in relation to perception of scrutiny in social anxiety disorder. *Psychiatry Res.* 202, 214–223.

Grimaldi G, Argyropoulos GP, Bastian A, et al. (2016). Cerebellar transcranial direct current stimulation (ctDCS): A novel approach to understanding cerebellar function in health and disease. *Neuroscientist* 22, 83–97.

Holmes SE, Scheinost D, DellaGioia N, et al. (2018). Cerebellar and prefrontal cortical alterations PTSD: Structural and functional evidence. *Chronic Stress*, 2, 10.

Hou JM, Zhao M, Zhang W, Song LH, Wu WJ, Wang J, Zhou DQ, Xie B, He M, Guo JW, Qu W, Li HT (2014). Resting-state functional connectivity abnormalities in patients with obsessive-compulsive disorder and their healthy first-degree relatives. *J. Psychiatry Neurosci.* 39, 304–311.

Hu X, Du M, Chen L, Li L, Zhou M, Zhang L, Liu Q, Lu L, Mreedha K, Huang X, Gong Q (2017). Meta-analytic investigations of common and distinct grey matter alterations in youths and adults with obsessive-compulsive disorder. *Neurosci. Biobehav. Rev.* 78, 91–103.

Jaeger D (2013). Cerebellar nuclei and cerebellar learning. In: Manto M, Schmahmann JD, Rossi F, Gruol DL, Koibuchi N (eds) *Handbook of the cerebellum and cerebellar disorders*. Dordrecht: Springer.

Kattoor J, Thürling M, Gizewski ER, Forsting M, Timmann D, Elsenbruch S (2014). Cerebellar contributions to different phases of visceral aversive extinction learning. *Cerebellum* 13, 1–8.

Ke J, Zhang L, Qi R, et al. (2016). A longitudinal fMRI investigation in acute post-traumatic stress disorder (PTSD). *Acta Radiol.* 57, 1387–1395.

Kolesar TA, Bilevicius E, Wilson AD, Kornelsen J (2019). Systematic review and meta-analyses of neural structural and functional differences in generalized anxiety disorder and healthy controls using magnetic resonance imaging. *NeuroImage Clin.* 24, 102016.

Lange I, Kasanova Z, Goossens L, et al. (2015). The anatomy of fear learning in the cerebellum: A systematic meta-analysis. *Neurosci. Biobehav. Rev.* 59, 83–91.

LeDoux J (1996). *The emotional brain: The mysterious underpinnings of emotional life.* New York: Simon & Schuster.

LeDoux J (2012). Rethinking the emotional brain. *Neuron* 73, 653–676.

62 Disorders of fear and anxiety

Lin CS (2018). Meta-analysis of brain mechanisms of chewing and clenching movements. *J. Oral Rehabil.* 45, 627–639.

Linden DJ (2003). From molecules to memory in the cerebellum. *Science* 301, 1682–1685.

Makovac E, Fagioli S, Watson DR, Meeten F, Smallwood J, Critchley HD, Ottaviani C (2019). Response time as a proxy of ongoing mental state: A combined fMRI and pupillometry study in generalized anxiety disorder. *NeuroImage* 191, 380–391.

Mapelli L, Pagani M, Garrido JA, D'Angelo E (2015). Integrated plasticity at inhibitory and excitatory synapses in the cerebellar circuit. *Front. Cell. Neurosci.* 9, 169.

Marr D (1969). A theory of cerebellar function. *J. Physiol.* 202, 437–470.

Mobbs D, Petrovic P, Marchant JL, Hassabis D, Weiskopf N, Seymour B, Dolan RJ, Frith CD (2007). *When fear is near: Threat imminence elicits prefrontal-periaqueductal gray shifts in humans. Science* 317, 1079–1083.

Moers-Hornikx VM, Vles JS, Lim LW, Ayyildiz M, Kaplan S, Gavilanes AW, Hoogland G, Steinbusch HW, Temel Y (2011). Periaqueductal grey stimulation induced panic-like behaviour is accompanied by deactivation of the deep cerebellar nuclei. *Cerebellum* 10, 61–69.

Monti DA, Tobia A, Stoner M, et al. (2018). Changes in cerebellar functional connectivity and autonomic regulation in cancer patients treated with the Neuro Emotional Technique for traumatic stress symptoms. *J. Cancer Surviv.* 12, 145–153.

Morris JS, Öhman A, Dolan RJ (1999). A subcortical pathway to the right amygdala mediating 'unseen' fear. *Proc. Natl. Acad. Sci. U.S.A.* 96, 1680–1685.

Morris MC, Compas BE, Garber J (2012). Relations among posttraumatic stress disorder, comorbid major depression, and HPA function: A systematic review and meta-analysis. *Clin. Psychol. Rev.* 32, 301–315.

Murre JM (1996). TraceLink: A model of amnesia and consolidation of memory. *Hippocampus* 6, 675–684.

Nakao T, Sanematsu H, Yoshiura T, Togao O, Murayama K, Tomita M, Masuda Y, Kanba S, Nakao T, et al. (2011). fMRI of patients with social anxiety disorder during a social situation task. *Neurosci Res.* 69, 67–72.

Öhman A (1986). Face the beast and fear the face: Animal and social fears as prototypes for evolutionary analyses of emotion. *Psychophysiology* 23, 123–145.

Öhman A, Mineka S (2001). Fears, phobias, and preparedness: Toward an evolved module of fear and fear learning. *Psychol. Rev.* 108, 483–522.

Oldrati V, Schutter DJLG (2018). Targeting the human cerebellum with transcranial direct current stimulation to modulate behavior: A meta-analysis. *Cerebellum* 17, 228–236.

Opitz A, Paulus W, Will S, Antunes A, Thielscher A (2015). Determinants of the electric field during transcranial direct current stimulation. *NeuroImage* 109, 140–150.

Pagliaccio D, Luby JL, Bogdan R, et al. (2014). Stress-system genes and life stress predict cortisol levels and amygdala and hippocampal volumes in children. *Neuropsychopharmacology* 39, 1245–1253.

Pan X, Wang Z, Wu X, Wen SW, Liu A (2018). Salivary cortisol in post-traumatic stress disorder: a systematic review and meta-analysis. *BMC Psychiatry* 18, 324.

Rabellino D, Densmore M, Théberge J, McKinnon MC, Lanius RA (2018). The cerebellum after trauma: Resting-state functional connectivity of the cerebellum in post-traumatic stress disorder and its dissociative subtype. *Hum. Brain Mapp.* 39, 3354–3374.

Ramnani N, Yeo CH (1996). Reversible inactivations of the cerebellum prevent the extinction of conditioned nictitating membrane responses in rabbits. *J. Physiol.* 495, 159–168.

Reiman EM, Fusselman MJ, Fox PT, Raichle ME (1989). Neuroanatomical correlates of anticipatory anxiety. *Science* 243, 1071–1074.

Sacchetti B, Scelfo B, Tempia F, Strata, P (2004). Long-term synaptic changes induced in the cerebellar cortex by fear conditioning. *Neuron* 42, 973–982.

Sánchez MM, Young LJ, Plotsky PM, Insel TR (2000). Distribution of corticosteroid receptors in the rhesus brain: Relative absence of glucocorticoid receptors in the hippocampal formation. *J. Neurosci.* 20, 4657–4668.

Schunck T, Erb G, Mathis A, Gilles C, Namer IJ, Hode Y, Dema-ziere A, Luthringer R, Macher JP (2006). Functional magnetic resonance imaging characterization of CCK-4-induced panic attack and subsequent anticipatory anxiety. *NeuroImage* 31, 1197–1208.

Schutter DJ (2012). The cerebello-hypothalamic-pituitary-adrenal axis dysregulation hypothesis in depressive disorder. *Med. Hypotheses* 79, 779–783.

Schutter DJ (2013). Human cerebellum in motivation and emotion. M Manto, DL Gruol, JD Schmamhann, N Koibuchi, F Rossi (Eds.), *Handbook of the cerebellum and cerebellar disorders*. Dordrecht: Springer, pp. 1771–1782.

Shin LM, Israel Liberzon I (2010). The neurocircuitry of fear, stress, and anxiety disorders. *Neuropsychopharmacology* 35, 169–191.

Stoodley CJ, Schmahmann JD (2010). Evidence for topographic organization in the cerebellum of motor control versus cognitive and affective processing. *Cortex* 46, 831–844.

Strata P (2015). The emotional cerebellum. *Cerebellum* 14, 570–577.

Styliadis C, Ioannides AA, Bamidis PD, Papadelis C (2015). Distinct cerebellar lobules process arousal, valence and their interaction in parallel following a temporal hierarchy. *NeuroImage* 110, 149–161.

Talati A, Pantazatos SP, Schneier FR, Weissman MM, Hirsch J (2013). Gray matter abnormalities in social anxiety disorder: Primary, replication, and specificity studies. *Biol. Psychiatry* 73, 75–84.

Thompson RF (2005). In search of memory traces. *Annu. Rev. Psychol.* 56, 1–23.

Tillfors M, Furmark T, Marteinsdottir I, Fredrikson M (2002). Cerebral blood flow during anticipation of public speaking in social phobia: A PET study. *Biol. Psychiatry* 52, 1113–1119.

Timmann D, Musso C, Kolb FP, et al. (1998). Involvement of the human cerebellum during habituation of the acoustic startle response: a PET study. *J. Neurol. Neurosurg. Psychiatry.* 65, 771–773.

Vaghi MM, Vértes PE, Kitzbichler MG, Apergis-Schoute AM, van der Flier FE, Fineberg NA, Sule A, Zaman R, Voon V, Kundu P, Bullmore ET, Robbins TW (2017). Specific frontostriatal circuits for impaired cognitive flexibility and goal-directed planning in obsessive-compulsive disorder: Evidence from resting-state functional connectivity. *Biol. Psychiatry* 81, 708–717.

Van den Heuvel OA, van Wingen G, Soriano-Mas C, Alonso P, Chamberlain SR, Nakamae T, Denys D, Goudriaan AE, Veltman DJ (2016) . *Brain circuitry of compulsivity Eur. Neuropsychopharmacol.* 26, 810–827.

Warwick JM, Carey P, Jordaan GP, Dupont P, Stein DJ (2008). Resting brain perfusion in social anxiety disorder: a voxel-wise whole brain comparison with healthy control subjects. *Prog. Neuropsychopharmacol. Biol. Psychiatry* 32, 1251–1256.

Westenberg HG, Fineberg N, Denys D (2007). Neurobiology of obsessive compulsive disorder: Serotonin and beyond. *CNS Spectr.* 12, 14–27.

Zuchowski ML, Timmann D, Gerwig M (2014). Acquisition of conditioned eyeblink responses is modulated by cerebellar tDCS. *Brain Stimul.* 7, 525–531.

Chapter 4

The cerebellar basis of mood disorders

Mood disorders are characterized by disturbances in the person's emotional and cognitive states. Mood disorders can be subdivided into bipolar and unipolar disorders. Unipolar disorder is a mental condition characterized by a prolonged state for at least two weeks of depressive mood. Bipolar disorder is a mental condition characterized by moods that cycle between depression and mania.

Unipolar disorder or major depressive disorder is a common condition and a leading cause of disability worldwide. Major depressive disorder is associated with signs and symptoms that include persistent sadness; anxiety; feelings of hopelessness; irritability; feelings of guilt, worthlessness, or helplessness; loss of interest or pleasure in hobbies and activities; fatigue and moving or talking more slowly (i.e., psychomotor retardation); feeling restless; memory problems; difficulties in decision making; early-morning awakening; appetite and/or weight changes; suicide ideation or suicide attempts; and physical pains without a clear physical cause.

Evolutionary biologists have proposed that while low mood signals the individual to retreat and recuperate to restore energy levels following excessive stress of after encountering harmful events, depression can be considered the result of an adaptation that has gone awry, wherein the individual is locked in this state of low mood (Nesse, 2000). The phenomenological phenotype of depressive disorders is heterogenous, indicating that the neurobiological mechanisms contributing to depressive disorder are likely to be diverse as well. Also, the triggers for depression onset can vary greatly. Reactive forms of depression have a clear antecedent, like the loss of a loved one, or being the victim of physical or mental abuse. Endogenous forms of depression do not have a clear set-point, and there appears not to be an extreme stressful event involved as in reactive depression. It has been proposed that endogenous depression is more hardwired in the biological make-up, while reactive depression is caused by external events that exert their destructive influence on the psychological and physical well-being of the person.

In the extension of problems in the fronto-cortical regulatory control systems, hyperactive stress and punishment circuits and underactive reward regions, disbalances in various neurotransmitter systems, including serotonin,

The cerebellar basis of mood disorders 65

noradrenaline and dopamine, have been demonstrated. Even though the biological correlates do not enable us to infer a strong form of causality, the phenomenological and biological disturbances indicate a state characterized by abnormalities in the regulation of bodily homeostasis and endogenous biorhythms. It should therefore not come as a surprise that major depressive disorder warps the sense of time. A meta-analytics study evaluated the results from 16 previous reports on time perception in depression and included data of 433 depressive patients and 485 healthy control subjects. The analysis demonstrated a robust effect showing that people with depression experience the passing of time as more slowly than non-depressed controls (Thönes & Oberfelt, 2015). The results of time warping and the well-documented disturbances in biorhythms hint at problems with internal clocks and timing in depressive disorder.

Bipolar disorder is a common, life-long progressive illness that typically begins in adolescence, with a lifetime prevalence of 1.0 percent in adolescents (Lewinsohn et al., 1995). The illness is characterized by unusual and rather extreme shifts in mood, energy, activity levels, and the ability to carry out day-to-day tasks (https://www.nimh.nih.gov/health/topics/depression/index.shtml). The mood changes range from episodes of extreme elated and energized behavior (manic) to episodes of sadness, low energy, and hopelessness (depression).

Manic depressive disorders can subdivide in Bipolar I and II disorder. Bipolar I disorder is diagnosed when the person has a manic episode that lasts at least seven days, or immediate hospitalization is required due to the severity of the manic symptoms. The depressive episode typically lasts more than two weeks and sometimes showed mixed features of both depression and mania. Bipolar II disorder is defined by a pattern of depressive and hypomanic episodes that do not include the extreme manic symptoms as in Bipolar I disorder.

When a person suffers from numerous periods of depressive and hypomanic symptoms lasting for at least two years, but do not meet the diagnostic requirements for a depressive and hypomanic episode, he or she suffers from cyclothymic disorder. It should be noted that in the case of cyclothymic disorder, the person had an episode in at least one year during childhood. During a hypomanic episode, an individual may feel very good, be highly productive, and function well. The person may not feel that anything is wrong, in contrast to family and friends who notice deviations in the person's typical mood and behaviors.

This lack of awareness indicates faulty reality monitoring and may signal the presence of a psychosis, as will be further addressed in Chapter 5 on schizophrenia. The mental inability to make a distinction between internally generated thoughts and perceptions and sensory information from the external world can occur during manic and depressive phases. Initial symptoms of difficulties in communicating, reduced emotional expression, social withdrawal, suspicion of others, and anxiety can develop into full-blown psychotic symptoms that include incoherent or irrational thoughts and speech, delusions and hallucinations. People who have grandiose delusions may believe they are invincible or have special powers. This type of delusion is common during the manic episode.

Paranoia is a delusion that is more typical during the depressive episode and can includes false ideas of being persecuted or irrational feelings of guilt. Sometimes persons also hallucinate and have sensory experiences that are not real, like hearing voices or seeing things that are not there. Important differences between bipolar disorder and schizophrenia are that in schizophrenia psychosis constitutes a primary feature of the disease and are more severe as compared to bipolar disorder. The onset of a manic followed by a depressive episode is often triggered by stressful events, and unipolar disorder is indicative for discordant biological rhythms and homeostatic dysfunction. Over the last decades, studies on disturbances in the biogenic and catecholamine signaling pathways, the hypothalamic-pituitary-adrenal (HPA) stress axis and cortical executive circuits have been central to understanding the pathophysiology of both bipolar and unipolar disorder (Manji, 2003).

The cerebellar basis of mood disorders

The proposal that the cerebellum is involved in the experience and regulation of mood and emotions was posited more than half a century ago (Anand, 1959). The discovery of intimate afferent and efferent connections to the brainstem and limbic system, including the hypothalamus and amygdala, has provided a neuroanatomical substrate to this theory. One of the first reports to relate the cerebellum to emotional experience involved a patient who reported unpleasant feelings after electrical stimulation of the dentate nucleus and superior peduncle (Nashold & Slaugther, 1969). In line with the suggested role of the cerebellum in mood and behavior is the abundance of serotonergic and noradrenergic inputs to the cerebellum, and their ability to modulate the cerebellar circuitry, and to affect cerebellar learning and control mechanisms (Schweighofer et al., 2004). In fact, there is currently a large body of empirical evidence in support of cerebellar abnormalities on the molecular, structural, and functional level in mood disorders.

Molecular level

Even though the evidence is still limited and heterogenous, several studies have confirmed abnormalities on the molecular level in the cerebellum of patients with unipolar and bipolar disorder. Proton magnetic resonance spectroscopy (MRS) research has provided evidence for global reductions of gamma-aminobutyric acid (GABA) synthesizing proteins in cerebellar tissue of patients diagnosed with mood disorder, and also, as we will see in the next chapter, in patients with schizophrenia (Fatemi et al., 2005).

In this post-mortem study, glutamic acid decarboxylase (GAD) and reelin levels were examined in cerebellar tissue samples that were taking from patients with unipolar disorder (n = 15), bipolar disorder (n = 15) and control subjects (n = 15). GAD is an enzyme responsible for the conversion of excitatory neurotransmitter glutamate to the inhibitory neurotransmitter GABA. GAD is localized to GABAergic interneurons in numerous brain sites, including the cerebellar cortex. Reelin is a protein involved in guiding lamination during embryonic brain development that plays a role in synaptic plasticity in the adult brain. Like GAD, reelin is localized to GABAergic interneurons and found in the granular cell layer of the cerebellum. Results revealed lower levels of GAD proteins in patients with unipolar and bipolar disorder versus controls. Reelin was found to be significantly decreased in bipolar disorder.

As discussed in Chapter 1, the cerebellum contains several GABAergic interneurons located in the cortex and the deep cerebellar nuclei. Purkinje cells are inhibited by stellate and basket cells in the molecular layer of the cerebellar cortex. The same cells have collaterals to the parallel (axonal) fibers of granule cells. Moreover, Golgi cells receive excitatory input from parallel fibers and subsequently suppress granular cell activity, forming an inhibitory feedback loop. As such, deficiencies in GABAergic function in the cerebellum can have far-reaching consequences for the integrity of the finely tuned cerebellar circuits. In addition, GABAergic driven forms of plasticity, like rebound potentiation, may also become impaired. Rebound potentiation is a type of long-term potentiation that takes place at the inhibitory synapses between stellate and Purkinje cells and inhibits Purkinje cell activity (Hirano et al., 2016).

In sum, GABAergic dysregulation of the cerebellum can cause impairments in locomotion (ataxia), learning, endogenous biological rhythms, affective processing, and cognitive functions and can be anticipated. The deviations in reelin levels in bipolar disorder may have neuronal developmental significance. Evidence comes from microscopic examinations of the mouse brain showing that low reelin levels are linked to inverted cortical cell layers (lamina), wrongly positioned neurons, and abnormal orientation of cell bodies and fibers (Goffinet, 1992).

Further support for this idea comes from by another post-mortem study that found an association between reelin and impaired Purkinje cell expression and positioning during development in patients with bipolar disorder (Maloku et al., 2010). In this study, Purkinje neuron density in the Purkinje cell layer was examined in cerebellar tissue of patients with bipolar disorder (n = 23) and 20 controls (n = 20). Next to the anticipated decrease of reelin protein expression in granular, but not Purkinje cells, an average of 20 percent lower cell density was observed for patients with bipolar disorder in comparison with controls. The effect was independent from post-mortem interval, sex, medication use, and duration of illness. The negative effects of reelin on Purkinje cell density were confirmed by subsequent data from mice with a reelin expression insufficiency.

While numerous studies have found *in vivo* chemical abnormalities in the cortico-limbic network of patients, there is yet only marginal evidence for disturbances in the biochemistry of the cerebellum in patients with mood disorders. One line of research comes from work on proton magnetic resonance spectroscopy (MRS) in children aged 9–12-year-old (Cecil et al., 2003). MRS is a neuroimaging technique used to quantitatively assess regional biochemistry and can provide insights into neuron viability, metabolism and quality of cellular membranes. This study investigated possible neurochemical differences in the cerebellar vermis between children with bipolar disorder (n = 9) and healthy children with a genetic predisposition to bipolar disorder (n = 10). Analysis of MRS data showed an 8 percent lower concentrations of N-acetyl aspartate (NAA) and creatine in the vermis of affected children compared to healthy children at risk. NAA is an amino acid derivative, and lower than normal concentrations indicate disturbances in metabolic activity and potential neuronal loss. Creatine plays an important role in energy transfer and equilibrium within cells, as this molecule is utilized as an energy reservoir by buffering adenosine triphosphate (ATP). The deviations in NAA and creatine concentration hint toward altered cerebellar metabolism in the presence of clinical symptoms.

Lower than normal levels of myo-inositol in the cerebellum have also been found in major depressive disorder (Chen et al., 2014). Myo-inositol is a vitamin B-like molecule that is present in glial cells and supports signal regulation of neurons. Eight weeks of SSRI treatment improve depressive symptoms and normalized myo-inositol levels in bilateral cerebellar hemispheres. Furthermore, increased levels of choline, a chemical involved in cellular membrane metabolism, were observed in the right cerebellar cortex.

In a more recent study, MRS was used to examine metabolic changes in the cerebellum associated with post-stroke depression (Zhang et al., 2016). Symptoms severity of 20 depressed patients with an ischemic stroke in the basal ganglia positively correlated to the choline/creatine and choline/NAA ratio in the cerebellar hemisphere contralateral to the lesion. The authors proposed elevated choline levels may relate to cerebellar nerve cell renewal and changes in cellular membrane structure. Speculatively, the increased ratio could reflect a transneural plasticity-based compensation strategy. This implies that the compensation strategy in response to basal ganglia damage includes regions that are critical for reward motivation and seeking behavior (Panksepp, 1998). In other words, more cerebellar compensation with higher levels of depression marks a physiological effort to normalize disrupted brain processes.

In conclusion, the results support deviations from normal in cerebellar cellular architecture and metabolism in mood disorders.

Structural level

Abnormalities of the cerebellar vermis have been repeatedly demonstrated in patients with bipolar disorder. Early preliminary studies using computerized tomography (CT) scans reported reduced volumes of the cerebellar vermis in patients with bipolar disorder as compared to healthy controls (Hamilton et al., 1983; Lippmann et al., 1982; Nasrallah et al., 1981). The presence of

The cerebellar basis of mood disorders 69

confounding factors, such as differences in alcohol use and age between group and limited spatial resolution of CT scans, made the data difficult to interpret. The proposed link between the vermis and bipolar disorder was confirmed by a quantitative 1.5T MRI morphometry analysis in hospitalized bipolar patients (n = 30) and matched controls (n = 16) (DelBello et al., 1999). Specifically, lobules VIII–X of the vermis were significantly smaller in multiple-episode patients as compared to first-episode patients and matched controls. The data suggest that vermal degeneration is initially not part of the underlying causes of bipolar disorder but may start to play a role during the worsening of symptoms.

Consistent with the study from DelBello et al. (1999), a more recent study also did not find differences in the vermis between young patients and healthy controls (Monkul et al., 2008). Yet, an inverse correlation between number of episodes and volumes of lobules VI–VII of the vermis was found in male patients, adding further support for structural and possible progressive neuro-degenerative changes in cerebellar vermis over time.

Notably, a possible confound in the interpretation of patient studies concerns the effects of medication use. Certain types of medication at high dosages have been shown to exert a negative influence over brain volumes (Emsley et al., 2017), hence providing a possible alternative explanation for volumetric changes in the cerebellar vermis. In contrast, there is evidence that in the management of bipolar disorder, the often-prescribed drug lithium has neuroprotective proper-ties and increases cerebellar gray and white matter volumes (Berk et al., 2017; Heidari et al., 2012). According to the latter findings, the therapeutic success of pharmacological agents depends on how well drugs, like lithium, slow-down or perhaps even prevent cerebellar atrophy. In fact, medication use may even obscure subtle but clinically relevant anatomical deviations. In spite of the fact that the observed volumetric reductions may in some cases be confounded by medication use, the findings do support the idea that the vermis is part of a neural circuit that regulates mood.

In a prospective cohort study of people with Bipolar I disorder the effects of disease progression on structural brain abnormalities and neuropsychological functioning were investigated in 20 patients and 21 control subjects (Moorhead et al., 2007). Variations in gray and white matter density were estimated and compared with changes in cognitive function and clinical status. Results found that patients showed larger decreases in hippocampal and parahippocampal gray matter densities, as well as significant reductions in cerebellar gray matter over four years. Furthermore, the gray matter density reductions were correlated to worsening of cognitive function and illness. In contrast to changes in gray matter, white matter densities were spared and did not differ between patients and controls.

The observation that the gray matter decline is correlated to worsening of cognitive functioning and illness course fits prior indication of cerebellar vermal volume reductions. However, a number of other studies failed to demonstrate vermal volumetric reductions, and even found evidence for enlarged vermal volumes in bipolar patients in comparison to controls (Moorhead et al., 2007;

Adler et al., 2007). Whether medication can account for the increases in density remains undetermined.

Additional support for smaller cerebellar volumes in patients with bipolar disorder was more recently provided by a voxel-based morphometry study (Eker et al., 2014). Structural brain scans were obtained and analyzed of 28 euthymic patients with bipolar disorder and their healthy siblings and compared to 30 matched healthy non-relatives. Gray matter analysis revealed that the left orbitofrontal cortex of patients with bipolar disorder and healthy siblings was smaller as compared to healthy controls. Furthermore, the left dorsolateral prefrontal cortex was found to be larger in healthy siblings than in patients and healthy non-relatives. Finally, exploratory region-of-interest (ROI) analyses revealed abnormalities of the right cerebellar hemisphere of both patients and healthy siblings in comparison to healthy non-relatives.

As articulated by the authors, the volume reductions in the orbitofrontal regions may point towards a disruption in the automatic regulation of emotions. The left dorsolateral prefrontal cortex is involved in voluntary emotion regulation, and the larger volumes in healthy siblings may reflect a neural compensation/protection mechanism (Eker et al., 2014). As for the cerebellum, right-sided volumetric reductions in Crus II were observed in patients as compared to healthy non-relatives (Figure 4.1). Crus II is involved in higher mental cognitive functions through its projections to the dorsolateral prefrontal and

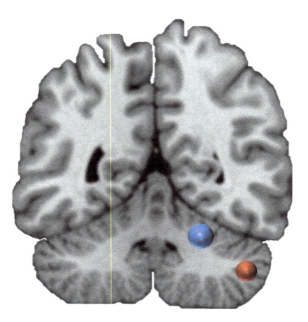

Figure 4.1. Significant differences in Crus II volume between patients and non-relative controls (in red) and between healthy siblings and non-relatives (in blue)

may point at issues in emotion regulation capacities. The contrast between healthy siblings and healthy non-relatives revealed volumetric reductions of lobules V–VI in healthy siblings (Figure 4.1). Interestingly, the latter volumetric difference may hint at a possible cerebellar predisposition to mood disorders.

Lobule V–VI are implicated in sensorimotor functions and emotional appraisal, but how the morphological difference translates to the function and behavior remains to be determined, but the cerebellar abnormalities contralateral to the cerebral cortical differences concur with the crossed cerebello-cerebral cortical connections (cf. Chapter 1 on neuro-anatomy) and the proposed role of the cerebellum in implicit emotion processing (medial cerebellum) and automatic emotion regulation (posterior cerebellum) (cf. Chapter 2 on emotions).

In a recent study, independent datasets containing different brain lesions and measures of depressive disorder (n = 461) were combined and voxel lesion symptom mapping was applied to isolate associations between lesion site and depressive symptoms (Padmanabhan et al., 2019). In addition, large connectome data comprised of resting state fMRI of 1,000 healthy volunteers were used to create lesion networks maps and search for links between depression and connected brain regions. Results showed large heterogeneity and that no single brain could be isolated to explain depression. Even though the lesion map study did not reveal a specific brain region, the researcher did find a common circuit that involved the left and right dorsolateral prefrontal cortex, left lateral occipital cortex, and right cerebellum.

These results may have implications for clarifying the neuro-anatomic basis for depression and treating depressive disorder not caused by a single isolated regional brain dysfunction (Padmanabhan et al., 2019). The findings may explain the efficacy of transcranial magnetic stimulation (TMS) treatment to the frontal cortex in the treatment of depressive disorder (Schutter, 2009, 2010) by stimulating a circuit that in addition to the cortical region, involves subcortical regions. Interestingly, the data provide further support for the proposed anti-depressant properties of non-invasive neuromodulation techniques targeting the cerebellum (Schutter & van Honk, 2005). However, a limitation is that the study did not consider compensatory network adaptations that sometimes occur after brain damage. Unrelated pre- and post-lesion factors including comorbidity of other disorders, psychosocial status and genetic make-up could also play a significant role in postlesion depression (Padmanabhan et al., 2019). Nonetheless, the cerebellar involvement in the lesion-based depression circuit is notable.

Next to deviations in gray matter volumes, deficiencies in white matter have also been reported in the cerebellum of patients with unipolar and bipolar disorders. The deficiencies provide an empirical basis for wiring abnormalities in the cerebellar circuitry and connectivity problems with other brain regions that are associated with mood disorders. In elucidating the presumed brain network dysfunctions associated with major depressive disorder, neural connectivity and

72 The cerebellar basis of mood disorders

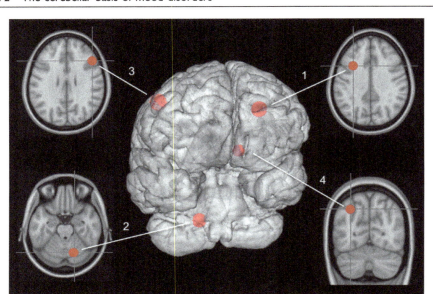

Figure 4.2. Four clusters within the lesion-based circuit associated with depression: (1) the left dorsolateral prefrontal cortex showed the largest peak association value (MNI coordinates: X = -32, Y = 12, Z = 34) followed by (2) the right cerebellum (MNI coordinates: X = 12, Y = -74, Z = -28), (3) right DLPFC (MNI coordinates: X = 48, Y = 24, Z = 28), and (4) left lateral occipital cortex (MNI coordinates: X = -32, Y = -70, Z = 48).

integrity of white matter tracts as indexed by fractional anisotropy (FA) were studied in young patients with treatment resistant major depressive disorder using diffusion tensor imaging (DTI) (Peng et al., 2013). DTI is a technique that detects the diffusion of water molecules along axonal fibers to examine the orientation and integrity of white matter tracts. Voxel-based analysis of the DTI scans showed significant decreases in the left middle frontal gyrus, left anterior extremity of the parahippocampal gyrus (uncus), and right cerebellum posterior lobe (Crus I). Furthermore, the three regional FA values correlated with depression severity and pointed towards deviations in cerebello-cortico-limbic connections in young adults with treatment resistant depression (Peng et al., 2013).

Lastly, the earlier discussed post-stroke depression study that found associations between heightened choline levels and depression severity, also looked at morphological changes in the cerebellum (Zhang et al., 2016). Analysis of the structural 3T MRI data demonstrated an inverse relation between cerebellar volumes and depression scores in patients suffering from post-stroke depression. The 1.5T DTI scans revealed reduced FA values in the cerebellum contralateral to the lesion location in the patient group with post-stroke depression as compared to patients without depression and healthy controls. The FA values of the patient group without depression and healthy controls did not differ.

Complementing the biochemical aberrations, morphological alterations are also found in the cerebellum of patients with post-stroke depression. Even though it can be concluded that this study found a link between cerebellar alterations and depression, interpretation of the results remains speculative at this point. Finally, abnormalities in cerebellar white matter microstructure in depressive disorder have recently been confirmed in a longitudinal study that examined data of nearly 19,000 subjects (Shen et al., 2019). Stable depressive symptoms including self-reported neuroticism assessed over a period of 6–10 years were associated with lower microstructural white matter integrity of projection fibers in the brain, and most prominently in the middle cerebellar peduncle. The meta-analytic results fit the idea of cerebello-extracerebellar misconnectivity in disrupted stress regulation circuits.

Functional level

Disease specific increases of resting state cerebellar activity have been observed in unipolar disorder (Fitzgerald et al., 2008; Guo et al., 2013b; Wang et al., 2014) and in women with premenstrual syndrome depressive disorder (Rapkin et al., 2011). In contrast, a meta-analysis provided evidence for decreases in cerebellar activity during reward processing in patients diagnosed with unipolar disorder (Zhang et al., 2013). The latter finding concurs with previous meta-analytic finding of abnormal cerebellar responses to emotional relevant information in unipolar disorder (Fitzgerald et al., 2008). Preliminary findings from a longitudinal study in older patients suggest that increased or decreased resting state cerebellar activity in unipolar disorder depends on whether patients are male or female, respectively (Dotson et al., 2009).

A number of studies have found reductions of local signal synchronization in the cerebellum of patients with unipolar and bipolar disorder (Liang et al., 2013; Liu et al., 2013). Interestingly, reduced local cerebellar signal synchronization has been shown to in particular differentiate between treatment resistance and treatment sensitivity in patients with unipolar disorder (Guo et al., 2013a). The decrease in local cerebellar signal synchronization in unipolar disorder are in line with diffusion tensor imaging findings showing abnormal white matter integrity and neural connectivity in the cerebellum of young treatment resistant patients with unipolar disorder (Peng et al., 2013). In fact, increases in local signal synchronization in the cerebellum have been linked to clinical improvement following antidepressant treatment (Wang et al., 2014).

On the network level, abnormalities in cerebellar functional connectivity to limbic and cortical regions is a reliable observation in patients with unipolar

74 The cerebellar basis of mood disorders

disorder (Gardner et al., 2014; Guo et al., 2015; Ma et al., 2013; Liu et al., 2012). In particular, abnormal cerebellar-cerebral resting-state functional connectivity has been found to discriminate depressive patients from healthy controls (Arnold et al., 2012). Both increased and decreased functional coupling of the cerebellum with the brain's cortical default mode network has been observed in unipolar disorder (Ma et al., 2013; Liu et al., 2012). Finally, a recent study showing functional decoupling of the cerebellum with the caudate nucleus lends further support for the proposed disturbances in cerebello-cortico-limbic circuits related to mood disorders (Gardner et al., 2014). Evidence from a number of studies indicates that abnormal cerebellar functional connectivity to the amygdala and hypothalamus normalizes following successful antidepressant treatment (Arnold et al., 2012; Yang et al., 2014). Table 4.1 provides an overview of the results showing cerebellar abnormalities in mood disorder as compared to healthy controls (Adamaszek et al., 2017).

In sum, results from studies on cerebellar biochemistry, morphology, and functional activity support the view of extending the limbic-cortical-striatal-thalamic network to include the cerebellum in the pathophysiology of unipolar and bipolar disorder. The functional significance of the cerebellum can be explained by disturbances in the regulation of biological rhythms and visceral signals coupled to internal bodily homeostatic functioning.

Chapter 1 mapped out the transsynaptic connections with the limbic system and anterior regions of the cerebral cortex together with the afferent feedback projections through the pons. This closed-loop circuit provides a neuro-anatomical blueprint foundation for the involvement of the cerebellum in affective experience and regulatory functions. As discussed in the previous section, there is substantial evidence for volumetric cerebellum deviations in patients with mood disorders. Disorders of mood can be conceptualized as the end-product of a progressive worsening of emotional and cognitive states. In line with the diathesis-stress model, the origins of mood disorders can be found in certain personality traits that make the person vulnerable to develop clinical symptoms when confronted with highly stressful events.

Neuroticism is such as personality trait that is typified by the natural tendency to experience negative thoughts and feelings accompanied by avoidant behavior (Eysenk, 1967). Typical of neuroticism is a lowered threshold for experiencing negative emotions to stressors and the long recovery time (McEwen, 1998). The fact that high neurotic individuals express behavioral avoidance and experience negative emotions even in the absence of stressors speaks in favor of neuroticism as a risk factor for mood disorders (Clark et al., 1994).

To test the hypothesis that neuroticism is inversely correlated to cerebellar volumes, structural 3T MRI scans and trait depression-anxiety scores of the revised NEO personality inventory were acquired in a sample of 38 non-clinical subjects (Schutter et al., 2012). As predicted, lower cerebellar volume corrected for total brain volume was associated with higher self-reported depressive-anxious personality traits. Differential contributions of gray and

Table 4.1. Selective overview of cerebellar abnormalities found in unipolar (UP) and bipolar (BP) disorder.

Analytic level	Main finding	Reference
Molecular	Abnormal GABA synthesizing proteins in UP and BP	Fatemi et al. (2005), Maloku et al. (2010)
	Disturbances in the metabolite N-acetylaspartate and choline ratio in BP	Cecil et al. (2003)
Structural	Reduced gray matter volumes of vermis in BP	Eker et al. (2014), Milles et al. (2005), Monkul et al. (2008)
	Volumetric reduction of posterior cerebellar vermis in BP	Kim et al. (2013)
	Smaller cerebellar volumes in BP	Baldaçara et al. (2011)
	Progressive gray matter loss in BP	Moorhead et al. (2007)
	Increased gray matter volume in BP	Adler et al. (2007)
	Smaller cerebellar volumes in UP	Frodl et al. (2008), Peng et al. (2011)
	White matter abnormalities in UP and BP	Abe et al. (2010), Mahon et al. (2009)
Functional	Increased resting state activity in UP	Guo et al. (2013), Rapkin et al. (2011), Wang et al. (2014)
	Decreased activity in reward processing	Zhang et al. (2013)
	Increased resting state activity in male patients and decreased resting state activity in female patients with UP	Dotson et al. (2009)
	Reduced local signal synchronization in UP and BP	Liang et al. (2013), Liu et al. (2013)
	Abnormal white matter integrity and neural connectivity in UP	Peng et al. (2013)
	Decreased functional connectivity with cerebral cortex in UP	Ma et al. (2013)
	Increased functional connectivity with cerebral cortex in UP	Liu et al. (2012)
	Decreased functional connectivity with caudate nucleus in UP	Gardner et al. (2014)

GABA: gamma-aminobutyric acid

white matter could not be confirmed. The overall pattern of findings not only fit the clinical observations discussed earlier but may suggest involvement of the cerebellum in the susceptibility to stress and experiencing negative emotions and mood states.

In a subsequent follow-up study, 149 healthy volunteers were included. Gray's behavioral inhibition scale (BIS) was added to test whether the earlier observed relation between the cerebellum and neuroticism would also be reflected in higher punishment sensitivity and behavioral avoidance. In addition to replicating the relation between cerebellar volumes and neuroticism, the BIS score was also found to inversely correlate to cerebellar volumes. In contrast to the previous study, this study was able to show differential contributions of gray and white matter. More specifically, reductions in gray matter reductions were responsible for the observed associations and fit reports of reduced cerebellar activity and smaller gray matter volumes in healthy volunteers with high levels of harm avoidance (O'Gorman et al., 2006). Harm avoidance is part of the neurotic personality style and correlates high with punishment sensitivity, worrying, lack of initiative, and shyness (Cloninger et al., 1993; De Fruyt et al., 2000).

Findings of both studies are in good agreement with the available clinical work and add to the findings of changes in cerebellar blood flow during negative mood states in non-clinical populations (Schraa-Tam et al., 2012). In understanding the specific regional contributions of the cerebellum in mood states, the vermis and paravermis have been shown to be directly coupled to affective processes in the limbic system. In concordance, fMRI studies have repeatedly demonstrated cerebellar midline activation during the experience of negative emotions (Stoodley & Schmahmann, 2010).

On the other hand, the posterior cerebellar hemispheres and their connections to the prefrontal cortex play a more prominent role in cognitive processes linked to emotion regulation and executive control. Reductions in functional connectivity between the cerebellum and the cerebral cortex, as shown in the patient studies, adhere to the explanation that mood disorders involve cognitive control dysfunction caused by impairments in the cerebello-thalamo-cortical loops. This explanation applies to patients with bipolar disorder and other mental disorders, indicative for a generic role of the cerebellum in the regulation of affective and cognitive processes. Instead of emphasizing the cognitive-oriented cortical interpretation of depression, the next section will discuss the idea that dysregulation of the forebrain's stress-axis results from abnormal reciprocal interactions with the cerebellum.

The cerebello-hypothalamic cross-talk dysregulation hypothesis

The hypothalamus is a vital brain region that regulates biorhythms, controls autonomic and endocrine activity, and regulates the immune system. The hypothalamic-pituitary-adrenal (HPA) axis is one of the four major neuroendocrine systems that controls the central and peripheral effects of stressors. Mood disorders are accompanied by disturbances in biorhythms and abnormal stress-related physiological reactivity, which is indicative of a systemic failure of internal homeostatic functioning (Kalisch et al., 2015). These observations point towards deficiencies in hypothalamic functioning that extends to the HPA-axis. The stress axis is made up of the paraventricular nucleus (PVN) of the hypothalamus that secretes corticotropic releasing hormone (CRH). CRH binds to receptors on cells located in the anterior pituitary gland and stimulate the release of adrenocorticotropic hormone (ACTH) in the bloodstream, the latter stimulating the productions of cortisol in the adrenal cortex. The inhibitory glucocorticoid receptor feedback loop to the anterior pituitary gland and hypothalamus allows for the control of ACTH and cortisol levels. Figure 4.3 illustrates the HPA-axis and its components.

Observations of atypical levels of the steroid hormone cortisol and hyperresponsivity of the central nervous system to stressors (Carpenter & Bunney, 1971; Cowen, 2010) have led to the idea of impaired HPA-axis functioning in

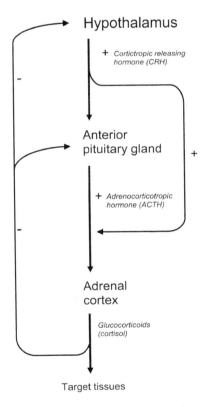

Figure 4.3. Structural and functional organization of the HPA-axis

major depressive disorder. A systematic review and meta-analysis published a few years ago showed that women with major depressive disorder exhibited blunted cortisol stress responses, whereas men with major depressive disorder showed an increased cortisol to psychosocial stress (Zorn et al., 2017). Activation of the HPA-axis is part of the complex physiological response pattern of the brain designed to mobilize the organism to deal with the stressor to restore internal homeostasis. Perhaps, the lower-than-normal responsivity by women and the higher-than-normal responses by men may indicate lack of engagement (cf. freezing) in women and overreacting (cf. fight-flight behavior) in men.

Melancholic and atypical forms of depression are more often associated with disturbed physiological parameters including hyper- and hypoactivation of the HPA axis, respectively (O'Keane et al., 2012). In addition, elevated levels of CRH as a result of increased activity of the PVN of the hypothalamus in patients suffering from depression have been confirmed in clinical studies (Thomson & Craighead, 2008). In sum, these findings show indicate suboptimal stress responses in at least a subset of individuals with major depressive disorder that marks problems in homeostatic regulation.

The monosynaptic projections between the cerebellum and paraventricular nucleus (PVN) of the hypothalamus provide the neuroanatomical and conceptual link between the cerebellum and hypothalamic dysfunction, in particular the HPA axis dysfunction in depressive disorder. Research devoted to studying the anatomical connections between the cerebellum and hypothalamus was initiated following repeated observations of visceral reactions to electric stimulation of the cerebellum (Zhu et al., 2006).

In the mid-80s, Dietrich and colleagues demonstrated both contralateral and ipsilateral projections from lateral, posterior, and dorsal nuclei of the hypothalamus to the cerebellum in the cat brain using retrograde labelling (Dietrichs, 1984). The projections consist of fibers that exclusively target the cerebellar cortex and deep cerebellar nuclei (DCN), and projections that branch and connect to both the cerebellar cortex and DCN. Similar connections were confirmed in various other mammalian species including the monkey brain. The reciprocity of the monosynaptic hypothalamic-cerebellar connection was established by a series of labelling studies demonstrating direct connections between the DCN to the hypothalamus (Haines et al., 1997). Viral tracing studies showed connections that traverse from the fastigial nucleus, nucleus interpositus, and dentate nucleus via the superior cerebellar peduncle to the lateral, posterior, dorsal, and paraventricular nuclei of the hypothalamus. Figure 4.4 depicts the monosynaptic hypothalamo-cerebellar and cerebello-hypothalamic connections.

Moreover, several studies suggest that as a direct result of the anatomical connections, the cerebellum has effects on the somatic-vegetative circuits, including the cardiovascular system, feeding, respiration, and motivation (Zhu et al., 2006). Even though the type of cerebello-hypothalamic projections remains unclear, findings from recent retrograde tracing studies in rats suggest

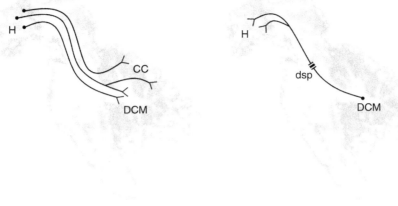

Figure 4.4. Monosynaptic hypothalamo-cerebellar and cerebello-hypothalamic connections CC: cerebellar cortex, DCN: deep cerebellar nuclei, dsp: decussation superior peduncle, H: hypothalamus.

that the cerebello-hypothalamic connections consist of both inhibitory (gamma-aminobutyric acid) and excitatory (glutamate) fibers (Lu et al., 2012; Wang et al., 2011). In addition to the direct coupling between the cerebellum and the stress circuit, immunohistochemistry has revealed dense concentrations of glucocorticoid (cortisol) receptors in the macaque cerebellar cortex (Sánchez et al., 2000). Especially, clusters of intensely immune-stained nuclei were found in the molecular cell layer in the vicinity of the Purkinje cell layer and, sporadically, in the Purkinje cell layer itself. In addition, low concentrations were seen in the rest of the molecular cell layer and very low numbers of immunoreactive cells in the granule cell layer (Sánchez et al., 2002).

Volumetric reductions of brain structures containing high density glucocorticoid receptors including the cerebellum in response to chronic stress have been reported (Pavlik et al., 1984). Indeed, the presence of high concentrations of glucocorticoid receptors in the cerebellum during perinatal cellular proliferation, high cortisol levels associated with, for example, stress can have a detrimental effect on the developing cerebellum (Pavlik et al., 1984). Functional connectivity analyses in healthy volunteers have revealed positive associations of daily cortisol levels with amygdala-centered functional connectivity to the hippocampus and cerebellum, while lowered functional connectivity between the amygdala and the ACC was observed during fearful face processing (Hakamata et al., 2017). The fact that cortisol predicts increases of functional amygdala connectivity with the hippocampus and cerebellum during threat processing suggests that cortisol sensitizes the subcortical stress circuit. In addition to further confirmation of the amygdala and hippocampus as regions implicated in HPA-axis regulation, this research also provides indirect evidence for the current hypothesis that the cerebellum is involved.

Resting state fMRI connectivity analyses revealed that pre-scan cortisol predicted decreased cross-network connectivity in healthy controls and increased cross-network connectivity in young adults with remitted major depressive disorder (rMDD) between the dorsal anterior cingulate, dorsomedial, and lateral prefrontal cortex, brain stem, and cerebellum. Furthermore, the pre-to-post change in cortisol levels was associated with a comparable pattern of findings. In the network analyses, cortisol predominantly predicted enhanced cross-network connectivity to cognitive control network regions, including the cerebellum, in rMDD (Peters et al., 2019). While the absolute cortisol levels did not differ between healthy controls and rMDD volunteers, the differential effects of cortisol on functional connectivity may be related to between-group variation in binding potential of cortisol to steroid responsive brain regions.

Cortisol's precursor CRH is another important central regulator of stress responses. CRF receptors are widely distributed throughout the brain. In addition to the hippocampus, particularly high expressions can be found in the cerebellar cortex and deep cerebellar nuclei (Reul & Holsboer, 2002). CRF is present in the climbing fibers and mossy fibers that constitute the main afferent systems that project to the cerebellar cortex (King et al., 1992). CRF is involved in the induction of long-term depression of Purkinje cell activity mediated by co-activation of climbing and parallel fibers (Miyata et al., 1999). This was shown by blocking LTD induction by introducing specific CRF receptor antagonists and restoring LTD by CRH replacement in the rat cerebellar cortex. The mossy fibre-granule cell relay allows for activation of granule cells whose axons (i.e., parallel fibers) in turn activate Purkinje cells (Eccles et al., 1966) and illustrate how CRF in mossy fibers can contribute to LTD at the parallel fiber-Purkinje cell synapse. The presence of glucocorticoid (GR) and CRF receptors in the cerebellum and direct involvement of CRF in cerebellar neuroplasticity lead to the question of whether glucocorticoids can influence CRF activity in the cerebellum. This question was addressed in a study that evaluated the effects of hormonal expression in the cerebellum, hippocampus, and hypothalamus to corticosterone injections in mice (Harlé et al., 2017).

On a side note, corticosterone is the main adrenal steroid in laboratory rodents, while the closely-related cortisol is the main adrenal steroid in humans (Raff, 2016). Rats and mice do not produce appreciable cortisol, because these animals lack the 17-α hydroxylase enzyme, which is necessary for the biosynthesis of cortisol. After six consecutive days of corticosterone administration, CRH gene transcription was downregulated in the hypothalamus and cerebellum. The hypothalamus showed upregulation of GR receptor gene expression that can be linked to the negative feedback loop of the HPA-axis. The cerebellum demonstrated a comparable upregulation, which can be taken as evidence for taking part in the negative feedback loop of the stress axis. In sum, the direct effects of stress hormones on cerebellar morphology and functionality further establish the role of the cerebellum in mood disorders.

Conclusion

The bidirectional anatomical connections form a reciprocal communication channel between the cerebellum and hypothalamus. Furthermore, the cortisol receptors in the cerebellar cortex yield an additional layer to the negative feedback loop of the HPA-axis, providing a second messenger system by which the cerebellum can interact with the stress circuit (Figure 4.5).

Together with other lines of research that have shown cerebellar abnormalities on the different levels of neural organization discussed in this chapter, cerebello-hypothalamic dysregulation may prove to be an important pathophysiological mechanism of mood disorder (Schutter, 2012).

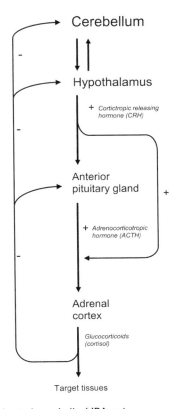

Figure 4.5. Modified hypothetical cerebello-HPA axis

References

Abe O, Yamasue H, Kasai K, et al. (2010). Voxel-based analyses of gray/white matter volume and diffusion tensor data in major depression. *Psychiatry Res.* 181, 64–70.

Adamaszek M, D'Agata F, Ferrucci R, et al. (2017). Consensus paper: Cerebellum and emotion. *Cerebellum* 16, 552–576.

Adler CM, DelBello MP, Jarvis K, Levine A, Adams J, Strakowski SM (2007). Voxel-based study of structural changes in first-episode patients with bipolar disorder. *Biol. Psychiatry* 61, 776–781.

Anand BK, Malhotra CL, Singh B, Dua S (1959). Cerebellar projections to limbic system. *J. Neurophysiol.* 22, 451–457.

Arnold JF, Zwiers MP, Fitzgerald DA, van Eijndhoven P, Becker ES, Rinck M, Fernández G, Speckens AE, Tendolkar I (2012). Fronto-limbic microstructure and structural connectivity in remission from major depression. *Psychiatry Res.* 204, 40–48.

Baldaçara L, Nery-Fernandes F, Rocha M, et al. (2011). Is cerebellar volume related to bipolar disorder? *J. Affect. Disord.* 135, 305–309.

Berk M, Dandash O, Daglas R, et al. (2017). Neuroprotection after a first episode of mania: A randomized controlled maintenance trial comparing the effects of lithium and quetiapine on grey and white matter volume. *Transl. Psychiatry* 7, e1011.

Carpenter Jr WT, Bunney Jr WE (1971). Adrenal cortical activity in depressive illness. *Am. J. Psychiatry* 128, 31–40.

Cecil KM, DelBello MP, Sellars MC, Strakowski SM (2003). Proton magnetic resonance spectroscopy of the frontal lobe and cerebellar vermis in children with a mood disorder and a familial risk for bipolar disorders. *J. Child Adolesc. Psychopharmacol.* 13, 545–555.

Chen HC, Lirng JF, Soong BW, et al. (2014). The merit of proton magnetic resonance spectroscopy in the longitudinal assessment of spinocerebellar ataxias and multiple system atrophy-cerebellar type. *Cerebellum Ataxias* 1, 17.

Clark LA, Watson D, Mineka S (1994). Temperament, personality, and the mood and anxiety disorders. *J. Abnorm. Psychol.* 103, 103–116.

Cloninger CR, Svrakic DM, Przybeck TR (1993) A psychobiological model of temperament and character. *Arch. Gen. Psychiatry* 50, 975–989.

Cowen PJ (2010). Not fade away: The HPA axis and depression. *Psychol. Med.* 40, 1–4.

De Fruyt F, Mervielde I, Hoekstra HA, Rolland JP (2000). Assessing adolescents' personality with the NEO PI-R. *Assessment* 7, 329–345.

DelBello MP, Strakowski SM, Zimmerman ME, Hawkins JM, Sax KW (1999). MRI analysis of the cerebellum in bipolar disorder: A pilot study. *Neuropsychopharmacology* 21, 63–68.

Dietrichs E (1984). Cerebellar autonomic function: Direct hypothalamocerebellar pathway. *Science* 223, 591–593.

Dotson VM, Beason-Held L, Kraut MA, Resnick SM (2009). Longitudinal study of chronic depressive symptoms and regional cerebral blood flow in older men and women. *Int. J. Geriatr. Psychiatry* 24, 809–819.

Eccles JC, Llinás R, Sasaki K (1966). The mossy fibre-granule cell relay of the cerebellum and its inhibitory control by Golgi cells. *Exp. Brain Res.* 1, 82–101.

Eker C, Simsek F, Yılmazer EE, et al. (2014). Brain regions associated with risk and resistance for bipolar I disorder: a voxel-based MRI study of patients with bipolar disorder and their healthy siblings. *Bipolar Disord.* 16, 249–261.

Emsley R, Asmal L, du Plessis S, Chiliza B, Phahladira L, Kilian S (2017). Brain volume changes over the first year of treatment in schizophrenia: relationships to antipsychotic treatment. *Psychol. Med.* 47, 2187–2196.

Eysenck HJ (1967). *The biological basis of personality.* Springfield, IL: Thomas.

Fatemi SH, Stary JM, Earle JA, Araghi-Niknam M, Eagan E (2005). GABAergic dysfunction in schizophrenia and mood disorders as reflected by decreased levels of glutamic acid decarboxylase 65 and 67 kDa and Reelin proteins in cerebellum. *Schizophr. Res.* 72, 109–122.

Fitzgerald PB, Laird AR, Maller J, Daskalakis ZJ (2008). A meta-analytic study of changes in brain activation in depression. *Hum. Brain Mapp.* 29, 683–695.

Frodl TS, Koutsouleris N, Bottlender R, et al. (2008). Depression-related variation in brain morphology over 3 year: Effects of stress? *Arch. Gen. Psychiatry* 65, 1156–1165.

Gardner A, Åstrand D, Öberg J, et al. (2014). Towards mapping the brain connectome in depression: Functional connectivity by perfusion SPECT. *Psychiatry Res.* 223, 171–177.

Goffinet AM (1992). The reeler gene: A clue to brain development and evolution. *Int. J. Dev. Biol.* 36, 101–107.

Guo W, Liu F, Liu J, et al. (2013a). Is there a cerebellar compensatory effort in first-episode, treatment-naive major depressive disorder at rest? *Prog. Neuropsychopharmacol. Biol. Psychiatry* 46, 13–18.

Guo W, Liu F, Xue Z, et al. (2013b). Abnormal resting-state cerebellar-cerebral functional connectivity in treatment-resistant depression and treatment sensitive depression. *Prog. Neuropsychopharmacol. Biol. Psychiatry* 44, 51–57.

Guo W, Liu F, Liu J, et al. (2015). Increased cerebellar-default-mode-network connectivity in drug-naive major depressive disorder at rest. *Medicine (Baltimore)* 94, e560.

Haines DE, Dietrichs E, Mihailoff GA, McDonald EF (1997). The cerebellar-hypothalamic axis: Basic circuits and clinical observations. *Int. Rev. Neurobiol.* 41, 83–107.

Hakamata Y, Komi S, Moriguchi Y, et al. (2017). Amygdala-centred functional connectivity affects daily cortisol concentrations: A putative link with anxiety. *Sci. Rep.* 7, 8313.

Hamilton NG, Frick RB, Takahashi T, Hopping MW (1983). Psychiatric symptoms and cerebellar pathology. *Am. J. Psychiatry* 140, 1322–1326.

Harlé G, Lalonde R, Fonte C, Ropars A, Frippiat JP, Strazielle C (2017). Repeated corticosterone injections in adult mice alter stress hormonal receptor expression in the cerebellum and motor coordination without affecting spatial learning. *Behav. Brain Res.* 326, 121–131.

Heidari Z, Mahmoudzadeh-Sagheb H (2012). Quantitative study of volumetric changes of cerebellum in male adult rat following lithium administration. *Int. J. High Risk. Behav. Addict.* 1, 66–70.

Hirano T, Yamazaki Y, Nakamura Y (2016). LTD, RP, and motor learning. *Cerebellum* 15, 51–53.

Kalisch R, Müller MB, Tüscher O (2015). A conceptual framework for the neurobiological study of resilience. *Behav. Brain Sci.* 38, e92.

Kim D, Cho HB, Dager SR, et al. (2013). Posterior cerebellar vermal deficits in bipolar disorder. *J. Affect. Disord.* 150, 499–506.

King JS, Cummings SL, Bishop GA (1992). Peptides in cerebellar circuits. *Prog. Neurobiol.* 39, 423–442.

Lewinsohn PM, Klein DN, Seeley JR (1995). Bipolar disorders in a community sample of older adolescents: Prevalence, phenomenology, comorbidity, and course. *J. Am. Acad. Child Adolesc. Psychiatry* 34, 454–463.

Liang MJ, Zhou Q, Yang KR, et al. (2013). Identify changes of brain regional homogeneity in bipolar disorder and unipolar depression using resting-state fMRI. *PLoS One* 8, e79999.

Lippmann S, Manshadi M, Baldwin H, Drasin G, Rice J, Alrajeh S (1982). Cerebellar vermis dimensions on computerized tomographic scans of schizophrenic and bipolar patients. *Am. J. Psychiatry* 139, 667–668.

Liu CH, Ma X, Wu X, et al. (2013). Regional homogeneity of resting-state brain abnormalities in bipolar and unipolar depression. *Prog. Neuropsychopharmacol. Biol. Psychiatry* 41, 52–59.

Liu L, Zeng LL, Li Y, Ma Q, Li B, Shen H, Hu D (2012). Altered cerebellar functional connectivity with intrinsic connectivity networks in adults with major depressive disorder. *PLoS One* 7, e39516.

Lu JH, Mao HN, Cao BB, Qiu YH, Peng YP (2012). Effect of cerebellohypothalamic glutamatergic projections on immune function. *Cerebellum* 11, 905–916.

Ma Q, Zeng LL, Shen H, Liu L, Hu D (2013). Altered cerebellar-cerebral resting-state functional connectivity reliably identifies major depressive disorder. *Brain Res.* 1495, 86–94.

Mahon K, Wu J, Malhotra AK, et al. (2009). A voxel-based diffusion tensor imaging study of white matter in bipolar disorder. *Neuropsychopharmacology* 34, 1590–1600.

Maloku E, Covelo IR, Hanbauer I, et al. (2010). Lower number of cerebellar Purkinje neurons in psychosis is associated with reduced reelin expression. *Proc. Natl. Acad. Sci. U.S.A.* 107, 4407–4411.

Manji HK, Quiroz JA, Payne JL, Singh J, Lopes BP, Viegas JS, Zarate CA. (2003). The underlying neurobiology of bipolar disorder. *World Psychiatry*, 2, 136–146.

McEwen BS (1998). Stress, adaptation, and disease. Allostasis and allostatic load. *Ann. N.Y. Acad. Sci.* 840, 33–44.

Miyata M, Okada D, Hashimoto K, Kano M, Ito M (1999). Corticotropin-releasing factor plays a permissive role in cerebellar long-term depression. *Neuron* 22, 763–775.

Monkul ES, Hatch JP, Sassi RB, et al. (2008). MRI study of the cerebellum in young bipolar patients. *Prog. Neuropsychopharmacol. Biol. Psychiatry* 32, 613–619.

Moorhead TW, McKirdy J, Sussmann JE, et al. (2007). Progressive gray matter loss in patients with bipolar disorder. *Biol. Psychiatry.* 62, 894–900.

Nashold BS, Slaughter DG (1969). Effects of stimulating or destroying the deep cerebellar regions in man. *J. Neurosurg.* 31, 172–186.

Nasrallah HA, Jacoby CG, McCalley-Whitters M. (1981). Cerebellar atrophy in schizophrenia and mania. *Lancet* 1, 110.

Nesse RM (2000). Is depression an adaptation? *Arch. Gen. Psychiatry* 57, 14–20.

O'Gorman RL, Kumari V, Williams SC, et al. (2006). Personality factors correlate with regional cerebral perfusion. *Neuroimage* 31, 489–495.

O'Keane V, Frodl T, Dinan TG (2012). A review of atypical depression in relation to the course of depression and changes in HPA axis organization. *Psychoneuroendocrinology* 37, 1589–1599.

Padmanabhan JL, Cooke D, Joutsa J, et al. (2019). A human depression circuit derived from focal brain lesions. *Biol. Psychiatry* 86, 749–758.

Panksepp J. (1998) *Affective neuroscience: The foundations of human and animal emotions.* New York: Oxford University Press.

Pavlík A, Buresová M (1984). The neonatal cerebellum: The highest level of glucocorticoid receptors in the brain. *Brain Res.* 314, 13–20.

Peng HJ, Zheng HR, Ning YP, et al. (2013). Abnormalities of cortical-limbic-cerebellar white matter networks may contribute to treatment-resistant depression: A diffusion tensor imaging study. *BMC Psychiatry* 13, 72.

Peng J, Liu J, Nie B, et al. (2011). Cerebral and cerebellar gray matter reduction in first-episode patients with major depressive disorder: A voxel-based morphometry study. *Eur. J. Radiol.* 80, 395–399.

Peters AT, Jenkins LM, Stange JP, et al. (2019). Pre-scan cortisol is differentially associated with enhanced connectivity to the cognitive control network in young adults with a history of depression. *Psychoneuroendocrinology* 104, 219–227.

Raff H (2016). CORT, Cort, B, corticosterone, and now cortistatin: Enough already! *Endocrinology* 157, 3307–3308.

Rapkin AJ, Berman SM, Mandelkern MA, Silverman DH, Morgan M, London ED (2011). Neuroimaging evidence of cerebellar involvement in premenstrual dysphoric disorder. *Biol Psychiatry* 69, 374–380.

Rapkin AJ, Berman SM, Mandelkern MA, Silverman DH, Morgan M, London ED (2011). Neuroimaging evidence of cerebellar involvement in premenstrual dysphoric disorder. *Biol Psychiatry* 69, 374–380.

Reul JM, Holsboer F (2002). Corticotropin-releasing factor receptors 1 and 2 in anxiety and depression. *Curr. Opin. Pharmacol.* 2, 23–33.

Sánchez MM, Young LJ, Plotsky PM, Insel TR (2000). Distribution of corticosteroid receptors in the rhesus brain: Relative absence of glucocorticoid receptors in the hippocampal formation. *J. Neurosci.* 20, 4657–4668.

Schraa-Tam CK, Rietdijk WJ, Verbeke WJ, et al. (2012). fMRI activities in the emotional cerebellum: A preference for negative stimuli and goal-directed behavior. *Cerebellum* 11, 233–245.

Schutter DJ (2009). Antidepressant efficacy of high-frequency transcranial magnetic stimulation over the left dorsolateral prefrontal cortex in double-blind sham-controlled designs: A meta-analysis. *Psychol. Med.* 39, 65–75.

Schutter DJ (2010). Quantitative review of the efficacy of slow-frequency magnetic brain stimulation in major depressive disorder. *Psychol. Med.* 40, 1789–1795.

Schutter DJ (2012). The cerebello-hypothalamic-pituitary-adrenal axis dysregulation hypothesis in depressive disorder. *Med. Hypotheses* 79, 779–783.

Schutter DJ, Koolschijn PC, Peper JS, Crone EA (2012). The cerebellum link to neuroticism: A volumetric MRI association study in healthy volunteers. *PLoS One* 7, e37252.

Schutter DJ, van Honk J (2005). The cerebellum on the rise in human emotion. *Cerebellum* 4, 290–294.

Schweighofer N, Doya K, Kuroda S (2004). Cerebellar aminergic neuromodulation: Towards a functional understanding. *Brain Res. Rev.* 44, 103–116.

Shen X, Adams MJ, Ritakari TE, Cox SR, McIntosh AM, Whalley HC (2019). White matter microstructure and its relation to longitudinal measures of depressive symptoms in mid- and late life. *Biol. Psychiatry* 86, 759–768.

Stoodley CJ, Schmahmann JD (2010). Evidence for topographic organization in the cerebellum of motor control versus cognitive and affective processing. *Cortex* 46, 831–844.

Thomson F, Craighead M (2008). Innovative approaches for the treatment of depression: targeting the HPA axis. *Neurochem. Res.* 33, 691–707.

Thönes S, Oberfeld D (2015). Time perception in depression: A meta-analysis. *J. Affect. Disord.* 175, 359–372.

Wang F, Cao BB, Liu Y, Huang Y, Peng YP, Qiu YH (2011). Role of cerebellohypothalamic GABAergic projection in mediating cerebellar immunomodulation. *Int. J. Neurosci.* 121, 237–245.

Wang L, Li K, Zhang Q, et al. (2014). Short-term effects of escitalopram on regional brain function in first-episode drug-naive patients with major depressive disorder assessed by resting-state functional magnetic resonance imaging. *Psychol. Med.* 44, 1417–1426.

Yang R, Zhang H, Wu X, et al. (2014). Hypothalamus-anchored resting brain network changes before and after sertraline treatment in major depression. *Biomed. Res. Int.*, 915026.

Zhang L, Sui R, Zhang L, Zhang Z (2016). Morphological and metabolic alteration of cerebellum in patients with post-stroke depression. *Cell Physiol. Biochem.* 40, 420–430.

Zhang WN, Chang SH, Guo LY, Zhang KL, Wang J (2013). The neural correlates of reward-related processing in major depressive disorder: A meta-analysis of functional magnetic resonance imaging studies. *J. Affect. Disord.* 151, 531–539.

Zhu JN, Yung WH, Kwok-Chong ChowB, ChanYS, WangJJ (2006). The cerebellarhypothalamic circuits: Potential pathways underlying cerebellar involvement in somatic–visceral integration. *Brain Res. Rev.* 52, 93–106.

Zorn JV, Schür RR, Boks MP, Kahn RS, Joëls M, Vinkers CH (2017). Cortisol stress reactivity across psychiatric disorders: A systematic review and meta-analysis. *Psychoneuroendocrinology* 77, 25–36.

Chapter 5

Cerebellum and affective dysmetria in schizophrenia

Schizophrenia is a life-disabling chronic brain disorder that affects approximately one percent of the general population. Schizophrenia is derived from the Greek words 'skhízein' (to split) and 'phrén' (mind) and was coined by Euger Bleuler to stress the pervasive disruption of mental processes in these patients (Andreasen, 1999). Schizophrenia literally means 'a mind that is ripped apart' and is thus not about having a split personality or multiple personalities.

The lack of coherence in mental processes is expressed in so-called negative and positive symptoms. Negative symptoms refer to a marked reduction or even absence of 'normal' behaviors. These can include loss of interest in daily life activities, neglect of personal hygiene, social withdrawal, apathy, and lethargy. Positive symptoms are characterized by an excess or distortion of behaviors, like hallucinations and delusions. In addition, individuals with schizophrenia demonstrate severe cognitive and affective disturbances including disorganized thoughts, memory problems, anxiety and depression.

Schizophrenia is typically associated with the presence of positive symptoms that relate to psychosis. Psychosis is a general term for describing abnormal states of the mind that is primarily caused by difficulties in determining what is real and what is not. In other words, hallucinations and delusions result from compromised reality monitoring processes in which the person is not able to make a distinction between external information that reaches the conscious mind through the senses and the internal information processes. For example, according to the 'dream intrusion' hypothesis, visual hallucinations may be caused by activation of the pontine-geniculate-occipital cortex pathway that is involved in the onset of rapid eye movements (REM) and dreaming (Waters et al., 2016). The complexity of the disorder lies in the fact that symptoms can vary considerably between individuals and share commonalities with other mental disorders including anxiety and depression.

On the conceptual level, schizophrenia has been designated as a misconnection syndrome that can be understood as the 'loosening of associations' as indicated by the disorganized neural processing within and between brain circuits (Friston, 1998; Andreasen, 1999). Meta-analyses have confirmed the widespread structural abnormalities of white matter, providing aggregated support for the 'wiring' problems in the brain of schizophrenic patients (Dong et al., 2017). Further evidence for the proposed ineffective and aberrant communication of brain signals was provided by a Chinese research team that evaluated white-matter functional connectivity in a sample of 97 schizophrenia patients and 126 healthy controls (Jiang et al., 2017). Ten large-scale white-matter cortical and subcortical networks were identified by a cluster analysis of voxel-based white-matter functional connectivity. Subsequent analyses showed deviations of functional connectivity in patients as compared to non-schizophrenic controls. In addition, the cerebellum was identified among the regions extensively involved among the affected networks.

In the wake of redefining schizophrenia to be a collection of symptoms, the term cognitive dysmetria was coined to emphasize the importance of the dysfunctional cognitive processes underlying the symptoms. Interestingly, cognitive dysmetria was also used to describe patients that suffered from cerebellar cognitive and affective syndrome (Schmahmann's syndrome) following damage to the cerebellum (Schmahmann, 2000).

Even though in the original writings the term cognitive was used to refer to intellectual as well as emotional aspects of mental activity (Andreasen, 1999), schizophrenia is mainly considered to be a disorder of thought, while the emotional dysfunctions in various neuronal levels are at least as important for understanding the etiology of schizophrenia. This assumption finds merit in neuroimaging studies that have established abnormalities in the subcortical emotion circuits of patients with schizophrenia (e.g., Paradiso et al., 2003), which has led some researchers to propose that deficits in affective functioning are the actual core deficits of schizophrenia (Lane, 2003). From this perspective, schizophrenia can be conceptualized as a schism between the cortical cognitive and subcortical emotion circuits.

The cortico-cerebellar-thalamic-cortical circuit

The cerebellum is well known for its involvement in the timing and coordination of complex and fine-grained motor acts. It does so in close conjunction with the cerebral cortex wherein closed feedback mediated through the pons and feedforward loops that run via the thalamus allows for the fluid sequence of movements. The close interplay between the somatosensory and motor components in this cortico-cerebellar-thalamic-cortical (CCTC) circuit (Figure 5.1) makes up an important part of the brain's perception-action chain. Damage to the cerebellum results in various neurological signs associated with lack of coordination of fine-grained movements as exemplified by typical under- and overshoots of intended positions of the limbs (so-called endpoint errors). The impaired coordination is proposed to stem from deficits in timing and sequencing neural signals. This generic impairment in monitoring and coordination information processing streams, as predicted by the universal cerebellar transform hypothesis, can be applied to understand schizophrenia as a thought disorder. That is, the internal disorganization caused by miscommunication and dissociated cognitive and affective systems within the CCTC circuit results in impairments of thought and behavior, hence the term cognitive dysmetria.

Among the first lines of evidence confirming functional abnormalities of inter-regional connectivity within the CCTC circuit comes from an early study that used fMRI in a sample of 22 patients with schizophrenia and 11 matched controls (Honey et al., 2005). Functional brain scans were made during a continuous performance task to capture the deviating patterns of brain activity associated with attention deficits in the patient group. Results revealed that while both anterior cingulate and cerebellum demonstrated a task-specific correlation to the medial superior frontal gyrus in healthy volunteers, this statistical relationship turned out to be disrupted in schizophrenic patients (Honey et al., 2005).

In a subsequent DTI tractography study the cerebellar white matter architecture of schizophrenic patients was studied in search of a structural neuroanatomical basis for the earlier reported findings (Kanaan et al., 2009). The study confirmed microstructural abnormalities in the cerebellar tracts in

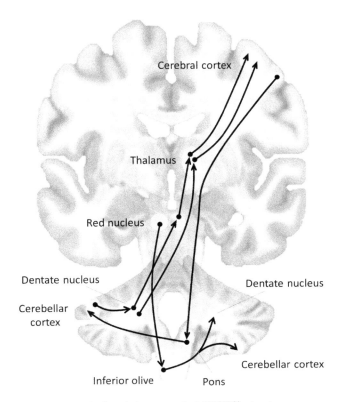

Figure 5.1. The cortico-cerebellar-thalamo-cortical (CCTC) circuit

patients, lending additional support for the cerebellar dysconnectivity theory of schizophrenia. Further analyses showed that deviations were present in all three major cerebellar tracts, indicative for deficits in the afferent (input) and efferent (output) channels of the cerebellum.

In another study, transcranial magnetic stimulation (TMS) was administered over the cerebellum to find deviations in signal transfer from the posterior cerebellar hemisphere to the contralateral motor cortex in schizophrenic patients (Daskalakis et al., 2005). As outlined in Chapter 1, the Purkinje cells in the cortex are the output cells of the cerebellum that send their inhibitory signals to the deep cerebellar nuclei (DCN). This inhibitory drive of the Purkinje cells in the posterior cerebellar hemisphere modulates the excitatory projections of the dentate and interposed nuclei to the motor cortex via the ventrolateral nucleus of the thalamus. Activating the Purkinje cells with a strong but short-lasting electromagnetic pulse applied over the posterior part of the head causes cerebellum mediated inhibition of cortico-spinal excitability. This reduction of corticospinal excitability can be measured by applying a suprathreshold TMS pulse to the motor cortex approximately 5 ms following the TMS pulse to the cerebellum (Figure 5.2). The degree of cerebellar inhibition was found to be significantly lower in schizophrenic patients as compared to healthy controls.

Activation of inhibitory Purkinje cells with TMS reduces the excitatory drive from the deep cerebellar nuclei to the motor cortex via the ventrolateral nucleus

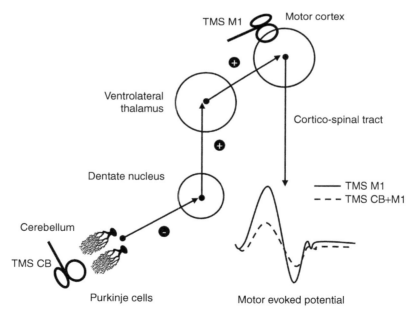

Figure 5.2. Experimental set-up for evaluating the functional integrity of the inhibitory cerebello-cerebro-cortical pathway using transcranial magnetic stimulation (TMS)

of the thalamus. The reduction in excitatory drive is evaluated by a second TMS pulse over the motor cortex that will activate the corticospinal tract and elicit a motor evoked potential in the hand muscle.

Post-mortem studies have found supporting evidence for reduced Purkinje cell densities in patients with schizophrenia (Tran et al., 1998), which provides an explanation for lowered cerebellar-related forward inhibition. In a more recent post-mortem study, no strong evidence was found for reduced Purkinje cell densities, but abnormalities were seen in the dendritic branches of the Purkinje cells in tissue samples of the cerebellar hemisphere from ten schizophrenic and control brains (Mavroudis et al., 2013). Finally, Nopoulos et al. (2001) suggested that decreased Purkinje inhibitory output results in an increased excitatory drive from the fastigial nucleus to mesencephalic dopaminergic neurons, resulting in a hyperdopaminergic state of midbrain, striatal, and limbic regions (Artiges et al., 2017). In particular, amygdala/hippocampus and putamen/pallidum were positively associated with hallucinations and paranoid feelings (Artiges et al., 2017).

Whether the Purkinje cell pathology is specific for schizophrenia remains an open question as morphological analyses have also demonstrated dendritic abnormalities in autosomal spino-cerebellar ataxia patients (Shintaku et al., 2009), chronic alcoholics (Ferrer et al., 1984) and elderly with Alzheimer's disease (Mavroudis et al., 2013). MRS studies have revealed decreased N-acetylaspartate and creatine in the anterior vermis and cerebellar cortex, which points to altered neuronal integrity of neurons, dendrites, and axons (Deicken et al., 2001; Ende et al., 2005). It has been proposed that the neurochemical deviations can be linked to glutamatergic deficits found in the cerebellum of schizophrenic patients. In particular, the NMDA receptor hypofunction and a GABAergic deficit may contribute to disruptions at the molecular and cellular levels, and cause problems in local signal processing and coordination.

Next to the abnormalities on the molecular level, a recent multisite analysis of 983 patients and 1,349 healthy controls established the cerebellum as a critical node in the neurocircuitry of schizophrenia (Moberget et al., 2018). The study was inspired by the heterogenous structural brain imaging reports in the scientific literature of volumetric abnormalities of the cerebellum in patients suffering from schizophrenia. This study examined the across-sample reproducibility, the regional specificity, and the relative effect sizes of the cerebellum as compared to other brain structures, as well as interdependencies between cerebellar and cerebral morphology in understanding the clinical signs and symptoms of schizophrenia (Moberget et al., 2018). Structural MRI data were collected from 14 institutes and analyzed using a standardized procedure.

Results from the meta-analysis showed significantly reduced cerebellar gray matter volumes in schizophrenic patients relative to healthy controls. Voxel-based analyses of cerebellar gray matter volume confirmed that the most pronounced reductions in volumes were located in the posterior cerebellar regions.

Notably, the significant difference in the anterior cerebellar regions observed between patients and controls may provide an account for the neurological soft signs observed in schizophrenia. These soft signs include body sway and eyeblink reflexes. Furthermore, the magnitude of the effect sizes of the cerebellum were comparable to the effect sizes of the most consistently documented cerebral (e.g., frontal cortex) and subcortical (e.g., hippocampus and amygdala) regional abnormalities found in schizophrenia. Finally, the cerebellar gray matter reduction in schizophrenic patients was already observed in young adults and remained fairly consistent across the age range. These results suggest that cerebellar volume reductions have neurodevelopmental rather than neurodegenerative origin (Moberget et al., 2018).

Support that cerebellar abnormalities in schizophrenia may already occur very early in life was found in a post-mortem study that examined the gyrification of the cerebellum of schizophrenic patients (Schmitt et al., 2011). Results showed that gyrification of the vermis was significantly reduced as compared to healthy controls, while no reliable differences were observed in the cerebellar hemispheres. The process of forming the characteristic folds of the cerebellar cortex that allows for a larger surface area to fit within the posterior fossa occurs mainly during the perinatal period (Schmitt et al., 2011). Behavioral symptoms indicative of abnormalities in the early development of the cerebellum and cortical maturation are delays in the infant's motor and language skills, such as smiling, vocalization, laughter, balance, smooth eye pursuit, and moving objects from hand-to-hand.

For understanding the neurodevelopmental trajectory of schizophrenia, genome-wide-association studies (GWAS) have discovered the involvement of complex transcriptional programs that contribute to brain development (Kang et al., 2011). A computer-based gene analysis program and integrated genomic databases were recently used to show that genes for schizophrenia were predominantly expressed in the cerebral cortex, medulla oblongata, thalamus, hypothalamus, and cerebellum (Sundararajan et al., 2018). Interestingly, several genes overlapped with genes found in bipolar disorder, autism spectrum disorder, attention deficit-hyperactivity disorder, and addiction.

In addition to genes that are implicated in the regulation of dopaminergic neurotransmission, the most replicable finding in GWAS studies of schizophrenia was the region on the genome that contains several genes that play a substantial role in the immune system. The discovery of shared genes between autoimmune diseases and schizophrenia adds further support to the inflammation theory (Eaton et al., 2010). In addition, exposure to viral infections has been shown to activate the maternal immune system and increase the risk of schizophrenia and autism (Knuesel et al., 2014). Indeed, infection with human roseoloviruses has been associated with reduced Purkinje cell size as shown in post-mortem brain tissue (Knuesel et al., 2014).

Disturbances in white matter integrity were associated with elevated peripheral interleukins, a group of proteins important for immune responses, in schizophrenia (Fu et al., 2019). As such, it is not unlikely that inflammatory processes contribute to the problems in signal transfer and functional connectivity between brain areas (Okugawa et al., 2005). The issue of dysconnectivity problems in the cortico-cerebellar-thalamic-cortical networks of schizophrenic brains has, similar to studies on major depressive disorder discussed in Chapter 4, been examined by investigating the cross-correlation of vascular activity across brain areas (i.e., a surrogate marker for functional connectivity) with resting state functional magnetic resonance imaging (fMRI).

Recently, a data-driven resting state functional connectivity analysis was used to identify networks associated with anhedonia and amotivation in schizophrenia (Brady et al., 2019). A specific breakdown of functional connectivity in a dorsolateral prefrontal cortex-to-cerebellum network correlated to the severity of these negative symptoms. Follow-up analysis indicated that the reduction in connectivity was strongest between the midline cerebellum and right dorsolateral prefrontal cortex. Next, transcranial magnetic stimulation (TMS) applied over the midline vermis and the resulting change in cerebellar-dorsolateral prefrontal cortex connectivity was associated with a reduction in negative symptoms (Brady et al., 2019). According to the authors, the cerebellar TMS related (causal) change in dorsolateral prefrontal cortex activity appears consistent with the dysmetria of thought hypothesis, which states that the cerebellum is involved in orchestrating higher mental and cognitive functions.

While this 'cognitive' interpretation is certainly conceivable, an interpretation along the lines of a change in the subcortical affective circuits seems equally probable. As discussed in Chapter 1, the midline areas of the cerebellum (vermis) project to the spinal cord and the limbic system, while the posterior-lateral cerebellar hemispheres project to the prefrontal cortex. Activation of the cerebellar-limbic networks is more closely related to the studied negative symptoms, which rely heavily on motivation and emotion (i.e., amotivation and anhedonia). This interpretation also fits the discussed findings in Chapter 4 about the relation between midline TMS and mood disorders. As such, the change in the dorsolateral prefrontal cortex may present a secondary effect to the primary modulation of the subcortical motivation circuits. Irrespective of the mechanism of action, the study provides compelling evidence for a role of the cerebellum in schizophrenia.

Moreover, the fact that exogenous applied electromagnetic fields to the cerebellum can modulate associated networks contributes to the idea of a new treatment alternative. This idea is inspired by an earlier proof of principle study that found indications of midline cerebellar TMS being able to attenuate negative symptoms (Demirtas-Tatlidede et al., 2010). Additionally, a randomized controlled trial provided further clinical support by showing improvements in negative symptoms and depression following ten sessions of midline cerebellar TMS (Garg et al., 2016).

The release of dopamine in frontal networks following direct electric stimulation of the deep cerebellar nuclei in rats may provide a biochemical explanation for the symptom improvement in human subjects (Mittleman et al., 2008). In a more recent animal study, optogenetic stimulation was used to address the question of how cerebellar circuits interact with frontal networks and influence mental processes (Parker et al., 2017). Optogenetics is a method that uses light to modulate activity in living tissue that has been engineered to express light sensitive ion channels on the cell's membrane. Stimulation of thalamic synaptic terminals of deep cerebellar nuclei projections was able to restore abnormal timing performance and activate the medial frontal cortex in a rodent model of schizophrenia-related frontal dysfunction (Parker et al., 2017).

The importance of the cerebellum as evidenced by the intervention studies is further substantiated by demonstrations of disturbances in resting state functional connectivity (FC) patterns. For example, a network-based approach to investigate the FC of the cerebellum in patients with schizophrenia found distinct cerebellar-thalamic disconnections associated with abnormalities of the brain's cognitive and affective networks, and symptom severity (Chen et al., 2013). Furthermore, there is some evidence showing the first-degree relatives of schizophrenia patients who are unaffected also exhibit deviations in cerebellar connectivity and underscore a developmental contribution to the disease (Guo et al., 2014).

In an additional study in patients with first-episode, drug-naive schizophrenia patients, unaffected siblings of schizophrenia patients, and healthy controls, patients and siblings shared increased default mode network consisting of the medial prefrontal cortex, posterior cingulate cortex, and superior parietal cortex–right Crus II connectivity compared to the controls. Compared with the controls, these patients exhibited a decreased right default attention network (DAN), which comprises the frontal eye fields, parietal cortex, and extrastriate visual regions, and bilateral cerebellum connectivity. In contrast, the unaffected siblings showed increased signal correlations between the right DAN and cerebellum relative to the controls. No significant relations were observed for the abnormal signal correlation and clinical variables. Perhaps, the increase in functional connectivity reflects a compensatory mechanism, but this is an assumption that deserves further research.

A subsequent study using a hypothesis-free approach aimed at identifying differences in cerebellar connectivity between patients and healthy controls also found evidence for abnormalities of the cerebellar hub and cerebello-subcortico-cortical loops in schizophrenia. To identify commonalities of cerebellum deviations across published studies, the interrelations between diagnosis, overall symptom severity, and regional gray matter volumes in the brain were examined in a large multicenter study (Gupta et al., 2015). Structural brain scans of 784 individuals with schizophrenia and 936 controls across 23 scanning sites in Europe and the United States were analyzed. The majority of individuals with schizophrenia were on antipsychotic medications and were clinically stable at the time of scanning.

Results revealed several independent clusters of diagnosis-related differences. The involved regions of gray matter abnormalities formed networks of anterior

Cerebellum in schizophrenia 95

temporal, insular, and medial prefrontal regions, as well as parts of the frontal cortex, posterior brain regions, brainstem, and cerebellar networks (Gupta et al., 2015). Two clusters located in the cerebellum showed reduced volumes in patients as compared to controls, and consisted of the culmen and declive of the vermis and bilateral lobules IX. A third cluster involving bilateral lobules Crus I–II showed relatively larger volumes in patients than controls. Figure 5.3 depicts locations that show deviations in individuals with schizophrenia as compared to healthy controls.

Why these regions showed relatively larger gray matter volumes remain unclear. The authors hinted at a possible false positive, since this particular finding could not be replicated with another analysis (Gupta et al., 2015). Perhaps these findings suggest local disruptions in the neural organization of non-motor related cerebellar areas that mature relatively late during development. For example, neural apoptosis is a highly conserved cellular mechanism of programmed cell death and plays a critical role in the formation and fine-tuning of functional circuits (Burek & Oppenheim, 1996). Notably, the frontal lobe dysfunctions in schizophrenia may share a relation with deviations in the posterolateral cerebellar regions and abnormal signal transfer in the cerebello-cortical loops. The overall pattern of findings confirms the presence of cerebellar volumetric deviations in cerebellar gray matter in schizophrenia, and together with the cortical and subcortical clusters may serve as endophenotypes for schizophrenia (Gupta et al., 2015).

A recent meta-analysis of structural and voxel-based morphometry and resting state fMRI studies in 783 patients and 704 matched healthy controls largely

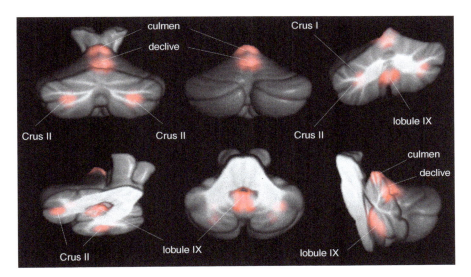

Figure 5.3. Localization of cerebellar regions associated with abnormal gray matter volumes in individuals with schizophrenia

confirmed the deviations found in the previous study (Ding et al., 2019). Aggregate results showed the presence of structural and functional cerebellar abnormalities in the vermian lobules IV/V/VII, left hemispheric lobules IV/V/IX, and left Crus I/II and right Crus I/lobule VIII of the posterior-lateral hemispheres. Figure 5.4 indicates the schematic surface locations of cerebellar deviations in schizophrenic patients based on the systematic analysis of studies.

What may be interesting to mention is that neuroanatomical-based pattern classification methods have shown the feasibility of an early diagnosis of psychosis onset both in clinical and familial high-risk populations. The discriminative neuroanatomical pattern underlying the classification consists of many regions, with an emphasis on the cerebellum together with frontal and temporal areas (Gupta et al., 2015; Zarogianni et al., 2019).

The next question that arises is to what extent cerebellar deviations correlate to living standards. As already mentioned, individuals with schizophrenia suffer from impairments in the socio-emotional and cognitive domains, which have a significantly negative impact on daily life functioning and overall quality of life. To address the neural correlates of functional outcome ranging from social functioning to resource needs to independent living was examined in a systematic review and meta-analysis that included 1,631 individuals with schizophrenia who were involved in 37 structural and 16 functional brain imaging studies (Wojtalik et al., 2017).

Analysis of the structural brain data revealed that better functioning was associated with smaller lateral ventricles and larger gray matter volumes of the

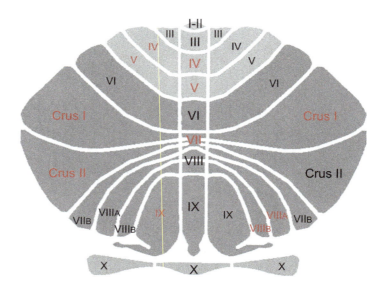

Figure 5.4. Cerebellar topography depicting the structural and functional abnormalities of the vermis and cerebellar hemispheres in schizophrenia

parahippocampal gyrus, dorsal cingulate cortex, and cerebellum. As global gray matter loss is a well-established finding in schizophrenia, the findings may indicate a positive effect on functioning that is associated with relative sparing of gray matter in the latter brain regions. The functional brain data also showed that better functioning correlates to greater activation of the anterior cingulate cortex, dorsolateral prefrontal cortex, and superior temporal gyrus (Wojtalik et al., 2017). The observed structural region, including the cerebellum, and functional region coincide with the brain's socio-emotional and cognitive networks that may be less affected in individuals with schizophrenia who function relatively well.

Possible mechanisms of action

While neuroscientific research has now established that the cerebellum and its parts are implicated in the negative and positive symptoms of schizophrenia, the specific role of each area underlying the cognitive and affective processes that give rise to symptoms remains unknown. Despite the limited mechanistic insights, several models of cerebellar function to explain the diversity of symptoms in schizophrenia have been postulated (Andreasen & Pierson, 2008).

The first model relies on conventional theories that conceptualize the cerebellum as a motor and associative learning machine (Marr–Albus). More specifically, the cerebellum accommodates three computational primitives necessary for learning (Strick et al., 2009; D'Angelo & Casali, 2013): (1) an internal forward model that is able to predict/anticipate the consequences of actions, (2) an internal feedback model (efferent copy) capable of comparing and detecting mismatches between predicted and actual outcomes, and (3) predictive minimization routine that actively modifies the internal forward and feedback models to optimize action-response predictions. On the neurophysiological level, the climbing fibers provide an error correction feedback signal that is transmitted to the DCN, basal ganglia, and cerebral cortex indicating the need to correct an executed motor movement. Much like a servo-controller, the cybernetic-like processes subserving feedback processing, internal updating, and adjusting output are intrinsic to procedural (motor) learning.

On the more generic level the cerebellum can be considered a structure that builds internal models of causal inference (entanglement) in which a particular behavior (action) is predictive for a certain outcome (reaction). In line with Thorndike's Law of Effect, reward (positive emotions) and punishment (negative emotions) signals shape the links between action and consequences. More specifically, an action that produces a reward in a particular situation becomes more likely to occur again in that situation, while the opposite holds for actions that result in punishment. Issues in the processing of reward and punishment signals (Kim et al., 2009) together with functional impairments of the cerebellum may prevent the construction of a coherent internal model of the world. As a result, individuals with schizophrenia experience disorganized patterns of thoughts and emotions. This conceptual framework may also provide an explanation for the high prevalence of comorbid anxiety and mood disorders in schizophrenia (Karpov et al., 2016; Upthegrove et al., 2017). For a discussion on cerebellum theories about anxiety and mood, see Chapters 4 and 5.

Disorganized thought and the proposed schism between the emotional and cognitive systems can be further understood by introducing the role of the cerebellum in time-keeping. Cluster analyses of neuroimaging studies indicate overlapping regions of cerebellar activation related to temporal reproduction timing, emotional processing, and executive functions (Keren-Happuch et al., 2014). The joint activation of the right lobule VI as depicted across all these domains provides evidence to support time-keeping as an essential function of the cerebellum and in the coordination of information processing streams. From this viewpoint, the cerebellum represents an internal clock function and operates as an internal timing device of neural processing streams. The direct reciprocal connections to the hypothalamus as a key player in the regulation of biorhythms further hint at the involvement of the cerebellum in the temporal coordination of internal physiology and behavior.

An alternative model proposes that the cerebellum with its uniform cellular organization as described in Chapter 1, is a 'general purpose modulator' that consists of countless units, called microcomplexes. These microcomplexes enable the cerebellum to process an array of functions to facilitate cortical cerebral processing. The idea of a 'general purpose modulator' is further articulated in the universal cerebellar transform (UCT) hypothesis by Jeremy Schmahmann and colleagues who write: '...integrating multiple internal representations with external stimuli and appropriate responses, the UCT maintains behavior around a homeostatic baseline, automatically and without conscious awareness, serving as an oscillation dampener to optimize performance according to context' (Schmahmann et al., 2019, p. 3).

Failure of the UCT arguably causes conflict between different information processing streams that give rise to disorganized thoughts and emotional instability. Moreover, in line with the learning model described earlier, the cerebellum fulfills a source monitoring role and has access to both interoceptive signals, that is, referring to the internal state of the body, as well as exteroceptive signals, that is, relating to stimuli external to an organism. When the cerebellum is no longer able to make correct inferences about these signals, then the resulting dysfunctional reality monitoring may cause psychoses.

In the scientific literature, the proposed explanatory frameworks concerning the non-motor related aspects of schizophrenia show a strong focus on dysfunctions in the cognitive domain. This is, for example, illustrated by describing schizophrenia in terms like cognitive dysmetria and a disorder of thought. While behavioral and neuroscientific research have unquestionably demonstrated dysfunctions in executive functioning and other cognitive domains, motivation and emotion are far less well studied, often even discarded as secondary to the main cognitive impairments. Even the negative symptoms associated with lack of motivation and depressive mood tend to be explained in terms of abnormalities within the brain's cognitive (cortico-centered) systems. In fact, the well-documented disturbances in the brain's limbic circuit hold the possibility that the subcortical emotional circuits are, at least partially, responsible for the cognitive impairments seen in schizophrenic patients.

A fourth model proposes that the cerebellum serves as a pacemaker for activity of the forebrain structures that include the cerebral cortex, thalamus, and limbic system (Heath et al., 1980a). It has been proposed that cerebellar atrophy of the vermal regions in particular reduces inhibitory output on these regions. The resulting loss of integrity and overactivity in these structures correlate to emotional dysregulation, psychoses, and clinical seizures (Heath et al., 1980a). Impaired vermis inhibitory output to the fastigial nuclei has been associated with hyperactivity of dopaminergic neurons in subcortical regions in schizophrenia (Martin & Albers, 1995). In keeping with the UCT function of the cerebellum, vermal dysfunction may be less likely to be correlated to a specific sign or symptom, but rather causes a generalized disorder associated with emotion dysregulation (Heath et al., 1982). So analogous to the fine-grained coordination of the motor systems, the cerebellum fulfills a similar role in non-motor related functions and contributes to keeping the brain in a functional (adaptive) range.

The proposed concept of the cerebellum as the brain's pacemaker has been confirmed on the cellular level. The high precision of intrinsic pacemaking in Purkinje (output) cells is important for cerebellar function (Walter et al., 2006). Careful pharmacological experimentation has shown that interference with the Purkinje cell's intrinsic pacemaking properties causes motor disturbances and ataxia-like symptoms (Walter et al., 2006). These findings illustrate that the timing of pacemaking in Purkinje cells is among the critical aspects associated with proper motor as well as non-motor functions. The idea of the cerebellar pacemaker has been explored by examining the effects of chronic subdural electric stimulation of the vermis in schizophrenia.

While vermis stimulation appears to yield good results in patients whose cardinal symptom involves disturbances in the affective domain, results in schizophrenia have been more variable. Of the 15 schizophrenic patients who were studied, two patients showed significant improvement (i.e., off medication, no psychotic signs or symptoms), six patients demonstrated a moderate response (i.e., functioning outside the hospital, low dose of neuroleptics), three patients displayed minimal changes, and four patients did not show any notable changes at all. The neurological complexity of the disease and heterogeneity of signs and symptoms across patients simply imply that not all patients will benefit from a standardized treatment in the same way.

In addition, observations of cerebellar atrophy mentioned earlier could make electric simulation less effective in patients with more pronounced vermal degeneration. Anecdotal reports suggested that combining intracranial cerebellar stimulation with medication yielded considerably better results. This idea fits modern ideas of using invasive and non-invasive forms of electric and magnetic brain stimulation as an adjuvant in the treatment of neuropsychiatric disorders. Interestingly, the stimulation frequency that appeared to produce the best results was at 100 Hz (Heath et al., 1980b). Studies on the activity frequencies across the cerebellar cortical cells indicate that the 100 Hz stimulation frequency falls in the range of Purkinje cell activity (30–150 Hz) (De Zeeuw et al., 2011). This notion fits the importance of pacemaking Purkinje cells in precision timing and the hypothesized synchronization of local and distal information processing streams.

Alternatively, neurostimulation of Purkinje cells in the treatment of epilepsy has yielded inconsistent and variable results. The complex foliation of the cerebellar cortex together with the different functional zones combined with a spatially diffuse focal stimulation may contribute to the limited efficacy of cerebellar entrainment to inhibit seizures (Kros et al., 2015). Stimulation of the centrally located deep cerebellar nuclei (i.e., interposed and fastigial nuclei) has been suggested to provide a better target point for modulating thalamocortical oscillations associated with generalized seizure onset (Kros et al., 2015). Thus, direct stimulation of central cerebellar nuclei may be a more effective way of reaching relevant distal connections and areas related to the earlier mentioned dopaminergic overactivity in the basal ganglia, and the regulation of the hypothalamus, hippocampus, amygdala, and medial frontal cortex.

Cerebellum in sleep and psychosis

Hallucinations and delusions show several commonalities with dreaming, including the perceptual distortions and emotional intensity, that offers circumstantial evidence for disturbances in the sleep-wake cycle of patients with schizophrenia. While the 'dream intrusion' hypothesis remains to be critically tested, sleep disorders are commonly observed in patients with schizophrenia (Waters et al., 2016; Reeve et al., 2019).

Sleep is critical for a multitude of physiological (homeostatic) functions that, among many others, involve immune responses, energy conservation/restoration, brain waste clearance, and memory consolidation. The suprachiasmatic nucleus (SCN) plays a critical role in the regulation of the chronobiological process, and disruptions within this hypothalamic area affect the internal timing mechanisms causing bio-arrhythmias (Buijs et al., 2019). More specifically, SCN controls the release of melatonin (N-acetyl-methoxytryptamine) by the pineal gland, and this neurotransmitter is directly linked to the initiation and maintenance of sleep. Reductions in midnight plasma levels have been demonstrated in patients (Bastos et al., 2019) and have been found to positively relate to sleep disturbances and psychosis (Anderson & Maes, 2012). Hyperactivity of the mesolimbic dopamine circuit is suggested to provide common ground for sleep disturbances and psychosis. This is evidenced by animal and human data that sleep disruptions lead to elevated dopamine release and sensitivity (Yate, 2016).

The increased dopamine levels, in turn, contribute to the disruptions in sleep and circadian rhythms, causing a vicious cycle that further predisposes to emotional lability and psychosis.

Even though our knowledge about the role of the cerebellum in sleep is still in its infancy, the cerebello-hypothalamic connection provides a neuroanatomic basis for how cerebellum dysfunctions can alter the sleep-wake cycle and may even cause sleep disorders (Canto et al., 2017; DelRosso & Hoque, 2014). At the cellular level, the diurnal clockwork of the SCN involves an autoregulatory feedback mechanism as shown by the rhythmic expression of clock genes (Gritti, 2013). The discovery that diurnal oscillations of molecular clock components occur in the cerebellar cortex, some of which are controlled by the SCN, demonstrates the direct involvement of the cerebellum in the brain's chronobiology (Rath et al., 2012). Purkinje and granular cells express CLOCK (*circadian locomotor output cycles kaput*) genes that play a central role in the regulation of the circadian rhythm. Research has shown that the CLOCK gene expression in the cerebellum shows a near 24-hour rhythm. Lesions of the SCN changes gene expression rhythm, indicating that the cerebellar CLOCK gene expression depends on SCN input (Mordel et al., 2013). Patients with REM (dream-state) sleep behavior disorder have smaller cerebellar cortical volumes of the anterior lobe and reduced DCN volumes (Boucetta et al., 2016). Conversely, cerebellar damage can give rise to sleep disorders (DelRosso & Hoque, 2014).

In cats, it has been found that lesioning the vermis and cerebellar hemispheres prolongs the mean duration of non-REM and total amount of time spent in the REM phase, while at the same time the number of sleep periods throughout the sleep-wake cycle is reduced (Nir & Tononi, 2010). The increase of activity in the mossy-fiber-parallel pathway, together with heightened activity of especially the fastigial nucleus during the REM phase, demonstrate the importance of the cerebellum in mammalian sleep (Canto et al., 2017). In terms of functions, implicit processes related to motor learning and memory consolidation are considered to involve the cerebellum during sleep. From the biological homeostatic perspective, these proposed functions can be complemented to the affective domain that includes the downregulation of psychological and bodily stress, fear extinction, and reward-punishment learning. Finally, it is important to emphasize that psychosis constitutes a misperception colored by an intense emotion. Although hallucinations and delusions are also common in the general 'healthy' population, the affective tone constitutes the primary cause of distress and suffering.

Conclusion

Cerebellar anomalies are part of the complex pathophysiology of schizophrenia, in which neural information processing streams and signaling are not properly synchronized. Structural and functional aberrations in interareal neural communication are associated with a disrupted pacemaker function of the

References

Anderson G, Maes M (2012). Melatonin: An overlooked factor in schizophrenia and in the inhibition of anti-psychotic side effects. *Metab. Brain Dis.* 27, 113–119.

Andreasen NC (1999). A unitary model of schizophrenia: Bleuler's 'fragmented phrene' as schizencephaly. *Arch. Gen. Psychiatry* 56, 781–787.

Andreasen NC, Pierson R (2008). The role of the cerebellum in schizophrenia. *Biol. Psychiatry* 64, 81–88.

Artiges E, Leroy C, Dubol M, et al. (2017). Striatal and extrastriatal dopamine transporter availability in schizophrenia and its clinical correlates: A voxel-based and high-resolution PET study. *Schizophr. Bull.* 43, 1134–1142.

Bastos MA, Oliveira Bastos PR, Portella RB, Soares LFG, Conde RB, Rodrigues PM, Lucchetti G (2019). Pineal gland and schizophrenia: A systematic review and meta-analysis. *Psychoneuroendocrinology* 104, 100–114.

Boucetta S, Dadar M, Jones BE, Collins DL, Dang-Vu TT (2016). Structural brain alterations associated with rapid eye movement sleep behavior disorder in Parkinson's disease. *Sci. Rep.* 6, 26782.

Brady Jr RO, Gonsalvez I, Lee I, et al. (2019). Cerebellar-prefrontal network connectivity and negative symptoms in schizophrenia. *Am. J. Psychiatry* 176, 512–520.

Buijs RM, Guzmán Ruiz MA, Méndez Hernández R, Rodríguez Cortés B (2019). The suprachiasmatic nucleus: A responsive clock regulating homeostasis by daily changing the setpoints of physiological parameters. *Auton. Neurosci.* 218, 43–50.

Burek MJ, Oppenheim RW (1996). Programmed cell death in the developing nervous system. *Brain Pathol.* 6, 427–446.

Canto CB, Onuki Y, Bruinsma B, van der Werf YD, De Zeeuw CI (2017). The sleeping cerebellum. *Trends Neurosci.* 40, 309–323.

Chen YL, Tu PC, Lee YC, Chen YS, Li CT, Su TP (2013). Resting-state fMRI mapping of cerebellar functional dysconnections involving multiple large-scale networks in patients with schizophrenia. *Schizophr. Res.* 149, 26–34.

D'Angelo E, Casali S (2013). Seeking a unified framework for cerebellar function and dysfunction: From circuit operations to cognition. *Front. Neural Circuits* 6, 116.

Daskalakis ZJ, Christensen BK, Fitzgerald PB, Fountain SI, Chen R (2005). Reduced cerebellar inhibition in schizophrenia: A preliminary study. *Am. J. Psychiatry* 162, 1203–1205.

Deicken RF, Feiwell R, Schuff N, Soher B (2001). Evidence for altered cerebellar vermis neuronal integrity in schizophrenia. *Psychiatry Res.* 107, 125–134.

DelRosso LM, Hoque R (2014). The cerebellum and sleep. *Neurol. Clin.* 32, 890–893.

Demirtas-Tatlidede A, Freitas C, Cromer JR, et al. (2010). Safety and proof of principle study of cerebellar vermal theta burst stimulation in refractory schizophrenia. *Schizophr. Res.* 124, 91–100.

De Zeeuw CI, Hoebeek FE, Bosman LW, Schonewille M, Witter L, Koekkoek SK (2011). Spatiotemporal firing patterns in the cerebellum. *Nat. Rev. Neurosci.* 12, 327–344.

Ding Y, Ou Y, Pan P, Shan X, Chen J, Liu F, Zhao J, Guo W (2019). Cerebellar structural and functional abnormalities in first-episode and drug-naive patients with schizophrenia: A meta-analysis. *Psychiatry Res. Neuroimaging* 283, 24–33.

Dong D, Wang Y, Chang X, et al. (2017). Shared abnormality of white matter integrity in schizophrenia and bipolar disorder: A comparative voxel-based meta-analysis. *Schizophr. Res.* 185, 41–45.

Eaton WW, Pedersen MG, Nielsen PR, Mortensen PB (2010). Autoimmune diseases, bipolar disorder, and non-affective psychosis. *Bipolar Disord.* 12, 638–646.

Ende G, Hubrich P, Walter S, et al. (2005). Further evidence for altered cerebellar neuronal integrity in schizophrenia. *Am. J. Psychiatry* 162, 790–792.

Ferrer I, Fabregues I, Pineda M, Gracia I, Ribalta T (1984). A Golgi study of cerebellar atrophy in human chronic alcoholism. *Neuropathol. Appl. Neurobiol.* 10, 245–253.

Friston KJ (1998). The disconnection hypothesis. *Schizophr. Res.* 30, 115–125.

Fu G, Zhang W, Dai J, et al. (2019). Increased peripheral interleukin 10 relate to white matter integrity in schizophrenia. *Front. Neurosci.* 13, 52.

Garg S, Sinha VK, Tikka SK, Mishra P, Goyal N (2016). The efficacy of cerebellar vermal deep high frequency (theta range) repetitive transcranial magnetic stimulation (rTMS) in schizophrenia: A randomized rater blind-sham controlled study. *Psychiatry Res.* 243, 413–420.

Gritti I (2013). The cerebellum, hypothalamus and behaviour. *Natural. Sci.* 5, 832–834.

Guo W, Jiang J, Xiao C, et al. (2014). Decreased resting-state interhemispheric functional connectivity in unaffected siblings of schizophrenia patients. *Schizophr. Res.* 152, 170–175.

Gupta CN, Calhoun VD, Rachakonda S, et al. (2015). Patterns of gray matter abnormalities in schizophrenia based on an international mega-analysis. *Schizophr. Bull.* 41, 1133–1142.

Heath RG, Dempesy CW, Fontana CJ, Fitzjarrell AT (1980a). Feedback loop between cerebellum and septal-hippocampal sites: Its role in emotion and epilepsy. *Biol. Psychiatry* 15, 541–556.

Heath RG, Franklin DE, Walker CF, Keating Jr. JW (1982). Cerebellar vermal atrophy in psychiatric patients. *Biol. Psychiatry* 17, 569–583.

Heath RG, Llewellyn RC, Rouchell AM (1980b). The cerebellar pacemaker for intractable behavioral disorders and epilepsy: Follow-up report. *Biol. Psychiatry* 15, 243–256.

Honey GD, Pomarol-Clotet E, Corlett PR, et al. (2005). Functional dysconnectivity in schizophrenia associated with attentional modulation of motor function. *Brain* 128, 2597–2611.

Jiang Y, Duan M, Chen X, et al. (2017). Common and distinct dysfunctional patterns contribute to triple network model in schizophrenia and depression: A preliminary study. *Prog. Neuropsychopharmacol. Biol. Psychiatry* 79, 302–310.

Kanaan RA, Borgwardt S, McGuire PK, et al. (2009). Microstructural organization of cerebellar tracts in schizophrenia. *Biol. Psychiatry* 66, 1067–1069.

Kang HJ, Kawasawa YI, Cheng F, et al. (2011). Spatio-temporal transcriptome of the human brain. *Nature* 478, 483–489.

Karpov B, Joffe G, Aaltonen K, et al. (2016). Anxiety symptoms in a major mood and schizophrenia spectrum disorders. *Eur. Psychiatry* 37, 1–7.

Keren-Happuch E, Chen SH, Ho MH, Desmond JE (2014). A meta-analysis of cerebellar contributions to higher cognition from PET and fMRI studies. *Hum. Brain Mapp.* 35, 593–615.

Kim YT, Lee KU, Lee SJ (2009). Deficit in decision-making in chronic, stable schizophrenia: From a reward and punishment perspective. *Psychiatry Investig.* 6, 26–33.

Knuesel I, Chicha L, Britschgi M, et al. (2014). Maternal immune activation and abnormal brain development across CNS disorders. *Nat. Rev. Neurol.* 10, 643–660.

Kros L, Eelkman Rooda OHJ, De Zeeuw CI, Hoebeek FE (2015). Controlling cerebellar output to treat refractory epilepsy. *Trends Neurosci.* 38, 787–799.

Lane RD (2003). The neural substrates of affect impairment in schizophrenia. *Am. J. Psychiatry* 160, 1723–1725.

Martin P, Albers M (1995). Cerebellum and schizophrenia: A selective review. *Schizophr. Bull.* 21, 241–250.

Mavroudis IA, Manani MG, Petrides F, et al. (2013). Dendritic and spinal pathology of the Purkinje cells from the human cerebellar vermis in Alzheimer's disease. *Psychiatr. Danub.* 25, 221–226.

Mittleman G, Goldowitz D, Heck DH, Blaha CD (2008). Cerebellar modulation of frontal cortex dopamine efflux in mice: Relevance to autism and schizophrenia. *Synapse* 62, 544–550.

Moberget T, Doan NT, Alnæs D, et al. (2018). Cerebellar volume and cerebellocerebral structural covariance in schizophrenia: A multisite mega-analysis of 983 patients and 1349 healthy controls. *Mol. Psychiatry* 23, 1512–1520.

Mordel J, Karnas D, Pévet P, Isope P, Challet E, Meissl H (2013). The output signal of Purkinje cells of the cerebellum and circadian rhythmicity. *PLoS One* 8, e58457.

Nir Y, Tononi G (2010). Dreaming and the brain: From phenomenology to neurophysiology. *Trends Cogn. Sci.* 14, 88–100.

Nopoulos PC, Ceilley JW, Gailis EA, Andreasen NC (2001). An MRI study of midbrain morphology in patients with schizophrenia: Relationship to psychosis, neuroleptics, and cerebellar neural circuitry. *Biol. Psychiatry* 49, 13–19.

Okugawa G, Nobuhara K, Sugimoto T, Kinoshita T (2005). Diffusion tensor imaging study of the middle cerebellar peduncles in patients with schizophrenia. *Cerebellum* 4, 123–127.

Paradiso S, Andreasen NC, Crespo-Facorro B, et al. (2003). Emotions in unmedicated patients with schizophrenia during evaluation with positron emission tomography. *Am. J. Psychiatry* 160, 1775–1783.

Parker KL, Kim YC, Kelley RM, et al. (2017). Delta-frequency stimulation of cerebellar projections can compensate for schizophrenia-related medial frontal dysfunction. *Mol. Psychiatry* 22, 647–655.

Rath MF, Rode K, Moller M (2012). Circadian oscillations of molecular clock components in the cerebellar cortex of the rat. *Chronobiol. Int.* 29, 1289–1299.

Reeve S, Sheaves B, Freeman D (2019). Sleep disorders in early psychosis: Incidence, severity, and association with clinical symptoms. *Schizophr. Bull.* 45, 287–295.

Schmahmann JD (2000). The role of the cerebellum in affect and psychosis. *J. Neuroling.* 13, 189–214.

Schmahmann JD, Guell X, Stoodley CJ, Halko MA (2019). The theory and neuroscience of cerebellar cognition. *Annu. Rev. Neurosci.* 42, 337–364.

Schmitt A, Schulenberg W, Bernstein HG, et al. (2011). Reduction of gyrification index in the cerebellar vermis in schizophrenia: A post-mortem study. *World J. Biol. Psychiatry* 12, 99–103.

Shintaku M, Kaneda D (2009). Chromosome 16q22.1-linked autosomal dominant cerebellar ataxia: An autopsy case report with some new observations on cerebellar pathology. *Neuropathology* 29, 285–292.

Strick PL, Dum RP, Fiez JA (2009). Cerebellum and nonmotor function. *Annu. Rev. Neurosci.* 32, 413–434.

Sundararajan T, Manzardo AM, Butler MG (2018). Functional analysis of schizophrenia genes using GeneAnalytics program and integrated databases. *Gene* 641, 25–34.

Tran KD, Smutzer GS, Doty RL, Arnold SE (1998). Reduced Purkinje cell size in the cerebellar vermis of elderly patients with schizophrenia. *Am. J. Psychiatry* 155, 1288–1290.

Upthegrove R, Marwaha S, Birchwood M (2017). Depression and schizophrenia: Cause, consequence, or trans-diagnostic issue? *Schizophr. Bull.* 43, 240–244.

Walter JT, Alviña K, Womack MD, Chevez C, Khodakhah K (2006). Decreases in the precision of Purkinje cell pacemaking cause cerebellar dysfunction and ataxia. *Nat. Neurosci.* 9, 389–397.

Waters F, Blom JD, Dang-Vu TT, et al. (2016). What is the link between hallucinations, dreams, and hypnagogic-hypnopompic experiences? *Schizophr. Bull.* 42, 1010–1098.

Wojtalik JA, Smith MJ, Keshavan MS, Eack SM (2017). A systematic and meta-analytic review of neural correlates of functional outcome in schizophrenia. *Schizophr. Bull.* 43, 1329–1347.

Yates NJ (2016). Schizophrenia: The role of sleep and circadian rhythms in regulating dopamine and psychosis. *Rev. Neurosci.* 27, 669–687.

Zarogianni E, Storkey AJ, Borgwardt S, et al. (2019). Individualized prediction of psychosis in subjects with an at-risk mental state. *Schizophr Res.* 214, 18–23.

Chapter 6

The socio-emotional cerebellum in autism spectrum disorder

Autism spectrum disorder (ASD) was first articulated by psychiatrists Leo Kanner (1894–1981) (Kanner, 1943) and Hans Asperger (1906–1980) in the 1940s (Asperger, 1944). They considered deficiencies in social communication skills to be the cornerstones of ASD. The word autism stems from the Greek word 'autos,' meaning 'about the self.' Both psychiatrists stressed the inability to relate to others and the disconnection from the outside world. Disturbances in experiencing the surroundings as an integral part of the self stand in the way of attaining intuitive, as opposed to cognitive, forms of thinking and complex social interactions. Up to the present day, ASD is considered a condition related to how an individual perceives and socializes with others, causing difficulties in social interaction and communication. In addition, limited and repetitive patterns of behavior are additional features of ASD.

ASD is considered a (neuro)developmental disorder because symptoms of autism typically start to occur within the first years of a child's life. A small percentage of children initially show a normal development trajectory in the first year but enter a phase of regression between 18 and 24 months of age when they develop autism symptoms. Children who show early signs of ASD may exhibit reduced eye contact and indifference to caregivers, while children with the regressive form after the first year start to display internalizing (withdrawal) or externalizing (aggressive) behaviors, and/or lose their acquired language skills.

Each child with ASD shows more or less a unique pattern of behavior and level of severity ranging from low to high functioning. For example, some children display learning difficulties and signs of lower than normal intelligence, while other children have normal to high intelligence but show more pronounced problems in social communication and adjusting to social situations. As such, the term spectrum in ASD emphasizes continuity and more adequately covers the signs and symptoms of the disorder. This is in contrast to a categorical approach of low (autism) and high functioning individuals (Asperger syndrome). Children and adults with ASD showing deficits in social interactions and communication may display any of the following signs (source: https://www.mayoclinic.org):

The socio-emotional cerebellum in ASD   107

- inability to respond to his or her name or seem not to hear when being addressed
- strong preference for playing in solitude and appears to live in his or her own world
- avoids physical contact and resists cuddling and holding
- makes poor eye contact and shows reduced facial expressiveness
- doesn't speak or has delayed speech, or loses previous ability to say words or sentences
- problems in initiating and maintaining a conversation, and the tendency to make requests or label items
- speaks with an abnormal tone or rhythm
- repetition of words or phrases verbatim
- difficulty in understanding simple questions or directions
- issues with interpreting facial expressions, body postures, or vocal tone of others
- lowered expressiveness of emotions and feelings, and unaware of others' emotions and feelings
- context-inappropriate attitude (e.g., passive or aggressive) during social interactions.

In addition to impairments in social interactions and communication, the limited and repetitive patterns of behavior can be illustrated by any of the following signs (source: https://www.mayoclinic.org):

- repetitive movements, such as rocking, spinning, or hand flapping, biting and/or head-banging
- development of specific routines or rituals, and becomes disturbed at the slightest deviation
- problems in gross and fine motor coordination (e.g., clumsiness, walking on toes, and stiff or exaggerated body language)
- obsessed by details of an object or activity, but fails to grasp the meaning and purpose of that particular object or activity
- hypersensitivity to light, sound, or touch, but at the same time hyposensitivity to pain or temperature
- absence of imitative or imaginary play (i.e., mental stimulation).

Research in the neurosciences has made considerable progress in identifying molecular, structural, and functional brain correlates of ASD. Even though the pathophysiological underpinnings remain incomplete at this time, available evidence points toward an important role of the cerebellum (Becker & Stoodley, 2013).

The cerebellum is among the first regions to differentiate during brain development and continues to mature during the first years of the newborn. This extended developmental trajectory makes the cerebellum susceptible to pre- and postnatal environmental influences. It has been shown that cerebellar injury during prematurity causes a > 30-fold increase in the risk for developing ASD (Limperopoulos et al., 2007). Certain genetic predispositions combined with exposure to stressors, such as certain toxins, inflammation, or other harming conditions, presumably initiate the pathophysiological complexity associated with neurodevelopmental disorders. Although the exact mechanisms remain unknown, it is not surprising that genetic make-up and early gene-environment interactions have a pronounced and lasting influence on the molecular, structural, functional, and system's level of cerebellar organization and activity.

It was recently discovered that risk genes for ASD play an important role in cerebellar formation and morphology (Wang et al., 2019). During the first postnatal week, high expression of cadherins (subtypes Cdh9 and Cdh11), a molecule important for cell binding, was observed in Purkinje cells of mice. Expression of Cdh11 was observed in lobule VI/VII of the vermis and lateral hemispheres (Crus I and II). The high level of Cdh11 expression in lobules VI/VII of the vermis was also correlated to a low level of expression of the Purkinje cell marker calbindin.

Moreover, these results concur with observed histopathological findings in the post-mortem brains of persons with ASD. In fact, a lower number of Purkinje cells in the vermis and cerebellar hemispheres are the most consistent neuropathological findings in ASD (Becker & Stoodley, 2013). These latter findings can be attributed to early developmental defects (Wegiel et al., 2010). In addition to the abnormalities in the Purkinje cell layer of the cerebellar cortex, reductions in the number of granular cells have also been observed, while the cell densities of the basket and stellate interneurons appear to fall in the normal range (Allen, 2005).

Bergmann glial cells are a special type of astrocytes that locate their cell bodies around Purkinje cells as their fibers enclose synapses on the Purkinje cell dendrites (Verkhratsky et al., 2013). This loss is proposed to involve a defect of the Bergmann glial cells in programmed cell death (i.e., pruning) and regulation glutamate homeostasis in nutrition (Chrobak & Soltys, 2017). Bergmann glial cells also support the migration of granule cells, guiding the small neurons from the external granular layer to the internal granular layer of the cerebellar cortex (Yamada & Wantanabe, 2002). Furthermore, Bergmann glial cells subserve neuroprotective functions in terms of keeping cerebellar plasticity in a functional range by influencing pf-cf–mediated long-term depression (LTD), which is deficient in individuals with ASD (Chrobak & Soltys, 2017). Figure 6.1. depicts a cellular mechanism for LTD in the cerebellar cortex.

Research using genetically modified (IB2 KO) mouse models that mimic some behavioral aspects of ASD in humans, including impaired motor performance and learning, has further explored possible neurochemical-related abnormalities in cerebellar plasticity (Soda et al., 2019). Extensive study of the cerebellar

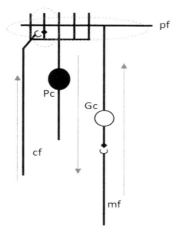

Figure 6.1. Pairing parallel fiber (pf) excitatory post-synaptic potentials with excitatory climbing fiber (cf) input causes a decrease of synaptic strength (LTD) between the parallel fibers (PFs) and Purkinje cells (PCs). Activity in parallel fibers is in part driving the background activity of PCs, and the modulation of this activity is instrumental for cerebellar learning processes.

glutamatergic N-methyl-D-aspartate (NMDA) receptor revealed evidence for hyperexcitability and hyperplasticity disruption of signal transfer in the granular cell layer and alteration of the response to mossy fiber input. Earlier demonstrations of delayed signal propagation at the climbing fiber-Purkinje cell synapse (Giza et al., 2010) may contribute to deficient timing that impairs the downregulation of excitability at the granular parallel-fiber Purkinje cells synapse (Soda et al., 2019). The temporal miscommunication identifies a plausible important cellular basis for cerebellar dysfunction in terms of hyperactivity that can at least account for a number of behavioral impairments found in ASD, and perhaps also in mood disorders (Chapter 4) and schizophrenia (Chapter 5).

Next to animal models, ^{1}H-magnetic resonance spectroscopy (^{1}H-MRS) provides a possible means to study neurochemical processes in humans. In the search for neurochemical deviations in ASD, a systematic literature search and meta-analysis were performed on 22 studies. Indices of N-acetyl aspartate (NAA), creatine, choline, myo-inositol, and glutamate/glutamine in frontal, temporal, parietal, amygdala-hippocampus complex, thalamus, and cerebellum were examined in relation to ASD. Significantly lower NAA levels for all the examined brain regions except for the cerebellum were observed in children with ASD as compared to typically developing children (Aoki et al., 2012).

According to the researchers, the earlier noted larger-than-normal brain size in conjunction with lowered NAA levels may indicate that transient volumetric expansion involves an increase in non-neuron tissues (e.g., glial cell proliferation) in children with ASD (Aoki et al., 2012). In addition, NAA levels normalize during development into adulthood. In contrast, another independent ^{1}H-MRS meta-analysis found significant reductions in NAA concentrations in the cerebellum of children with ASD (Ipser et al., 2012). The proposed increase in glial cell proliferation is also a sign of altered neurogenesis and can point at neuronal and axonal loss, and neuronal metabolic dysfunctions (Ipser et al., 2012).

Although both meta-analyses find consistent lower NAA levels throughout the brain, the regional specificity of the abnormalities remains variable, limiting the conclusions that can be drawn from these meta-analyses. A serious concern about meta-analyses on MRS studies is the heterogeneity of sampling (i.e., location of the voxel) in the regions of interest across the different studies (Ipser et al., 2012). Variability within the patient and control samples on demographics, for example, can also restrain the sensitivity (i.e., true positive) and specificity (i.e., true negative) of meta-analyses that include a relatively small set of studies. Overall, the animal and human studies provide evidence that cellular abnormalities in the brain that occur during early development contribute to the abnormalities and malformations seen in the cerebellum and other brain regions of individuals with ASD.

In one of the few exceptional studies performed on post-mortem cerebella in 13 persons with ASD, focal qualitative developmental defects were investigated to characterize regions that are prone to developmental alterations in ASD (Wegiel et al., 2010). Cerebellar flocculonodular dysplasia was found in six subjects (46%). Focal dysplasia and hypoplasia in the vermis was found in two consecutive subjects, suggesting local cerebellar developmental problems in eight of the 13 (62%) autistic subjects being examined. The broad spectrum of qualitative neuropathological developmental changes observed in 12 of 13 brains (92%) indicates multiregional impairments in neurogenesis, neuronal migration, and maturation in ASD (Wegiel et al., 2010). This broad variability concurs with the 1H-MRS meta-analytic findings and may contribute to the quantitative and qualitative diversity of the signs and symptoms.

Extreme male brain and male bias in ASD

The prevalence of ASD is fairly consistent across cultures (Mash & Barkley, 2003), as is the observation that the number of males with ASD significantly exceeds the number of females with ASD (ratio 3:1) (Haida et al., 2019).This latter finding has led to the 'extreme male brain' hypothesis of ASD (Baron-Cohen, 2002). The hypothesis lends indirect behavioral support from the observation that individuals with ASD prefer systemizing (male-dominant trait) over empathizing (female-dominant trait) (Baron-Cohen, 2002). Systemizing involves creating rules and ordering things according to a scheme. Empathizing is the ability to understand and share the emotions and feelings of others. Individuals with ASD are typically excellent in systematizing but have difficulties with emotive processes and social communication.

The male bias has been explained by females being underdiagnosed as they exhibit fewer atypical behaviors common to ASD, such as abnormal eating, temper tantrums, and self-injurious behavior (Tsakanikos et al., 2011). However, a large cohort study including more than 800 participants with ASD showed that even though typical sex differences for empathy weakened, they remained nonetheless present in adults with autism (Baron-Cohen et al., 2014). More recently, a mouse model of ASD was used to investigate sex-related neural and behavior differences of maternal immune activation (MIA) in response to infections. Results showed that males were more affected by MIA than females as male mice showed fewer social interactions and greater impairments in the motor domain as compared to female mice (Haida et al., 2019). Additionally, more extensive reductions in Purkinje cell densities accompanied by lower amounts of neurons in the motor cortex were found in the male mice.

While the basis for the male bias remains unknown, hormones may provide some hints for understanding male-female difference in immune responses. The primary female sex hormone estrogen has been shown to enhance immune responses, while the primary male sex hormone testosterone has immunosuppressive effects (Becker, 2012). There is some evidence suggesting that fetal testosterone levels as measured in amniotic fluid may be predictors of future ASD-related behaviors, but the exact effects of sex hormones during development are highly complex and need more study (Ferri et al., 2018). For example, inflammation during a critical post-natal period of Purkinje cell development in rats disrupts local estradiol production, resulting in attenuated growth of Purkinje dendritic trees and less juvenile social play behavior, but only in males (Hoffman et al., 2016).

Another possible explanation for the male bias in autism proposes the role of neuropeptides in sex differences, especially oxytocin and vasopressin. These peptides are synthesized in the hypothalamus and are regulators of anxiety, depression/sadness, anger, stress, and social behavior in a wide variety of mammals, including humans (Neumann & Landgraf, 2012).

Even though sex differences in these neuropeptides are still under scientific debate, there is evidence to suggest that oxytocin-related activity is altered in ASD (Dumais & Veenema, 2016). Oxytocin is associated with behaviors that are typically diminished in ASD, such as empathy, social attachment, and prosocial acts. In addition to the presence of oxytocin and vasopressin binding sites in the cerebellum together with the existing reciprocal connections to the hypothalamus, the Purkinje cell abnormalities observed may play a role in the relation between neuropeptide dysregulation and social-emotional functioning in ASD.

Deviations in cerebellar morphology

On the structural macroscopic level, there are numerous studies that report deviations of cerebellar volumes in ASD relative to matched controls. Recently, a systematic meta-analysis of the available literature was performed to more precisely quantify the proposed difference in cerebellar volumes and morphology (Traut et al., 2018). Results found no convincing evidence for differences between patients with ASD and control subjects. Total cerebellar volume and cerebellar white matter volume were marginally larger in ASD, while lobules VI and VII of the vermis were slightly smaller in ASD. However, the significance of the results did not survive statistical correction for multiple comparisons (Traut et al., 2018). It should be noted that the number of subjects that could be included in some of the more specific (subregion) analyses was limited, which increased the chance of a statistically underpowered meta-analysis and less reliable outcome. Furthermore, the categorical approach does not take ASD severity of, for example, social-emotional impairments, into account. This leaves open the possibility that cerebellar abnormalities are present in more severe cases, but the effect size regresses to the mean by less impaired individuals that have no clear cerebellar abnormalities. Notwithstanding, on the gross neuroanatomic level, MRI-based analyses do not support ASD-specific deviations in cerebellar volumes.

Hypoplasia of the vermis and the concomitant loss of inhibitory action were found to be associated with reduced seeking (approach) behavior in ASD (Courchesne, 1997). This observation has been confirmed in cerebellectomized rodents that expressed significantly less motivation to explore while their motor skills were left unchanged (Walker et al., 2007). Extensive research on regional gray matter and white matter of the cerebellum in ASD points towards disturbances associated with movement, language, social skills, mentalizing, and emotion regulation (D'Mello & Stoodley, 2015). Figure 6.2 shows a mapping of functions and their corresponding cerebellar locations in ASD.

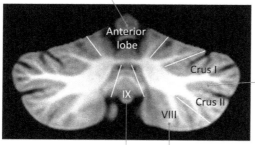

Figure 6.2. Overview of the relations between structural deviations of the cerebellum and behavioral symptoms in ASD (D'Mello & Stoodley, 2015)

Resting state functional activity

Resting state low frequency fluctuations in the blood-oxygen level dependent signals can be used to investigate the functional architecture of the brain. Resting state conditions arguably reflect the brain's internal homeostatic state and can be viewed as the functional backbone of task-related activity. Abnormalities in resting state activity has been demonstrated in many disorders, and a recent meta-analysis explored the evidence for disturbances in resting state activity in ASD (Wang et al., 2018). After careful screening, 15 datasets consisting of 382 patients and 348 controls were included in the meta-analysis. Results showed that patients with ASD as compared to controls showed patterns of hyperactivity in the motor cortical areas, frontal cortex, and bilateral cerebellar lobule VIII/IX. Hypoactivity was observed in temporal cortex, precuneus, cingulate cortex, and bilateral cerebellum Crus I. Peak activations are shown in Figure 6.3.

The inferior posterior lobe (lobule VIII–IX) is part of the so-called fractured somatotopic representation of the cerebellum. Fractured somatotopy refers to the pattern of topographical representation of different body parts, which is not situated continuously over an extensive portion of cerebellar cortex, but is divided into smaller, discrete patches (Manni & Petrosini, 2004). While the somatotopic organization of the cerebellum is still under scientific debate, the homunculi type representations are considered to be essential to the coupling between the sensory and motor systems. It is therefore not surprising that the

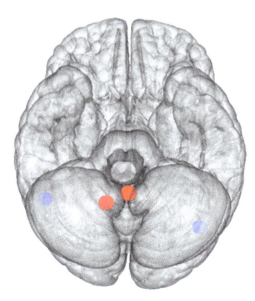

Figure 6.3. Lower resting state activity in bilateral Crus I (blue) and higher resting state activity in lobule IX (red) in ASD compared to non-ASD control subjects

cerebellum takes part in the processing of nociceptive stimuli and is related to the subjective experience of pain (Welman et al., 2018).

Furthermore, individuals with ASD appear to show a-typical responses to noxious (painful) stimuli (Chen et al., 2017). According to the embodiment theory of empathy, observing bodily sensations or emotions (e.g., faces) in another person causes neural activation patterns comparable to those that occur when one's self directly experiences those feelings (Keysers et al., 2011). The embodiment theory finds support in the clinical setting, where pain insensitivity is considered to be a specified diagnostic criterion of ASD (Vaughn et al., 2019). The meta-analyses also revealed robust underactivity in regions that are part of the default mode network (DMN) and in cerebellar Crus I (Wang et al., 2018). The DMN and posterolateral cerebellar hemispheres play an important role in various emotional and social processes, self-referential thought, and theory of mind. Together with possible alterations in sensory-based bodily and emotional experience involving the more medial parts of the cerebellum (Damasio, 2003), a role seems to be reserved for the cerebellum in empathy and social emotional functioning.

Cerebellum and the tempo-parietal junction (TPJ)

Understanding the social origin and purpose of the behaviors of others or the self (i.e., 'body' reading) as well as their state of mind (i.e., 'mind' reading or mentalizing) is an important mental ability of the human species (Van Overwalle et al., 2014). Results of an early large meta-analysis of more than 350 fMRI studies revealed activity in cerebellar areas associated with sensorimotor processing and executive functioning during social cognitive tasks. Initially, the findings were interpreted as domain-general processes linked to semantics, executive functioning, and abstract mentalizing (Van Overwalle et al., 2014).

Resting state fMRI research on the parcellation of cerebellar topography suggests that the cerebellum does carry out domain-specific computations when it comes to social and emotional-related mentalizing (Van Overwalle et al., 2015). In this particular research, cerebello-cortical functional connectivity was analyzed in 1,000 participants (Buckner et al., 2011). Results revealed that, in addition to the presence of at least two homotopic maps of the entire cerebral cortex in the cerebellum, lobules Crus I and II were part of the resting state DMN (Buckner et al., 2011). These results concur with other meta-analytic findings (Wang et al., 2018). The close correspondence between major areas of the DMN and social cognitive-dedicated cerebral cortical areas (e.g., temporo-parietal junction and dorsal medial prefrontal cortex) indicates that the posterolateral cerebellar hemispheres play a substantial role in various emotional and social processes, self-referential thought, and mentalizing (e.g., theory of mind).

These findings were confirmed in a functional neuroimaging study that examined cerebellar surface activation patterns in healthy volunteers during a theory of mind test. A typical theory of mind test focuses on the comprehension of false beliefs. In this particular context, a false belief is the ability of a person to predict the action of a second person in a particular situation, while the person knows that this second individual has an incorrect belief about this situation (Blijd-Hoogewys et al., 2008). Functional decomposition of cerebellar activation revealed activation patterns in Crus I–II, lobule IX, and the vermis VI–X when engaged in theory of mind (King et al., 2019). Theory of mind involves processes associated with language controlling for neural activity patterns induced by verb generation and word reading that leaves left-sided activity in Crus I–II, vermis, and bilateral lobules IX–X (Figure 6.4). This finding concurs with reduced connectivity between the right dorsal TPJ and the left Crus II in ASD, and supports the idea that disruptions of the posterolateral regions in cognitive processes and multimodal integration contribute to social deficits in ASD (Igelström et al., 2017). Activation of the vermis and lobules X–IX illustrates the importance of emotion and the autonomic nervous system in theory of mind, regions which have been reported atypical in ASD as well (Levitt et al., 1999).

In sum, these data further establish the involvement of the cerebellum in cognitive and affective functions that are compromised in ASD.

The cerebellar mapping study by Van Overwalle and Marien (2016) showed that, in accordance with the functional topography of the cerebellum discussed in Chapter 1, the evolutionary older anterior lobe and medial regions involved

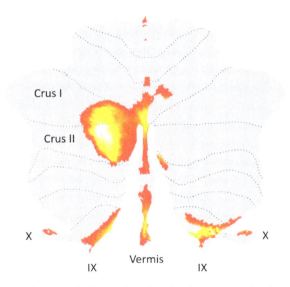

Figure 6.4. Flatmap of the cerebellar surface showing increased activation during theory of mind controlled for activation to verb generation and word reading (King et al., 2019) Source image: http://www.diedrichsenlab.org/imaging/AtlasViewer/viewer.html

in processing sensorimotor and affective inputs are engaged in simulation ('mirroring'). These areas interface the exteroceptive and interoceptive information processing streams. Social signals, like body posture and emotional facial expressions, are internalized to elicit a comparable mental state (affective empathy). The evolutionary younger lateral-posterior cerebellar hemispheres are more involved in mentalizing, such as cognitive deliberations on the context, autobiographical information, beliefs, intentions of the other, and selecting situation appropriate responses (cognitive empathy).

This ability to create and relate to mental states of others is called Theory of Mind (ToM). ToM is an important social skill that enables us to interpret and predict other people's behavior, and it forms the basis of social communication and affiliation. Impaired social communication skills of individuals with ASD have been attributed to a less well-developed ToM (Baron-Cohen et al., 1985). Central to ToM is the capacity to recognize and experience those states (internalization).

Problems in the brain's ability to simulate mental states of others are proposed to be important features of ASD. However, studies investigating mimicry responses to emotional facial expressions in 6–7-year-old children diagnosed with ASD do not show similar facial electromyographic responses as matched controls (Deschamps et al., 2015). So even though the person is responsive to social emotional signals, referencing the information to the self may be impaired, and mentalizing may not occur or result in attribution errors, like eliciting the wrong (emotional) mental state and/or assigning the wrong intentions of others.

Problems in keeping attention can interfere with ToM, in particular when social interactions are not perceived as rewarding or even seen as threatening. For example, the low social approach behavior and high social withdrawal tendencies seen in ASD may stem from disturbances in the brain's reward and punishment circuits (Dawson et al., 2005). In fact, lower or even absent reward responses to social contact, a phenomenon that can already be observed in neonates who appear less responsive to smiling and parental care, interfere with the development of ToM.

Within the framework of predictive coding, ToM involves the building and updating of internal mental models linked to social interactions and communication. These generative models serve as mental representations of causality that allow the person to order/construct a predictable social world. The ability to refine/update the models based on novel experiences provides the necessary mental flexibility to adjust to and cope with changing novel and typically stressful situations. Problems in the brain's predictive coding system, and particularly the cerebellum, may explain why individuals with ASD experience great stress and anxiety when confronted with novel or ambivalent situations that sometimes result in stereotypical responses. In addition, systematizing as one of the core features of ASD can be seen as a coping strategy to minimize uncertainty and avoid stress and anxiety. This could also partly explain the

The socio-emotional cerebellum in ASD 117

attentional focus on details and problems in acquiring knowledge without resorting to analytical (cognitive) reasoning (i.e., intuitive thinking).

A cerebello-vagal theory of autism

Mental inflexibility discussed in the previous section has been linked to disturbances that can already arise on the level of the autonomic nervous system (ANS). The ANS controls visceral bodily functions and innervates muscles and glands, and regulates homeostatic processes, including metabolism, heart rate, thermoregulation (sweating), and digestion (Porges et al., 2003). The ANS can subdivide in the sympathetic, parasympathetic, and enteric nervous system. The sympathetic nervous system is linked to the body's fight-flight system, whereas the parasympathetic nervous system is concerned with relaxation and recovery. In the vast majority of cases, these systems exert mutual antagonistic actions in which one system activates a physiological response and the other system inhibits it. The enteric nervous system is the intrinsic nervous system of the gastrointestinal (digestive) system, and it can function independently from the sympathetic and parasympathetic nervous system.

The vagus nerve, the 10th cranial nerve, represents a major component of the autonomic nervous system. The vagus nerve consists of mainly afferent fibers that relay sensory information about the state of the body's organs to the brain. The core nucleus of the vagal afferents is the nucleus of the solitary tract (NST), a series of clusters of nerve cell bodies that form a vertical column of gray matter in the medulla. Through the center of the solitary nucleus (SN) runs the solitary tract, a white bundle of nerve fibers that includes fibers from the facial, glossopharyngeal, and vagus nerve (Butt et al., 2020). The NST projects to neighboring brainstem regions, such as the locus coeruleus (noradrenaline) and raphe nuclei (serotonin), as well as to the reticular formation, hypothalamus, amygdala, thalamus, and cerebellum. The SN is the primary integrative center for cardiovascular control and other autonomic functions by stimulating the parasympathetic and inhibiting the sympathetic nervous system.

According to the Polyvagal Theory, the mammalian nervous system developed with specific neural and behavioral features that promote and maintain bodily homeostasis in response to environmental challenges (Porges, 2001, 2003). The vagus nerve has three distinct autonomic subdivisions that are associated with specific behavioral correlates (Porges, 2007). The phylogenetically oldest component is the unmyelinated dorsal motor nucleus of the vagus and is associated with immobilization (e.g., freezing). The initiation of fight-flight (mobilization) behavior is governed on the level of the spinal cortex and linked to the sympathetic adrenal system.

Finally, the evolutionary youngest myelinated ventral vagal complex (nucleus ambiguus) is involved in social communication and engagement (e.g., facial expressions and vocalization). The convergence of the vagal components and associated neural structures in the regulation of parasympathetic activity and social communication signals offers a correlate for an integrated social engagement system with facial and visceral components (Porges, 2001, 2003, 2007).

Respiratory sinus arrhythmia (RSA) is frequently used as a physiological proxy for measuring vagal (parasympathetic) tone. RSA indexes moment-to-moment variability in heart rate that occurs during each breathing cycle. In particular, heart rate accelerates when breathing in and decelerates when breathing out. Furthermore, RSA increases during resting state (relaxing) conditions and decreases during stress or tension.

RSA is facilitated by the myelinated ventral vagal complex, providing a mechanism for lowering sympathetic-adrenal activity (vagal brake). Lower-than-normal RSA during resting state has been observed in persons with ASD (Porges et al., 2013). Chronic depression of the myelinated vagal inhibitory action has been put forward as an explanation for the lower mental flexibility and attenuated stress regulation in ASD. The dysfunctional vagal brake arguably causes less social approach and engagement and gives rise to predominantly avoidance-related behaviors.

Support for this idea comes from a study that examined the interrelations between RSA and social behavior in ASD and typically-developing 4–7-year-old children (Patriquin et al., 2013). Resting state RSA amplitudes were positively associated with more conventional gestures, more instances of joint attention, and receptive language abilities in the children with ASD. Comparable to reports of typically developing children, ASD children with higher basal RSA amplitude showed more RSA suppression during an attention demanding task. These findings are in good agreement with other studies showing a positive correlation of RSA with emotion recognition, social skills, and less parent-reported behavioral problems (Bal et al., 2010; Van Hecke et al., 2009).

While there is no conclusive evidence that disturbances in vagal function can be causally linked to ASD, vagus nerve stimulation (VNS) has shown promising effects in overcoming insufficient vagal function and contributes to improving social functioning in ASD (Engineer et al., 2017). VNS is an FDA approved add-on therapy that is safe and effective in reducing seizure frequency and duration in individuals with epilepsy. Like a pacemaker, VNS innervates the vagal nerve by sending regular mild electrical pulses. The pulse generator is implanted in the upper side of the chest, and a thin flexible wire that connects the pulse generator to the vagal nerve is inserted through a small incision in the lower part of the neck.

The functional link between the cerebellum and vagus nerve in humans was highlighted in a positron emission tomography (PET) study that examined changes in blood flow in response to VNS (Henry et al., 1998). Ten patients with partial epilepsy underwent PET scans before and during left cervical VNS. Increases in blood flow were observed in the brainstem, hypothalamus, thalamus, insular cortex, and cerebellar hemispheres, while decreases in blood flow were found in the amygdala, hippocampus, and posterior cingulate. The findings indicate that the vagal nerve can directly innervate regions dedicated to autonomic activity and somatosensory information processing, as well as the limbic system (Henry et al., 1998).

In a more recent study VNS-related activation of these regions was found to be part of a network associated with good treatment efficacy (Yu et al., 2018). Studies using VNS in children with both epilepsy and ASD have shown that VNS reduces seizure frequency and improves affective and cognitive functioning in ASD (Levy et al., 2010). Even though, there are some indications that the effects of VNS on ASD symptoms are independent of the changes in seizure activity, clearly more research is needed to evaluate the specificity of VNS in ASD (van Hoorn et al., 2019).

Alternative non-invasive forms of VNS, including stimulation of the auricular branch of the ear (auricular neuromodulation), which is anatomically connected to the vagus nerve, are currently tested on their ability to influence vagal tone and behavior (Mercante et al., 2018). As demonstrated in a recent experimentally controlled fMRI study in healthy volunteers, auricular neuromodulation activates the afferent vagal pathways and increases regional blood flow in the left frontal cortex, cingulate cortex, striatum, and cerebellum (Badran et al., 2017). If transcutaneous vagal stimulation proves to elicit predictable physiological effects, then large-scale randomized controlled trials become more readily feasible to conduct. Figure 6.5 depicts the anatomical locations of cerebellar activation in response to electric stimulation of the auricular branch.

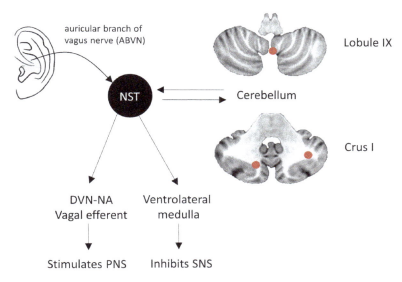

Figure 6.5. Transcutaneous auricular vagus nerve stimulation increases regional blood flow in bilateral Crus I and the nodular lobe (IX) of the vermis. Regions of interest overlap with peak activations as reported in the original study by Badran et al. (2017)

The findings in humans concur with animal studies that have isolated projections of vagal afferents via climbing fibers to the vermis (Okahara & Nisimaru, 1991). Indeed, closer examination of the climbing fiber representation of the vagal afferents to the cerebellum indicates that vagal input into the cerebellum has modulatory effects on the cerebellar somatosensory input (Tong et al., 1991).

In relation to ASD, epileptogenic (kindling)-like neural activity, including dysfunctions of the autonomic nervous system may be part of the pathophysiology of ASD. This could explain why ASD and epilepsy often co-occur (Jeste & Tuchman, 2015). Previous pioneering work by neurologists like Irving Cooper (Cooper & Upton, 1978) have demonstrated that subdural electric stimulation of the cerebellar cortical surface has anti-epileptic effects. Presumably owing to its modulatory effects on limbic and cerebral cortical regions, as well as the vagal nerve, the cerebellum may play a role in preventing uncontrollable electric disturbances in the central and peripheral nervous system. Moreover, electric stimulation of the rabbit cerebellar vermis has been shown to induce vagal-related changes in autonomic activity including effects on heart rate and blood pressure (Rocha et al., 2008). If the reciprocal cerebello-vagal pathway turns out to play a role in ASD, then targeting this pathway should, analogous to treating epilepsy, improve behavioral symptoms.

In addition to the vermis, deep cerebellar stimulation of the fastigial nucleus, a region that receives dense inhibitory projections from the vermis, produces cardiac arrhythmia in anesthetized cats (Al Senawi & Downman, 1983). As outlined in Chapter 1 on cerebellar neuroanatomy, the deep cerebellar nuclei are innervated by the Purkinje cell layer of the cerebellar cortex, but at the same time also receive collateral excitatory input from the mossy and climbing fibers.

On a final speculative account, reduced downstream inhibitory input in conjunction with upstream excitatory input from the ascending fibers may cause dysfunctional hyperactivity of the fastigial nucleus and disrupt cerebellar output to connected distal brain regions. Injecting high frequency electric currents or random electric noise into the fastigial nucleus may create a virtual lesion that will effectively works as a circuit breaker. This idea concurs with recent experimental modelling theories that predict that DCN stimulation is more effective in normalizing aberrant brain activity than cerebellar cortical stimulation (Kros et al., 2015). In sum, the available scientific work suggests that the modulation of cerebellar functioning may be one of the possible routes for developing novel ways to improve socio-emotional functioning in persons with ASD. Particularly, applying neuromodulation techniques as an adjuvant (priming) treatment to behavioral training programs may have added value for improving cognitive functioning, motor coordination, and social communicative skills in ASD.

Conclusion

The cerebellum in ASD shows disturbances on the cellular organization, structural deviances, and abnormal functional activity. Brain research has shown that the socio-emotional problems involve cerebellum-related dysregulation of autonomic functioning, mentalizing, and empathy. The cerebellum is a central node implicated in widely distributed and complex networks in the brain that are disorganized in ASD as a result of cerebellar dysfunction.

References

Allen G (2005). The cerebellum in autism. *Clin. Neuropsychiatry* 2, 321–337.

Al Senawi DE, Downman CB (1983). Cardiac arrhythmic response evoked by stimulation of fastigial nuclei in the anesthetized cat. *J. Auton. Nerv. Syst.* 8, 15–24.

Aoki Y, Kasai K, Yamasue H (2012). Age-related change in brain metabolite abnormalities in autism: a meta-analysis of proton magnetic resonance spectroscopy studies. *Transl. Psychiatry.* 2, e69.

Asperger H (1944). Die 'autistischen psychopathen' im kindesalter. *Arch. Psychiatr. Nervenkr.* 117, 76–136.

Bal E, Harden E., Lamb D, Van Hecke AV, Denver JW, Porges SW (2010). Emotion recognition in children with autism spectrum disorders: Relations to eye gaze and autonomic state. *J. Autism Dev. Disord.* 40, 358–370. Baron-Cohen S, Leslie AM, Frith U (1985). Does the autistic child have a 'theory of mind'? *Cognition* 21, 37–46.

Baron-Cohen S (2002). The extreme male brain theory of autism. *Trends Cogn. Sci.* 6, 248–254.

Baron-Cohen S, Cassidy S, Auyeung B, et al. (2014). Attenuation of typical sex differences in 800 adults with autism vs. 3,900 controls. *PLoS One* 9, e102251.

Becker KG (2012). Male gender bias in autism and pediatric autoimmunity. *Autism Res.* 5, 77–83.

Becker EB, Stoodley CJ (2013). Autism spectrum disorder and the cerebellum. *Int. Rev. Neurobiol.* 113, 1–34.

Blijd-Hoogewys EM, van Geert PL, Serra M, Minderaa RB (2008). Measuring theory of mind in children. Psychometric properties of the ToM Storybooks. *J. Autism Dev. Disord.* 38, 1907–1930.

Buckner RL, Krienen FM, Castellanos A, Diaz JC, Yeo BT (2011). The organization of the human cerebellum estimated by intrinsic functional connectivity. *J. Neurophysiol.* 106, 2322–2345.

Butt MF, Albusoda A, Farmer AD, Aziz Q (2020). The anatomical basis for transcutaneous auricular vagus nerve stimulation. *J. Anat.* 236, 588–611.

Chen C, Hung AY, Fan YT, Tan S, Hong H, Cheng Y (2017). Linkage between pain sensitivity and empathic response in adolescents with autism spectrum conditions and conduct disorder symptoms. *Autism Res.* 10, 267–275.

Chrobak AA, Soltys Z (2017). Bergmann glia, long-term depression, and autism spectrum disorder. *Mol. Neurobiol.* 54, 1156–1166.

Cooper IS, Upton AR (1978). Use of chronic cerebellar stimulation for disorders of disinhibition. *Lancet* 1, 595–600.

Courchesne E (1997). Brainstem, cerebellar and limbic neuroanatomical abnormalities in autism. *Curr. Opin. Neurobiol.* 7, 269–278.

Damasio A (2003). Feelings of emotion and the self. *Ann. N.Y. Acad. Sci.* 1001, 253–261.

Dawson G, Webb SJ, McPartland J (2005). Understanding the nature of face processing impairment in autism: insights from behavioral and electrophysiological studies. *Dev. Neuropsychol.* 27, 403–424.

D'Mello AM, Stoodley CJ (2015). Cerebro-cerebellar circuits in autism spectrum disorder. *Front. Neurosci.* 9, 408.

Dumais KM, Veenema AH (2016). Vasopressin and oxytocin receptor systems in the brain: Sex differences and sex-specific regulation of social behavior. *Front. Neuroendocrinol.* 40, 1–23.

Engineer CT, Hays SA, Kilgard MP (2017). Vagus nerve stimulation as a potential adjuvant to behavioral therapy for autism and other neurodevelopmental disorders. *J. Neurodev. Disord.* 4, 20.

Ferri SL, Abel T, Brodkin ES (2018). Sex differences in autism spectrum disorder: A review. *Curr. Psychiatry Rep.* 20, 9.

Giza J, Urbanski MJ, Prestori F, Bandyopadhyay B, Yam A, Friedrich V, et al. (2010). Behavioral and cerebellar transmission deficits in mice lacking the autism-linked gene islet brain-2. *J. Neurosci* 30, 14805–14816.

Haida O, Al Sagheer T, Balbous A, Francheteau M, Matas E, Soria F, Fernagut PO, Jaber M (2019). Sex-dependent behavioral deficits and neuropathology in a maternal immune activation model of autism. *Transl. Psychiatry* 9, 124.

Henry TR, Bakay RA, Votaw JR, Pennell PB, Epstein CM, Faber TL, et al. (1998). Brain blood flow alterations induced by therapeutic vagus nerve stimulation in partial epilepsy: I. Acute effects at high and low levels of stimulation. *Epilepsia* 39, 983–990.

Hoffman JF, Wright CL, McCarthy MM (2016). A critical period in Purkinje cell development is mediated by local estradiol synthesis, disrupted by inflammation, and has enduring consequences only for males. *J. Neurosci.* 36, 10039–10049.

Igelström KM, Webb TW, Graziano MSA (2017). Functional Connectivity Between the Temporoparietal Cortex and Cerebellum in Autism Spectrum Disorder. *Cereb. Cortex* 27, 2617–2627.

Ipser JC, Syal S, Bentley J, Adnams CM, Steyn B, Stein DJ (2012). 1H-MRS in autism spectrum disorders: A systematic meta-analysis. *Metab. Brain Dis.* 27, 275–287.

Jeste SS, Tuchman R (2015). Autism spectrum disorder and epilepsy: Two sides of the same coin? *J. Child Neurol.* 30, 1963–1971.

Kanner L (1943). Autistic disturbances of affective contact. *Nerv. Child.* 2, 217–250.

Keysers C, Thioux M, Gazzola V. (2011). Mirror neuron system and social cognition. In: J Decety & JT Cacioppo (Eds), *Handbook of Social Neuroscience.* New York: Oxford University Press.

King M, Hernandez-Castillo CR, Poldrack RA, Ivry RB, Diedrichsen J (2019). Functional boundaries in the human cerebellum revealed by a multi-domain task battery. *Nat. Neurosci.* 22, 1371–1378.

Kros L, Eelkman Rooda OHJ, De Zeeuw CI, Hoebeek FE (2015). Controlling cerebellar output to treat refractory epilepsy. *Trends Neurosci.* 38, 787–799.

Levitt JG, Blanton R, Capetillo-Cunliffe L, Guthrie D, Toga A, McCracken JT (1999). Cerebellar vermis lobules VIII-X in autism. *Prog Neuropsychopharmacol Biol Psychiatry.* 23, 625–633.

Levy ML, Levy KM, Hoff D, Amar AP, Park MS, Conklin JM, et al. (2010). Vagus nerve stimulation therapy in patients with autism spectrum disorder and intractable epilepsy: results from the vagus nerve stimulation therapy patient outcome registry. *J. Neurosurg. Pediatr.* 5, 595–602.

Limperopoulos, C., Bassan, H., Gauvreau, K., Robertson, R.L., Jr., Sullivan, N.R., Benson, C.B., et al. (2007). Does cerebellar injury in premature infants contribute to the high prevalence of long-term cognitive, learning, and behavioral disability in survivors? *Pediatrics* 120, 584–593.

Manni E, Petrosini L (2004). A century of cerebellar somatotopy: A debated representation. *Nat. Rev. Neurosci.* 5, 241–249.

Mash EJ, Barkley RA (2003). *Child psychopathology.* New York: Guilford Press.

Mayo Clinic. Autism spectrum disorder. https://www.mayoclinic.org/diseases-conditions/autism-spectrum-disorder/symptoms-causes/syc-20352928.

Mercante B, Deriu F, Rangon CM (2018). Auricular neuromodulation: The emerging concept beyond the stimulation of vagus and trigeminal nerves. *Medicines (Basel)* 5, 10.

Neumann ID, Landgraf R (2012). Balance of brain oxytocin and vasopressin: implications for anxiety, depression, and social behaviors. *Trends Neurosci.* 35, 649–659.

Okahara K, Nisimaru N (1991). Climbing fiber responses evoked in lobule VII of the posterior cerebellum from a vagal nerve in rabbits. *Neurosci. Res.* 12, 232–239.

Patriquin MA, Scarpa A, Friedman BH, Porges SW (2013). Respiratory sinus arrhythmia: a marker for positive social functioning and receptive language skills in children with autism spectrum disorders. *Dev. Psychobiol.* 55, 101–112.

Porges SW (2001). The polyvagal theory: Phylogenetic substrates of a social nervous system. *Int. J. Psychophysiol.* 42, 123–146.

Porges SW (2003). The polyvagal theory: Phylogenetic contributions to social behavior. *Physiol. Behav.* 79, 503–513.

Porges SW (2007). The polyvagal perspective. *Biol. Psychol.* 74, 116–143.

Porges SW, Macellaio M, Stanfill SD, McCue K, Lewis GF, Harden ER, et al. (2013). Respiratory sinus arrhythmia and auditory processing in autism: Modifiable deficits of an integrated social engagement system? *Int. J. Psychophysiol.* 88, 261–270.

Rocha I, Gonçalves V, Bettencourt MJ, Silva-Carvalho L (2008). Effect of stimulation of sublobule IX-b of the cerebellar vermis on cardiac function. *Physiol. Res.* 57, 701–707.

Soda T, Mapelli L, Locatelli F, Botta L, Goldfarb M, Prestori F, D'Angelo E (2019). Hyperexcitability and hyperplasticity disrupt cerebellar signal transfer in the IB2 KO mouse model of autism. *J. Neurosci.* 39, 2383–2397.

Traut N, Beggiato A, Bourgeron T, Delorme R, Rondi-Reig L, Paradis AL, et al. (2018). Cerebellar volume in autism: Literature meta-analysis and analysis of the autism brain imaging data exchange cohort. *Biol. Psychiatry* 83, 579–588.

Tsakanikos E, Underwood L, Kravariti E, Bouras N, McCarthy J (2011). Gender differences in co-morbid psychopathology and clinical management in adults with autism spectrum disorders. *Res. Autism Spect. Dis.* 5, 803–808.

Van Hecke AV, Lebow J, Bal E, Lamb D, Harden E, Kramer A, et al. (2009). Electroencephalogram and heart rate regulation to familiar and unfamiliar people in children with autism spectrum disorders. *Child Dev.* 80, 1118–1133.

Van Hoorn A, Carpenter T, Oak K, Laugharne R, Ring H, Shankar R (2019). Neuromodulation of autism spectrum disorders using vagal nerve stimulation. *J. Clin. Neurosci.* 63, 8–12.

Van Overwalle F, Baetens K, Mariën P, Vandekerckhove M (2014). Social cognition and the cerebellum: A meta-analysis of over 350 fMRI studies. *NeuroImage* 86, 554–572.

Van Overwalle F, Baetens K, Mariën P, Vandekerckhove M (2015). Cerebellar areas dedicated to social cognition? A comparison of meta-analytic and connectivity results. *Soc. Neurosci.* 10, 337–344.

Van Overwalle F, Mariën P (2016). Functional connectivity between the cerebrum and cerebellum in social cognition: A multi-study analysis. *NeuroImage* 124, 248–255.

Vaughan S, McGlone F, Poole H, Moore DJ (2019). *A quantitative sensory testing approach to pain in autism spectrum disorders*. *J. Autism Dev. Disord.* 50, 1607–1620. doi:10.1007/s10803-019-03918-0.

Verkhratsky A, Butt, AM (2013). *Glial Physiology and Pathophysiology*. New York: John Wiley and Sons, Inc.

Walker BR, Diefenbach KS, Parikh TN (2007). Inhibition within the nucleus tractus solitarius (NTS) ameliorates environmental exploration deficits due to cerebellum lesions in an animal model for autism. *Behav. Brain Res.* 176, 109–120.

Wang C, Pan YH, Wang Y, Blatt G, Yuan XB (2019). Segregated expressions of autism risk genes Cdh11 and Cdh9 in autism-relevant regions of developing cerebellum. *Mol. Brain* 12, 40.

Wang W, Liu J, Shi S, Liu T, Ma L, Ma X, et al. (2018). Altered resting-state functional activity in patients with autism spectrum disorder: A quantitative meta-analysis. *Front. Neurol.* 9, 556.

Wegiel J, Kuchna I, Nowicki K, Imaki H, Wegiel J, Marchi E, et al. (2010). The neuropathology of autism: Defects of neurogenesis and neuronal migration, and dysplastic changes. *Neuropsychol. Rev.* 119, 755–770.

Welman MFH, Smit AE, Jongen JLM, Tibboel D, van der Geest JN, Holstege JC (2018). Pain experience is somatotopically organized and overlaps with pain anticipation in the human cerebellum. *Cerebellum* 17, 447–460.

Yamada K, Watanabe M (2002). Cytodifferentiation of Bergmann glia and its relationship with Purkinje cells. *Anat. Sci. Int.* 77, 94–108.

Yu R, Park HJ, Cho H, Ko A, Pae C, Oh MK, et al., (2018). Interregional metabolic connectivity of 2-deoxy-2[18 F]fluoro-D-glucose positron emission tomography in vagus nerve stimulation for pediatric patients with epilepsy: A retrospective cross-sectional study. *Epilepsia* 59, 2249–2259.

Chapter 7

Emotionally explosive minds

A cerebellum-oriented theory on reactive aggression

Cesare Lombroso (1835–1909) was best known and infamous for his theory of anthropological criminology. He postulated the idea that criminality and anti-social behavior was inherited and could be identified on the basis of physical characteristics. In his search for validity for his theory, he made acquaintance with the notorious bandit Giuseppe Villela. After Villela's death, Lombroso was assigned to perform postmortem examination. Abduction of the brain revealed a greatly enlarged cerebellar vermis which led to the impression that malformation of the cerebellum contributed to antisocial behavior. In addition to being among the first people to advocate the idea that criminality could result from neurophysiological problems, Lombroso was among the first to recognize a possible link between disruptive behavioral disorders and the cerebellum.

Disruptive behavioral disorders (DBD) refer to a group of disorders that can be observed in children and adolescents. DBDs include oppositional defiant disorder (ODD), conduct disorder (CD), and intermittent explosive disorders (IED) (APA, 2013). Kleptomania and pyromania also fall under this group of disorders but are rare conditions and will not be further considered here.

Children with ODD often lose their temper, are easily annoyed, and are often angry and resentful. This irritable mood is complemented by behaviors associated with frequent arguing with authority figures, refusing to comply with requests or rules, deliberately annoying others, and blaming others for their mistakes. Holding grudges and seeking revenge (vindictiveness) are also symptoms of ODD. These symptoms are more severe than normal misbehavior and upset the individual or others around him/her, thereby causing problems at school, work, and/or social activities.

CD is a more serious disorder than ODD and involves more extreme forms of misbehavior. The child or adolescent behaves aggressively toward people and/or animals and may engage in bullying, physical fights, use of a weapon, torturing animals, destroying other people's property on purpose, lying or stealing, or violating important rules (such as running away overnight or skipping school before age 13) (APA, 2013). These behaviors cause significant problems in school and social activities. CD is only diagnosed in children and

126 Emotionally explosive minds

youth up to 18 years of age. Adults with similar symptoms may be diagnosed with antisocial personality disorder (APA, 2013). In particular, the presence of callous-unemotional traits (i.e., lack of empathy, no remorse, shallow affect) often is accompanied by severe aggression and antisocial behavior and is a predictor for the development of psychopathy in adults.

Persons with IED have frequent impulsive, aggressive, angry outbursts. These outbursts can be either verbal or physical aggression and are directed toward property, animals, or other people. Importantly, the rage-like outbursts are out of proportion to the event or incident that triggered them and cause much distress for the person, often leading to problems at work or home. IED is not diagnosed in children under age 6 (APA, 2013), and individuals who have experienced physical and emotional trauma as a child or teenager are at greater risk of developing

Forty percent of children and adolescents with conduct disorder also meet criteria for an anxiety or mood-related disorder (Lahey et al., 2002). It has been proposed that individuals with DBDs show disturbances in two distinct neural circuits (Blair, 2013). The first (bottom-up) emotional system is implicated in the processing and regulations of emotions in which the subcortical limbic circuit plays a leading role. The second (top-down) cognitive system more specifically involves the striatum and the prefrontal cortex, which are dedicated to action monitoring, working memory, and response inhibition (Blair, 2013).

In particular a hypersensitive emotional system has been linked to anger outbursts and impulsive aggression. Indeed, a person in a state of rage is devoid from the capacity for rational thought and reasoning. Anger attacks may reach a point of no return ('seeing red'), whereby the subject engages in violence and aggressive acts until the individual is incapacitated or the source of their rage has been eliminated. The urgency and the 'instantaneous' affective phenomenological experience is typical of rage. When an organism is frustrated, threatened, or otherwise irritated and preparing to remove an obstacle or subdue an attacker, it will initiate strong activation of the sympathetic nervous system. The most notable changes involve a rise in blood pressure, increased muscle tone, and heart rate acceleration. Notably, the behaviors associated with rage show remarkable similarities both within and across the mammalian species, like a rodent, a dog, a monkey, or a human jumping on or striking out at an adversary (Panksepp & Biven, 2012; Panksepp, 2016). In humans, rage is also associated with less archetypal expressions, such as pounding on an uncooperative vending machine, making a sarcastic comment, or rude and offensive gestures.

Neuroscientific evidence has shown that the internally experienced motivation linked to extreme anger and rage originates from the instinctual action system located in the subcortical circuits of the mammalian brain (Panksepp & Biven, 2012). Indeed, electric stimulation of the anger neurocircuits in a mammal evokes autonomic (sympathetic) arousal, hissing, growling, and aggressive behavior towards anything in its direct surroundings.

Elaborate anatomical research has identified several crucial regions that comprise the anger circuit. The amygdala is a collection of nuclei dedicated to the detection of threat. The amygdala works like a switch that directly signals the hypothalamus when a potential threat is being perceived. The medial hypothalamus is central to the regulation of the autonomic system and has a gain function to prepare the body for action. From there, fibers run to specific locations in the periaqueductal gray (PAG) of the midbrain, which are concerned with the commands to execute rage-like behavior (output) (Panksepp, 1998). This form of aggression elicited by this so-called rage circuit involves a sharp rise in sympathetic nervous system activity and is known as affective attack or defensive rage (Panksepp & Biven, 2012). As will be discussed later in this chapter, animal and human studies have verified associations between anger attacks and immediate automatic activation of the sympathetic *FIGHT* mode governed by hypothalamic-centered steroid-responsive networks under the supervision of the cerebellum (Panksepp & Biven, 2012; Schutter, 2013; van Honk & Schutter, 2006; van Honk et al., 2010). Figure 7.1. shows the subcortical circuit associated with rage and affective (reactive) aggression.

In contrast, predatory aggression is more instrumental, premeditated, and appetitive. In cats, predatory aggression can be evoked by stimulating the lateral hypothalamus, which is part of the brain's dopaminergic reward (seeking)

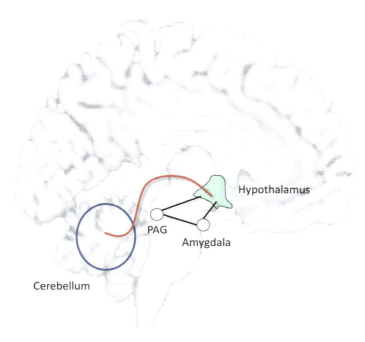

Figure 7.1. Cerebello-subcortical rage circuit

system that also includes the striatum (e.g., nucleus accumbens) and cerebral cortex (e.g., prefrontal cortex) (Panksepp & Zellner, 2004). Moreover, reward-initiated approach behavior is facilitated by low punishment sensitivity that effectively downplays the *FLIGHT* modus. For example, hyposensitivity to punishment can already be demonstrated in DBD children who show poor fear conditioning to aversive stimuli as compared to matched controls (Gao et al., 2010).

Feelings of anger can be mitigated in animals and humans whose brains are equipped with a sophisticated cognitive system. Extensive research has shown that anger attacks and aggression involve dysfunction of the brain's cognitive control system. More specifically, the prefrontal cortex (PFC) is considered the seat of high-level cognitive functioning that modulates activity of the motivation-dedicated subcortical limbic regions that include the amygdala and hypothalamus (Bartholow, 2018). The supervisory role of the PFC is expressed by evaluating and anticipating the consequences of future actions. As such, actions like anger outbursts and aggressive behaviors that are most likely to bring higher costs (e.g., incarceration) than benefits (e.g., emotional tension relief) should be avoided, and these subcortical motivational tendencies should be inhibited.

However, these cerebral cortical oriented top-down regulation models are less suitable to explain the rapid onset and escalation of rage and aggressive outbursts to allow any form of conscious rational-based intervention or cognitive control (Mobbs et al., 2007). This phenomenon can be understood by differences in temporal processing of the subcortical and cortical pathways. While the subcortical route processes information quickly (~15 ms), processing in the cortical pathway takes considerably more time (i.e., hundreds of ms) (Davidson, 2000; LeDoux, 2000; van Honk et al., 2010; Bartholow, 2018). From this viewpoint, anger and aggression can thus be evoked by a (1) hypersensitive rage circuit, (2) hyperreactive reward circuit, (3) hyposensitive punishment system, and (4) hypoactive cortical control circuit, or a combination of the four.

The cerebellum in rage and impulsive aggression

From neuropsychological research, we now know that lesions to the cerebellum can cause affective and cognitive disturbances, including impairments in emotion regulation, impulsivity, and unexplainable anger (Schmahmann & Sherman, 1998; Hoche et al., 2018). These clinical observations concur with studies during the 1970s in which, similar to the concept of a pacemaker, intracranial electric stimulation of the cerebellum normalized behavior in severely disordered patients suffering from rage and aggression (Heath, 1977; Heath, Llewellyn et al., 1980; Heath, Dempsey et al., 1980). Another important lead for cerebellar involvement in rage and aggression comes from animal studies that found a causal link between perturbing cerebellar activity and eliciting rage and aggressive behavioral displays (Berman et al., 1978; Heath et al., 1977).

An activation-likelihood estimation meta-analysis (GingerALE 2.3.6, www.brainmap.org) of functional neuroimaging studies (search criteria: 'fMRI' and 'anger' and/or 'aggression') to weigh the evidence of the available human data. Coordinates of cerebellum activation of 17 studies in healthy participants were entered in a standard cluster-level based analysis ($p = 0.05$). The null distribution of the ALE statistic at each voxel was determined with a permutation test (1,000 permutations). These p values were then used to calculate the activation threshold (false discovery rate was set at $p = 0.001$). Results revealed several activation clusters in the cerebellum associated with anger and aggressive tendencies (Figure 7.2).

Research in the affective neurosciences has shown that the vermis (paleocerebellum) is linked to the affective (visceral) experience, the anterior lobe is concerned with somatosensory representation and motor preparation/commands, and the (neocerebellar) posterior lobe serves a regulatory function (Stoodley & Schmahmann, 2018). A systematic review and ALE meta-analysis of structural and functional neuroimaging revealed no evidence for cerebellum abnormalities in children with either ODD or CD (Noordermeer et al., 2016).

In contrast, some indication was found for smaller cerebellar volumes in ODD/CD with comorbid attention deficit hyperactivity disorder (ADHD). Findings from another meta-analysis of volumetric region-of-interest (ROI) studies indicates that lower volumes of total cerebellum and vermian lobules VIII–X in ADHD are able to account for the observed effect by the former meta-analysis (Valera et al., 2007). Functional neuroimaging studies have further complemented the structural findings by demonstrating patterns of cerebellar hypoactivation during expectancy violation (Durston et al., 2007), as well as lower resting state functional connectivity in fronto-striatal-cerebellar circuits (Konrad & Eickhoff, 2010). These observations suggest that impairments

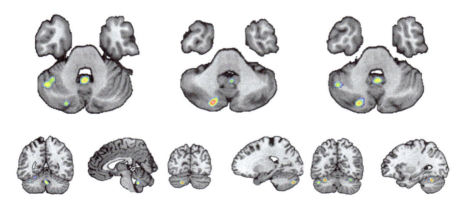

Figure 7.2. Clusters of bilateral activation of the anterior (lobule VI) and posterior lobes (Crus I) of the cerebellum and cerebellar vermis (IX-nodular lobe) associated with anger and motivational tendencies associated with aggressive behavior.

130 Emotionally explosive minds

predicting temporal and contextual cues in the environment interfere with behavioral flexibility and adaptation. Furthermore, soft signs of compromised cerebellar functions have repeatedly been demonstrated in individuals with ADHD and include increased postural sway and behavioral impairments sensorimotor timing (Hove et al., 2015; Hove et al., 2017).

While there appear to be no cerebellar disturbances in ODD/CD only, deviations of regional cerebellar activity have been documented in a male adolescent group with CD (Wu et al., 2017). Assessment of the temporal synchrony of regional blood oxygen level-dependent (BOLD) signals, together with similarities in spontaneous neural activity, showed deviations in temporal-parietal-limbic regions and cerebellum as compared to matched controls. For the cerebellum in particular, lower signal synchrony was observed in the left anterior (lobule V) and right posterior (lobule VI) regions. As shown in Figure 7.2, lobule VI is among the regions that are activated during the emotion anger, and the current deviations found in CD may hint at altered processing and regulation of aggression-related emotions.

The possible contributions of ADHD symptoms to the deviations of spontaneous neural activity in the CD group were not examined, which leaves open the possibility that the regional deviations are not specific for CD. On the other hand, ADHD and DBD share several symptoms (e.g., impulsivity), so a categorical division between the two conditions may in fact be misleading and even incorrect.

In adults, cerebellar abnormalities have been demonstrated in individuals diagnosed with antisocial personality disorder (APD) (Moreno-Rius, 2019). Large volumetric gray matter reductions have been observed in the right lobule VI of the posterior cerebellum in violent offenders with psychopathic, as compared to non-psychopathic, tendencies as assessed with the Hare Psychopathy Checklist-revised (PCL-R) and non-offenders (Kolla et al., 2014). Interestingly, results once again pinpointed lobule VI as one of the cerebellar regions that showed consistent abnormalities. Electric stimulation of the cerebral face area in monkeys elicited neural responses in posterior regions of the anterior lobe and lobule VI (Snider & Eldred, 1952). Even though the functional significance of lobe VI activity remains to be elucidated, the latter findings may hint at a possible distortion in the face representation areas of the cerebellum in APD, which, in turn, may impair face perception. The perception of negative emotional faces, including those that depict anger, sadness, disgust, and fear, are interpersonal communication signals, which are crucial for theory of mind, empathy, and interpreting social (correction) signals, which are arguably compromised in APD (Blair, 2013; van Honk et al., 2010).

Examination of intrinsic functional connectivity patterns in the human brain has revealed that lobule IV largely maps to cerebral networks associated with premotor cortex and the supplementary motor area, regions associated with motor control and response selection (Buckner et al., 2011). These findings may reveal abnormalities in parts of the neural circuit supposedly involved in affective attack/defensive rage. Disrupted functional connectivity patterns between posterior parts of the cerebellum and cortical association areas linked to the DMN and attention networks in violent offenders further point towards problems in aligning interoceptive and exteroceptive information (Tang et al., 2013). Additionally, violent offenders as compared to controls also show enhanced cerebellar-amygdala and lower cerebellar-PFC functional connectivity (Leutgeb et al., 2016). These findings indicate heightened emotionality involving the anteromedial parts of the cerebellum and reduced regulation capacity associated with the posterolateral cerebellar hemispheres.

In addition to issues with the cerebello-dentato-thalamic cortical pathway, a recent animal study found causal evidence for involvement of the vermis in aggression. In this study, optogenetic methods were used to modulate activity of cerebellar Purkinje cells in lobule VII of the vermis to examine aggressive behavior (e.g., biting attacks) in mice (Jackman et al., 2020). Optogenetics is a technique that uses light to control activity of genetically modified living cells that produces light-sensitive proteins called opsins. Results showed that increasing the inhibitory Purkinje cell activity in the vermis lowered the frequency of biting attacks in a so-called resident-intruder paradigm, whereas optogenetic inhibition of the same cells significantly enhanced biting attacks. The effects were specific as motor performance and other behaviors, including self-grooming by the resident and social interactions, were not affected. Optogenetic stimulation of Purkinje cells in Crus II did not influence aggressive behavior. These findings add to the existing literature that the vermis are implicated in aggressive behavior and a special role is reserved for the inhibitory output of Purkinje cells to the fastigial nucleus. These results imply that the vermis is particularly involved in the regulation of defensive affective (reactive) forms of aggression located in the subcortical system, while the posterolateral hemispheres may be more implicated in predatory (proactive) forms of aggression involving the cerebello-cortical loops.

The study by Kolla et al. (2014) reported a similar rate of substance use disorders between extreme and less extreme APD groups, suggesting that the volumetric reduction is not due to the deleterious effects of drugs. What may be notable in this respect are findings of smaller gray matter volumes of superior frontal, cingulate, and parahippocampal gyri, amygdala, thalamus, and right cerebellum (lobule V) in individuals at high-risk for alcohol dependence (Benegal et al., 2007). Since the reductions were positively associated with the presence of externalizing symptoms, these results were taken as evidence in support of abnormalities in regions that play a role in reward seeking and approach-related behavior (Benegal et al., 2006). The fact that substance abuse and dependence is common in persons with APD may hint at a sensitive predatory aggression circuit in people with severe impulse control issues. Demonstrations of bilateral activation of lobule V to appetitive pictures in convicted criminal psychopaths (PCL-R score > 30) further support the proposed role of this region in reward-related arousal and subjective experience (Müller et al., 2003).

The right-lateralized involvement of the cerebellum and its contralateral projections to the left cerebral cortical hemisphere supplements the cerebral cortical asymmetry of motivational direction (Harmon-Jones, 2013; Schutter & Harmon-Jones, 2013). The balance between activity in the left and right frontal cortex, commonly referred to as asymmetric frontal cortical activity, has served as a proxy for an organism's approach and avoidance-related motivational tendencies. In particular, many studies have examined the influence of the manipulation of motivational direction on asymmetrical frontal cortical activity and found results consistent with the idea that greater relative left frontal cortical activity is associated with approach motivation and anger (Kelley et al., 2017).

These manipulation studies are complemented by previous observations of dominant left-sided frontal electric cortical asymmetries in psychopathic individuals, providing a neural correlate that could in part explain the approach-motivation related lifestyle that includes sensation seeking, risk-taking, and aggression (Hecht, 2011). The findings have been independently replicated in a sample of imprisoned violent offenders by showing that the direction and degree of left-sided anterior brain activity was positively associated with aggressive behavior (Keune et al., 2012). Whether an analogous but opposite asymmetry exists on the level of the cerebellum remains to be tested, but based on what is currently known about the crossed cerebello-cortical connections, lateralized involvement of the right and left cerebellar hemispheres in approach- and withdrawal-related motivation, respectively, can be expected.

To further explore the cerebellar regions activated during anger and aggression, a coordinate-based activation likelihood estimation meta-analysis was performed on 28 fMRI studies reporting 57 cerebellar activation foci from 819 participants (Klaus & Schutter, 2020). Results showed significant activation clusters in the right anterior as well as left anterior lobules V and VI, and Crus I–II of the left posterior cerebellar hemisphere. In addition, aggressive behavior following provocation activated lobules V and VI and Crus I, while cerebellar activity during passive viewing of anger-related stimuli was restricted to left-hemispheric lobules VIIIA and VIIIB.

Based on earlier magnetoencephalography (MEG) research that mapped out the temporal dynamics of the different cerebellar regions during emotion processing (Styliadis et al., 2015), and what is currently known about the functional topography of the cerebellum, the observed activation pattern fits a provocation-related perception-action loop. Figure 7.3 shows a neurofunctional framework of aggression depicting the suggested involvement of the specified cerebellar regions in the different processing stages in aggression (Klaus & Schutter, 2020).

The contributions of the cerebellum in predatory (proactive) aggression versus affective (reactive) aggression can be traced back to its connections to the cerebral cortex and limbic system, respectively. The connections of the posterolateral cerebellar areas to the frontal cortex support the premeditated

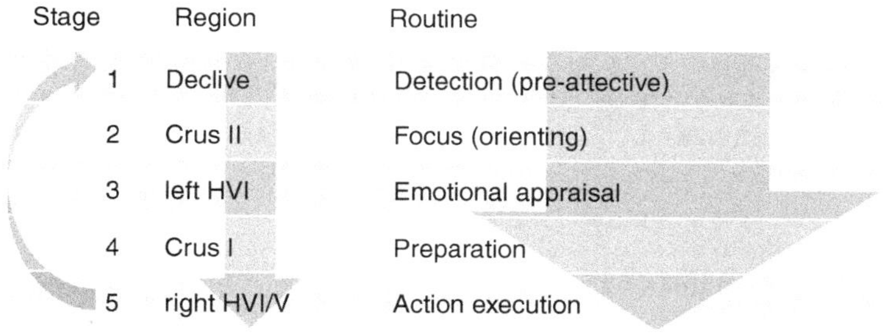

Stage	Region	Routine
1	Declive	Detection (pre-attective)
2	Crus II	Focus (orienting)
3	left HVI	Emotional appraisal
4	Crus I	Preparation
5	right HVI/V	Action execution

Figure 7.3. Functional compartmentalization of the cerebellum in aggression

(cognitive) forms of aggression, while the connections of the medial cerebellar regions to the limbic system subserve the affective forms of aggression.

In the following paragraph, a neuroanatomic model will be presented that provides a starting point for understanding the role of the cerebellum in extreme anger, disruptive behaviors, and uncontrollable forms of aggressive behavior.

A cerebellum-hypothalamic road to rage and aggression

Observations of sham rage and aggressive attacks in animals in response to electric stimulation has put the hypothalamus at the forefront of candidate regions in the modulation of the brain's basic FIGHT (approach)-FLIGHT (avoidance) systems (Barbosa et al., 2017). Between the 1960s and 1980s, several independent groups published satisfactory results on the hypothalamus as a psychosurgical target ('hypothalamotomy') to treat refractory violent behavior (for a review see Barbosa et al., 2017). More recently, the development of deep brain stimulation and modern stereotactic techniques has caused a renewed interest in the hypothalamus as a target for ethically more accepted psycho-surgical interventions. Interestingly, deep brain stimulation (DBS) studies targeting the hypothalamus enabled scientists to further establish the role of the hypothalamus in the autonomic and emotion circuits (Rizzi et al., 2017).

At the same time, studies have repeatedly demonstrated that electric stimulation of the cerebellum causes visceral (autonomic) responses (Zhu et al., 2006), indicative for a possible functional anatomical link between the cerebellum and hypothalamus. In support, monosynaptic reciprocal connections between the cerebellum and hypothalamus in the animal brain were discovered after a series of viral tracing studies (Dietrichs, 1984; Haines et al., 1997). This discovery concurs with an earlier study in which decorticated cats show autonomic effects, including large increases in arterial blood pressure, and outbursts of rage in response to electric stimulation of the fastigial nuclei and in surrounding fibers (Zanchetti & Zoccolini, 1954). Indeed, efferent pathways from the fastigial nucleus to the hypothalamus, together with the fastigio-reticular

134 Emotionally explosive minds

tract and the connections of the fastigial nucleus to the brain stem reticular formation, can explain these autonomic and behavioral findings (Zanchetti & Zoccolini, 1954). Contrary to electric stimulation of the deep cerebellar fastigial nuclei, electric stimulation of the superficial cerebellar cortex does not cause any notable changes in autonomic activity.

Interestingly, when the hypothalamus is electrically innervated causing strong, autonomic reactions, such as elevations of heart rate and blood pressure, subsequent stimulation of the anterior cerebellar cortex suppresses these hypothalamic induced visceral responses (Lisander & Martner, 1971). This latter observation can be understood by the efferent inhibitory projections of the Purkinje cells to the deep cerebellar nuclei exerting a dampening effect on the fastigial nuclei and related extracerebellar regions, including the hypothalamus involved in autonomic activity.

A recent optogenetic study in mice showed that the paraventricular nucleus of the hypothalamus plays a leading role in autonomic activity associated with defense-like (FIGHT-FLIGHT) behaviors (Mangieri et al., 2019). Non-invasive cerebellar brain stimulation, albeit indirectly, further supports the link between the cerebellum and hypothalamus, and its involvement in visceral, emotive, and control-related processes in humans (Ferrari et al., 2018; Grimaldi et al., 2016; Schutter & van Honk, 2006; Schutter & van Honk, 2009).

Cerebellum on steroids

Psychoneuroendocrinological studies have shown that the ratio between the (catabolic) stress hormone cortisol and (anabolic) androgen hormone testosterone is predictive for aggression (Popma et al., 2007; Johnson et al., 2014; Rosell & Siever, 2015). Cortisol and testosterone are the end-products of the hypothalamus-pituitary-adrenal (HPA) and hypothalamus-pituitary-gonadal (HPG) axis, respectively, and govern bodily homeostasis and affect. In Chapter 4, the proposed role of the cerebellum in the regulation of the hypothalamus and the HPA-axis in mood was introduced. The monosynaptic projections from the fastigial nucleus and interposed nuclei (i.e., globose and emboliform nucleus) and to the paraventricular nucleus (PVN) of the hypothalamus (Haines et al., 1997) provide a direct gateway to the modulation of steroid hormonal levels and subsequent regulation of autonomic functions.

As illustrated in Figure 7.4, the paraventricular nucleus of the hypothalamus plays a crucial role in controlling the HPA-axis and HPG-axis by releasing corticotropic (CRH) and gonadotropic releasing hormone (GnRH), respectively. CRH and GnRH subsequently activate the anterior pituitary gland which, in turn, releases adrenocorticotropic hormone (ACTH), luteinizing hormones (LH), and follicle stimulating hormone (FSH) in the bloodstream. ACTH that binds to the adrenal cortex will cause cortisol release, while binding of LH and FS in the gonads will cause the release of sex steroids.

Emotionally explosive minds 135

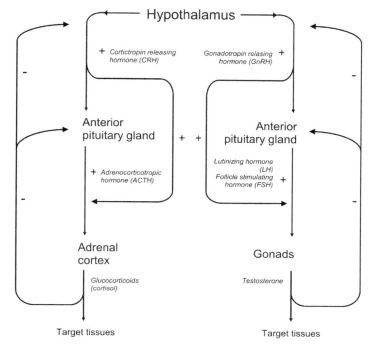

Figure 7.4. The hypothalamic-pituitary-adrenal (HPA) and hypothalamic-pituitary-adrenal (HPG) axis in the production of the steroids cortisol and testosterone

The sex steroid testosterone can inhibit activity of the HPA axis (Viau, 2002) by androgen receptor binding on the anterior extension of the hypothalamus and the medial preoptic area, particularly in the context of stress/provocation (Viau et al., 1996). In addition, other animal studies have shown that HPA hormones can inhibit HPG axis activity, suggestive of a mutually antagonistic working mechanism (Rivier & Rivest, 1991; Viau, 2002). Acute increases of endogenous testosterone levels sensitize the hypothalamus and midbrain structures and FIGHT-related motivational tendencies associated with anger (Hermans et al., 2008).

In contrast, cortisol downregulates the activational effects of testosterone and desensitizes the subcortical rage-aggression brain structures (Hermans et al., 2008). This reciprocal mechanism of action can be explained by the existing reciprocal inhibitory connection between the HPA-axis and HPG-axis (Johnson et al., 1992; Viau, 2002). The steroids cortisol and testosterone bind to the limbic steroid-responsive subcortical circuits (Wood, 1996) through which they exert their effects on the brain's FIGHT (testosterone) or FLIGHT (cortisol) modus when confronted with environmental challenges (Schulkin, 2003). Experimentally lowering the cortisol (C)/testosterone (T) ratio by single

136 Emotionally explosive minds

administrations of testosterone in healthy volunteers sensitizes the FIGHT system as evidenced by increases in approach-related motivation and anger during provocation (Terburg et al., 2009; van Honk & Schutter, 2006).

In further support, a moderating effect of cortisol on the relationship between testosterone and overt aggression has been observed in delinquent male adolescents (Popma et al., 2007). Specifically, lower levels of cortisol may contribute positively to the correlation between T and aggressive behavior, while the opposite is observed when cortisol levels are relatively high. In addition, lower C/T ratios were also found to predispose to more aggressive behavior in healthy volunteers (Platje et al., 2015). Functional neuroimaging showed that the psychological effects associated with anger can be explained by an increase in responsivity of the neural aggression (FIGHT) circuits a direct consequence of shifting the C/T ratio to a single administration of testosterone (Hermans et al., 2008).

There is evidence that both axes can also work in parallel and that the interactions between the two axes are not necessarily based on mutual inhibition (Dismukes et al., 2015). In a study with incarcerated adolescents from a maximum-security detention and treatment facility, adolescents with higher levels of testosterone also demonstrated higher levels of cortisol and dehydroepiandrosterone (DHEA) levels. DHEA is endogenous steroid hormone precursor and end-product of the adrenal cortex and gonads that can act both as an androgen and stress hormone. Adolescents who had experienced greater life adversity demonstrated an even higher positive correlation between the HPG and HPA hormones (Dismukes et al., 2015). Speculatively, the hormonal coupling may bear a relationship with defensive (reactive) aggression in which stress/threat-related responses more readily elicit frustration, anger, and aggression (FIGHT) rather than anxiety and worry (FLIGHT).

A significant positive correlation between testosterone and cortisol levels was observed in adolescents showing high on interpersonal affect (e.g., grandiose sense of self, manipulation) and antisocial behavior (e.g., poor anger control, criminal versatility) on the Hare Psychopathy Checklist. The researchers speculated that when testosterone is high in these individuals, HPG-axis functioning 'hijacks' the HPA-axis and makes the stress-axis operate in an androgenergic manner (Johnson et al., 2014). Similar to the previous study, stressors in this group are more likely to elicit approach-related motivation and anger instead of apprehension and feelings of anxiety.

In contrast, males high on CU traits (e.g., cold-heartedness, lack of remorse) with high levels of testosterone showed lower DHEA and cortisol activity (Johnson et al., 2014), which fits the inhibitory HPG-HPA axis cross-talk model (Viau et al., 2002). CU traits are associated with higher rates of delinquency and aggression and linked to hypoactive amygdala responses to fearful faces (Lozier et al., 2014). This fits Lykken's original concept of fearlessness as a core feature of psychopathy (Lykken, 1957). In addition to lower- than-normal amygdala responsivity, Lozier et al. (2014) found associations between cerebellar activity in response to fearful faces and externalizing behavior (i.e., rule-breaking, aggressive

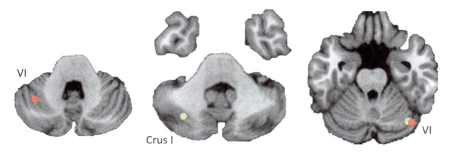

Figure 7.5. Regional cerebellar activity showing positive (red) and negative associations (green) with externalizing behavior in conduct disorder

behavior) in adolescents with conduct disorder. Results showed that bilateral activation of lobule IV was positively correlated to externalizing behavior, while more right-sided activity of lobule IV and left Crus I was related to less externalizing behavior (Figure 7.5).

Hypothetically, bilateral activity of lobule VI can be interpreted along the lines of arousal and emotional appraisal and immediate (approach-related) motor actions, while the joint activation of right lobule IV and left Crus I reflects inhibitory regulatory processes following arousal and emotional appraisal. Notably, activation of left Crus I is in line with the contralateral projections of the posterolateral cerebellar regions to the right-sided cortical 'avoidance' system. The cerebellum is not only sensitive to steroid hormones, as discussed in Chapter 4 on mood disorders, but is also a steroidogenic structure that expresses steroidogenic enzymes and produces neurosteroids (Yarim & Kabakci, 2004), the cerebellar connections with the HPG and HPA axes in the context of anger and aggression, and psychopathology is a topic that requires further research.

In addition to regulating steroid hormone levels, the PVN controls body fluid balance through the secretion of oxytocin and vasopressin and plays a role in gastrointestinal and cardiovascular functions. Interestingly, the peptide vasopressin is implicated in individual survival and defensive behaviors that include mobilization and aggression during threat (Carter, 2017). Oxytocin is a peptide that within the context of safety downregulates the vasopressin mediated defensive functions enabling prosocial human behaviors, including social attachment and care. It is therefore hardly surprisingly that synthetic administrations of oxytocin are currently being investigated as a possible anti-aggressive agent in humans (De Jong & Neumann, 2018). Neural activation patterns to peripheral injections of oxytocin injections and oxytocin directly infused in the brain via the lateral ventricle were studied with 7T fMRI in awake rats (Ferris et al., 2015). In contrast to brain regions with high density oxytocin receptors, centrally administered oxytocin did not activate the cerebellum. The

138 Emotionally explosive minds

absence of activation concurs with the low number of oxytocin binding sites in the cerebellum.

Interestingly, peripheral oxytocin injections on the hand did elicit cerebellar activity in multiple lobules. The cerebellum may be coordinating the autonomic response to the interoceptive environment activated by peripheral OT acting on peripheral organs, like the heart and blood vessels, that contain oxytocin receptors. Since the cerebellum receives visceral information from many sources, including the hypothalamus and vagus nerve, the cerebellum is able to monitor and regulate autonomic functions (Cavdar et al., 2001).

The well-established neural structures implicated in the steroid-controlled feedback regulation of the HPA-axis and HPG-axis of the FIGHT circuit include the medial frontal cortex, hippocampus, and amygdala (Panksepp & Biven, 2012). The high corticoid receptor densities (Sánchez et al., 2000) together with the androgen receptors (Koibuchi, 2008) and their direct connections to the hypothalamus arguably make the cerebellum an intrinsic part of the latter circuit as a region contributing to the initiation, experience, and regulation of anger and aggression. In particular, the interplay between the cerebellum and hypothalamus arguably reflects an important facet of the neural dynamics, which reduced tonic and phasic cerebellar inhibition of the hypothalamus. Circumstantial evidence shows that peptides and steroid hormone play a role in (de)sensitizing the cerebellar-subcortical rage circuit. During provocation and/or frustration (i.e., stressors), the lowered inhibition may cause rapid escalation of activity ('limbic kindling') in the anger circuit and elicit aggression (Fragkaki et al., 2018).

Importantly, the functionality of the cerebellum also depends on input from the limbic and cortical regions, so dysfunctions within these areas can compromise the signals that are sent to the cerebellum. A similar case holds for signals from the autonomic nervous system that are relayed to the cerebellum. Reduced autonomic sympathetic (electrodermal) activity in anticipation of, and in response to, an aversive stimulus can already be observed in psychopathy-prone adolescent boys (Fung et al., 2005). The low sensitivity to negative and potentially harming stimuli contributes to poor fear conditioning and further biases the organism to respond with FIGHT (anger) rather than FLIGHT (fear) behaviors during stress. In fact, poor fear conditioning in young children is a risk factor for developing aggressive and criminal behavior (Fung et al., 2005) and further substantiates the proposed role of the cerebellum in extreme anger and aggression. It should be noted that while low fear and anxiety are considered to be protective in terms of outbursts of anger and aggression, this does not rule out defensive forms of anger and aggression that arise from extreme anxiety/panic states, as was discussed in Chapter 3.

Findings of low central nervous system activity are further strengthened by results of a large prospective, population-based birth cohort study showing that lower resting heart rate is a robust correlate of violent crimes for males (Murray et al., 2016). On the phenomenological level, low autonomic arousal is associated with unpleasant feelings of lethargy, irritability, and boredom. This effect can already be observed in young children who prefer to watch video clips depicting extreme anger and have lower heart rate levels as compared to peers who choose to watch video clips with mild anger (El-Sheikh et al., 1994). Thus, unpleasant states arising from low autonomic arousal contribute to sensation (reward) seeking that can include risk taking, rule breaking, and violence. Moreover, the degree of sensation seeking is likely to be mediated by fearlessness. As noted, low sympathetic activity and reactivity to aversive stimuli, and poor fear conditioning are positively associated with anger and aggression. These findings concur with increased reward dependency, low punishment sensitivity, and reduced cognitive control.

Moreover, the physiological hyporesponsivity has been associated with callous-unemotional (CU) personality traits. CU traits are characterized by shallow affect and lack of empathy. CU traits in children relate to persistent aggressive behavior and are predictive for serious antisocial behavior and psychopathic tendencies in adulthood. In a functional magnetic resonance (fMRI) imaging study, neural responses to pictures depicting other people in pain were evaluated in a sample of children with conduct problems (n = 37) and matched controls (n = 18) (Lockwood et al., 2013). In comparison to the matched controls, children with conduct problems demonstrated lower oxygen level-dependent responses to others' pain in the insula, anterior cingulate cortex, and inferior frontal gyrus. In line with previous studies, these regions fit the neural structures associated with emotional sensitivity and empathy.

Additionally, another brain area that was left undiscussed showed significant deviations in several loci, namely the cerebellum. Children with conduct problems as compared to matched controls showed significantly less activity in the centralis of the vermis and right lobule VI and Crus I when viewing pictures of other individuals in pain. In contrast, increased activity was observed in the culmen section of the vermis. The lower activation patterns in the right cerebellar hemisphere concur with other research that has linked the right cerebellum to the bilateral temporo-parietal junction (TPJ) in theory of mind (Van Overwalle et al., 2019).

Abnormal activity in the vermis, along with reduced activity in the right cerebellar hemisphere, suggest impairments in emotional sensitivity and understanding the mental states of others. Less cerebellar engagement in social situations could contribute to a predisposition of a person to respond with aggression when being provoked. In further support, a recent study showed a comparable pattern of motor-corrected right-lateralized cerebellar activity, as depicted in Figure 7.6, when healthy volunteers performed a task in which they had to indicate whether short stories contains true or false belief (King et al., 2019).

Although this task has been criticized for tapping into just one aspect of people's understanding of the mental state of others (Bloom & German, 2000), the pattern of cerebellar activity is nonetheless consistent across the different studies. In addition, theory of mind is suggested to involve language processes (Corballis, 2017), which could in part explain the right-sided cerebellar activity.

140 Emotionally explosive minds

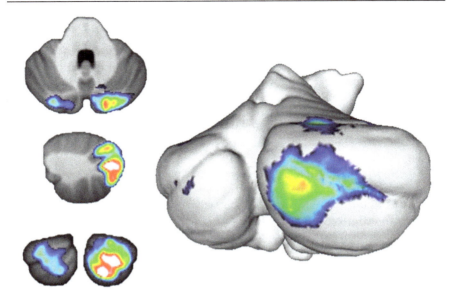

Figure 7.6. Motor-corrected cerebellar neural responses and surface-based representation of activity in theory of mind using a spatially unbiased atlas template of the cerebellum and brainstem (Diedrichsen, 2006; Diedrichsen et al., 2009; Diedrichsen & Zotow, 2015)

In sum, these data indicate that the cerebellum plays a role in externalizing aggressive behavior associated with callous-unemotional traits.

The cerebellum and addiction

Sensation seeking behavior sometimes involves the use of psycho-active substances, including alcohol, nicotine, marijuana, cocaine, and heroin. It is therefore not surprising that the combination of increased reward and reduced punishment sensitivity, and lower cognitive regulation makes a person vulnerable to the development of substance use disorder. Substance use disorder or drug addiction is a condition in which a person loses the ability to control drug use and becomes physiologically and mentally dependent on the drug.

Substance use disorders involve Thorndike's law of effect in which reinforcement learning takes place on the basis of the rewarding (pleasurable) effects associated with the drugs. In addition to the well-documented role of the cerebellum in associative learning as discussed in Chapter 3 on fear and anxiety-related disorders, the cerebellar cortex modulates dopamine release in the brain's reward circuit, including the ventral tegmental area (VTA) and medial frontal cortex.

Notably, an increase in cerebellar activity can be observed when an anticipated reward is provided, while a decrease in cerebellar activity occurs when the anticipated reward does not become available (prediction violation). The proposal that the cerebellum is particularly involved in prediction processes of drug availability fits the idea of reinforcement learning. This idea is supported by neuro-anatomical research showing that the vermis receives input from the VTA as demonstrated in the rat brain (Ikai et al., 1992). The VTA transfers reward signals to the cerebellum to facilitate associative learning and promote addictive behaviors (Miquel et al., 2016). Neural plasticity in the cerebellum is in part mediated by glutamate and endocannabinoid-dependent cellular mechanisms, and addictive drugs have been shown to interfere with cerebellar glutamate and endocannabinoid functioning (Palomino et al., 2014).

Drugs with addictive properties typically cause behavioral sensitization, a phenomenon characterized by a progressive increase in drug-induced stimulating and incentive effects. For example, chronic cocaine administration followed by a one-week withdrawal period led to reductions in the Purkinje cell-related inhibition of the DCN neurons in the rodent cerebellum (Miquel et al., 2016). Interestingly, destruction of the interposed nuclei, that is the nucleus globose and emboliform nucleus, interferes with drug-induced habit formation (Callu et al., 2007), which is a key feature in the transition to addiction (Everitt and Robbins, 2005).

On the system's level, aberrant patterns of neural activity and disadvantageous risky decision making have been found in an inpatient group of abstinent heavy cannabis users (Bolla et al., 2005). Compared to non-drug users, the inpatient group showed increased activation in lobule VI and Crus I of the left cerebellum, while the cortical regions associated with executive functioning were less activated during the Iowa Gambling Task psychological test (Bolla et al., 2005). The increased cerebellar activity may be explained in terms of reward-focused reinforcement learning and a failed attempt to form correct predictions based on punishment signals (e.g., somatic markers), which are crucial for performing well on the gambling task. Indeed, somatic markers convey important physiological information associated with negative outcomes that are used to adjust and optimize behavior and involve the hypothalamus as well as the cerebellum.

A serotonergic link to reactive aggression?

Next to the proposed role of steroid hormones, preclinical research supports a role of serotonin in aggression and impulsivity. In humans, evidence for associations between serotonergic activity, anger, and psychopathic behavior has also been found (Da Cuncha-Bang et al., 2017). In this particular study using incarcerated violent offenders and healthy controls, the serotonergic binding potential with PET was examined in the anterior cingulate cortex, orbitofrontal cortex, and striatum. Increased binding was found in these regions in the violent offenders, which correlated to anger and psychopathic traits. Although the physiological meaning of neurotransmitter binding potential remains a topic of research, high serotonergic binding may reflect lower availability of this neurotransmitter in the synapse. This interpretation is supported by preclinical data and observations of reduced serotonin levels found in post-mortem brain studies of suicide victims (Mann et al., 1989).

Rodent research has shown that serotonergic fibers are the third main afferent fibers into the cerebellum and innervate granular cells, Purkinje cells, and interneurons (Oostland & Van Hooft, 2013). In addition, serotonin is suggested to be involved in the postnatal development of the cerebellum by contributing to dendritic growth and the formation of synapses (Oostland & Van Hooft, 2013). The raphe nuclei located in midline of the brainstem are the primary sources of serotonergic neurons projecting throughout the brain. PET and MRI based resting state functional connectivity analyses in healthy volunteers revealed positive correlations between the raphe nuclei to the anterior cingulate cortex, amygdala, insula, hippocampus, basal ganglia, and cerebellum (Beliveau et al., 2015). While research across the different neurobiological and psychological domains is still in its initial phase, available studies have shown that the cerebellum-serotonin link adds to the importance of the little brain in aggression related disorders, as well as other neuropsychiatric condition disorders, such as major depressive disorder and addiction, that involve serotonergic dysfunctions.

Conclusion

This chapter covered empirical research involving both animals and humans that points towards cerebellar contributions to reactive aggression and impulsive-related behaviors. A cerebello-subcortical framework has been introduced that provides a theoretical neural account for emotional outbursts of anger and sensation seeking behavior. While unravelling the exact mechanisms on the molecular, structural, and functional level remain a topic for future research, it may be time to broaden our neuroscientific research focus and move beyond the classic cortico-limbic models of aggression and antisocial behavior.

References

American Psychiatric Association (2013). *Diagnostic and statistical manual of mental disorders* (5th ed.). Arlington: American Psychiatric Association Publishing.

Barbosa DA, de Oliveira-Souza R, Monte Santo F, de Oliveira Faria AC, Gorgulho AA, De Salles AA (2017). The hypothalamus at the crossroads of psychopathology and neurosurgery. *Neurosurg. Focus* 43, E15.

Bartholow BD (2018). The aggressive brain: Insights from neuroscience. *Curr. Opin. Psychol.* 19, 60–64.

Beliveau V, Svarer C, Frokjaer VG, Knudsen GM, Greve DN, Fisher PM (2015). Functional connectivity of the dorsal and median raphe nuclei at rest. *NeuroImage* 116, 187–195.

Benegal V, Antony G, Venkatasubramanian G, Jayakumar PN (2007). Gray matter volume abnormalities and externalizing symptoms in subjects at high risk for alcohol dependence. *Addict. Biol.* 12, 122–132.

Berman AF, Berman D, Prescott JW (1978). The effect of cerebellar lesions on emotional behavior in the rhesus monkey. In IS Cooper, M Riklan, RS Snider (Eds.), *The cerebellum, epilepsy and behavior* (pp. 277–284). New York: Plenum. Adapted and reprinted as Berman, AJ (1997). Amelioration of aggression: Response to selective cerebellar lesions in the rhesus monkey. In JD Schmahmann (Ed.), The cerebellum and cognition. *Int. Rev. Neurobiol.* 41, 111–119.

Blair RJ (2013). The neurobiology of psychopathic traits in youths. *Nat. Rev. Neurosci.* 14, 786–799.

Bloom P, German TP (2000). Two reasons to abandon the false belief task as a test of theory of mind. *Cognition* 16, 25–31.

Bolla KI, Eldreth DA, Matochik JA, Cadet JL (2005). Neural substrates of faulty decision-making in abstinent marijuana users. *NeuroImage* 26, 480–492.

Buckner RL, Krienen FM, Castellanos A, Diaz JC, Yeo BT (2011). The organization of the human cerebellum estimated by intrinsic functional connectivity. *J. Neurophysiol.* 106, 2322–2345.

Callu D, Puget S, Faure A, Guegan M, El Massioui N (2007). Habit learning dissociation in rats with lesions to the vermis and the interpositus of the cerebellum. *Neurobiol. Dis.* 27, 228–237.

Carter CS (2017). The oxytocin-vasopressin pathway in the context of love and fear. *Front. Endocrinol.* 8, 356.

Cavdar S, San T, Aker R, Sehirli U, Onat F (2001). Cerebellar connections to the dorsomedial and posterior nuclei of the hypothalamus in the rat. *J. Anat.* 198, 37–45.

Corballis MC (2017). Language evolution: A changing perspective. *Trends Cogn. Sci.* 214, 229–232.

Da Cunha-Bang S, Hjordt LV, Perfalk E, et al. (2017). Serotonin 1B receptor binding is associated with trait anger and level of psychopathy in violent offenders. *Biol. Psychiatry* 82, 267–274.

Davidson RJ, Putnam KM, Larson CL (2000). Dysfunction in the neural circuitry of emotion regulation: A possible prelude to violence. *Science* 289, 591–594.

De Jong TR, Neumann ID (2018). Oxytocin and aggression. *Curr. Top. Behav. Neurosci.* 35, 175–192.

Diedrichsen J (2006). A spatially unbiased atlas template of the human cerebellum. *NeuroImage* 33, 127–138.

Diedrichsen J, Balsters JH, Flavell J, Cussans E, Ramnani N (2009). A probabilistic atlas of the human cerebellum. *NeuroImage* 46, 39–46.

Diedrichsen J, Zotow E (2015). Surface-based display of volume-averaged cerebellar data. *PLoS One* 7, e0133402.

Dietrichs E (1984). Cerebellar autonomic function: Direct hypothalamocerebellar pathway. *Science* 223, 591–593.

Dismukes AR, Johnson MM, Vitacco MJ, Iturri F, Shirtcliff EA (2015). Coupling of the HPA and HPG axes in the context of early life adversity in incarcerated male adolescents. *Dev. Psychobiol.* 57, 705–718.

Durston S, Davidson MC, Mulder MJ, et al. (2007). Neural and behavioral correlates of expectancy violations in attention-deficit hyperactivity disorder. *J. Child. Psychol. Psychiatry* 48, 881–889.

El-Sheikh M, Ballard M, Cummings EM (1994). Individual differences in preschoolers' physiological and verbal responses to videotaped angry interactions. *J. Abnorm. Child Psychol.* 22, 303–320.

144 Emotionally explosive minds

Everitt BJ, Robbins TW (2005). Neural systems of reinforcement for drug addiction: from actions to habits to compulsion. *Nat. Neurosci.* 8, 1481–1489.

Ferrari C, Oldrati V, Gallucci M, Vecchi T, Cattaneo Z (2018). The role of the cerebellum in explicit and incidental processing of facial emotional expressions: A study with transcranial magnetic stimulation. *Neuroimage* 169, 256–264.

Ferris CF, Yee JR, Kenkel WM, et al. (2015). Distinct BOLD activation profiles following central and peripheral oxytocin administration in awake rats. *Front. Behav. Neurosci.* 9, 245.

Fragkaki I, Cima M, Granic I. (2018). The role of trauma in the hormonal interplay of cortisol, testosterone, and oxytocin in adolescent aggression. *Psychoneuroendocrinology* 88, 24–37.

Fung MT, Raine A, Loeber R, et al. (2005). Reduced electrodermal activity in psychopathy-prone adolescents. *J. Abnorm. Psychol.* 114, 187–196.

Gao Y, Raine A, Venables PH, Dawson ME, Mednick SA (2010). Reduced electrodermal fear conditioning from ages 3 to 8 years is associated with aggressive behavior at age 8 years. *J. Child Psychol. Psychiatry* 51, 550–558.

Grimaldi G, Argyropoulos GP, Bastian A, et al. (2016). Cerebellar transcranial direct current stimulation (ctDCS): A novel approach to understanding cerebellar function in health and disease. *Neuroscientist* 22, 83–97.

Haines DE, Dietrichs E, Mihailoff GA, McDonald EF (1997). The cerebellar-hypothalamic axis: basic circuits and clinical observations. *Int. Rev. Neurobiol.* 41, 83–107.

Harmon-Jones E (2003). Clarifying the emotive functions of asymmetrical frontal cortical activity. *Psychophysiology* 40, 838–848.

Heath RG (1977). Modulation of emotion with a brain pacemaker. Treatment for intractable psychiatric illness. *J. Nerv. Ment. Dis.* 165, 300–317.

Heath RG, Dempesy CW, Fontana CJ, Fitzjarrell AT (1980). Feedback loop between cerebellum and septal-hippocampal sites: Its role in emotion and epilepsy. *Biol. Psychiatry* 15, 541–556.

Heath RG, Llewellyn RC, Rouchell AM (1980). The cerebellar pacemaker for intractable behavioral disorders and epilepsy: Follow-up report. *Biol. Psychiatry* 15, 243–256.

Hecht D (2011). An inter-hemispheric imbalance in the psychopath's brain. *Pers. Individ. Diff.* 51, 3–10.

Hermans EJ, Ramsey NF, van Honk J (2008). Exogenous testosterone enhances responsiveness to social threat in the neural circuitry of social aggression in humans. *Biol. Psychiatry* 63, 263–270.

Hoche F, Guell X, Vangel MG, Sherman JC, Schmahmann JD (2018). The cerebellar cognitive affective/Schmahmann syndrome scale. *Brain* 141, 248–270.

Hove MJ, Gravel N, Spencer RMC, Valera EM (2017). Finger tapping and pre-attentive sensorimotor timing in adults with ADHD. *Exp. Brain Res.* 235, 3663–3672.

Hove MJ, Zeffiro TA, Biederman J, Li Z, Schmahmann J, Valera EM (2015). Postural sway and regional cerebellar volume in adults with attention-deficit/hyperactivity disorder. *NeuroImage Clin.* 8, 422–428.

Ikai Y, Takada M, Shinonaga Y, Mizuno N (1992). Dopaminergic and nondopaminergic neurons in the ventral tegmental area of the rat project, respectively, to the cerebellar cortex and deep cerebellar nuclei. *Neurosci.* 51, 719–728.

Jackman SL, Chen CH, Offermann, HL, et al. (2020). Cerebellar Purkinje cell activity modulates aggressive behavior. *BioRvix*, doi:10.1101/2020.01.06.891127.

Johnson MM, Dismukes AR, Vitacco MJ, Breiman C, Fleury D, Shirtcliff EA (2014). Psychopathy's influence on the coupling between hypothalamic-pituitary-adrenal and -gonadal axes among incarcerated adolescents. *Dev. Psychobiol.* 56, 448–458.

Kelley NJ, Hortensius R, Schutter DJ, Harmon-Jones E (2017). The relationship of approach/avoidance motivation and asymmetric frontal cortical activity: A review of studies manipulating frontal asymmetry. *Int. J. Psychophysiol.* 119, 19–30.

Keune PM, van der Heiden L, Várkuti B, Konicar L, Veit R, Birbaumer N (2012). Prefrontal brain asymmetry and aggression in imprisoned violent offenders. *Neurosci. Lett.* 515, 191–195.

King M, Hernandez-Castillo CR, Poldrack RA, Ivry RB, Diedrichsen J (2019). Functional boundaries in the human cerebellum revealed by a multi-domain task battery. *Nat. Neurosci.* 22, 1371–1378.

Klaus J, Schutter DJ (2020). *Functional topography of anger and aggression in the human cerebellum.* Manuscript submitted for publication.

Koibuchi N (2008). Hormonal regulation of cerebellar development and plasticity. *Cerebellum* 7, 1–3.

Kolla NJ, Gregory S, Attard S, Blackwood N, Hodgins S (2014). Disentangling possible effects of childhood physical abuse on gray matter changes in violent offenders with psychopathy. *Psychiatry Res.* 221, 123–126.

Konrad K, Eickhoff SB (2010). Is the ADHD brain wired differently? A review on structural and functional connectivity in attention deficit hyperactivity disorder. *Hum. Brain Mapp.* 31, 904–916.

Lahey BB, Loeber R, Burke J, Rathouz PJ, McBurnett K (2002). Waxing and waning in concert: Dynamic comorbidity of conduct disorder with other disruptive and emotional problems over 7 years among clinic referred boys. *J. Abnorm. Psychol.* 111, 556–567.

LeDoux JE (2000). Emotion circuits in the brain. *Annu. Rev. Neurosci.* 23, 155–184.

Leutgeb V, Wabnegger A, Leitner M, et al. (2016). Altered cerebellar-amygdala connectivity in violent offenders: A resting-state fMRI study. *Neurosci. Lett.* 610, 160–164.

Lisader B, Martner J (1971). Cerebellar suppression of the autonomic components of the defence reaction. *Acta Physiol. Scand.* 81, 84–95.

Lockwood PL, Sebastian CL, McCrory EJ, et al. (2013). Association of callous traits with reduced neural response to others' pain in children with conduct problems. *Curr. Biol.* 23, 901–905.

Lozier LM, Cardinale EM, VanMeter JW, Marsh AA (2014). Mediation of the relationship between callous-unemotional traits and proactive aggression by amygdala response to fear among children with conduct problems. *JAMA Psychiatry* 71, 627–636.

Lykken DD (1957). A study of anxiety in the sociopathic personality. *J. Abnorm. Psychol.* 55, 6–10.

Mangieri LR, Jiang Z, Lu Y, Xu Y, Cassidy RM, et al. (2019). Defensive behaviors driven by a hypothalamic-ventral midbrain circuit. *eNeuro* 6, ENEURO.156–119. 2019.

Mann JJ, Arango V, Marzuk PM, Theccanat S, Reis DJ (1989). Evidence for the 5-HT hypothesis of suicide. A review of post-mortem studies. *Br. J. Psychiatry Suppl.* 8, 7–14.

Miquel M, Vazquez-Sanroman D, Carbo-Gas M, et al. (2016). Have we been ignoring the elephant in the room? Seven arguments for considering the cerebellum as part of addiction circuitry. *Neurosci. Biobehav. Rev.* 60, 1–11.

Mobbs D, Petrovic P, Marchant JL, et al. (2007). When fear is near: Threat imminence elicits prefrontal-periaqueductal gray shifts in humans. *Science* 317, 1079–1083.

Moreno-Rius J (2019). Is there an 'antisocial' cerebellum? Evidence from disorders other than autism characterized by abnormal social behaviours. *Prog. Neuropsychopharmacol. Biol. Psychiatry* 89, 1–8.

Müller JL, Sommer M, Wagner V, et al. (2003). Abnormalities in emotion processing within cortical and subcortical regions in criminal psychopaths: Evidence from a functional magnetic resonance imaging study using pictures with emotional content. *Biol. Psychiatry* 54, 152–162.

Murray J, Hallal PC, Mielke GI, Raine A, Wehrmeister FC, Anselmi L, Barros FC (2016). Low resting heart rate is associated with violence in late adolescence: A prospective birth cohort study in Brazil. *Int. J. Epidemiol.* 45, 491–500.

Noordermeer SD, Luman M, Oosterlaan J (2016). A systematic review and meta-analysis of neuroimaging in oppositional defiant disorder (ODD) and conduct disorder (CD) Taking attention-deficit hyperactivity Disorder (ADHD) into account. *Neuropsychol. Rev.* 26, 44–72.

Oostland M, van Hooft JA (2013). The role of serotonin in cerebellar development. *Neurosci.* 248, 201–212.

Palomino A, Pavón FJ, Blanco-Calvo E, et al. (2014). Effects of acute versus repeated cocaine exposure on the expression of endocannabinoid signaling related proteins in the mouse cerebellum. *Front. Integr. Neurosci.* 8, 22.

Panksepp J (1998). *Affective neuroscience: The foundations of human and animal emotions.* New York: Oxford University Press.

Panksepp J (2016). The cross-mammalian neurophenomenology of primal emotional affects: From animal feelings to human therapeutics. *J. Comp. Neurol.* 524, 1624–1635.

Panksepp J, Biven L (2012). *The archaeology of mind: Neuroevolutionary origins of human emotions.* New York: WW Norton & Company Inc.

Panksepp, J, Zellner, M. (2004). Toward a neurobiologically based unified theory of aggression. *Rev. Int. Psycholog. Soc.* 17, 37–61.

Platje E, Popma A, Vermeiren RR, Doreleijers TAH, Meeus WHJ, et al. (2015). Testosterone and cortisol in relation to aggression in a non-clinical sample of boys and girls. *Aggress. Behav.* 41, 478–487.

Popma A, Vermeiren R, Geluk CA, et al. (2007). Cortisol moderates the relationship between testosterone and aggression in delinquent male adolescents. *Biol. Psychiatry* 61, 405–411.

Rivier C, Rivest S (1991). Effect of stress on the activity of the hypothalamic-pituitary-gonadal axis: Peripheral and central mechanisms. *Biol. Reprod.* 45, 523–532.

Rizzi M, Trezza A, Messina G, De Benedictis A, Franzini A, Marras CE (2017). Exploring the brain through posterior hypothalamus surgery for aggressive behavior. *Neurosurg. Focus* 43, E14.

Rosell DR, Siever LJ (2015). The neurobiology of aggression and violence. *CNS Spectr.* 20, 254–279.

Sánchez MM, Young LJ, Plotsky PM, Insel TR (2000). Distribution of corticosteroid receptors in the rhesus brain: Relative absence of glucocorticoid receptors in the hippocampal formation. *J. Neurosci.* 20, 4657–4668.

Schmahmann JD, Sherman JC (1998). The cerebellar cognitive affective syndrome. *Brain* 121, 561–579.

Schulkin J (2003). Allostasis: A neural behavioral perspective. *Horm. Behav.* 43, 21–30.

Schutter DJ (2013). Human cerebellum in motivation and emotion. In: M Manto, DL Gruol, JD Schmahmann, N Koibuchi, F Rossi (Eds), *Handbook of the cerebellum and cerebellar disorders.* Dordrecht: Springer Science Business Media, pp. 1771–1783.

Schutter DJ, Enter D, Hoppenbrouwers SS (2009). High-frequency repetitive transcranial magnetic stimulation to the cerebellum and implicit processing of happy facial expressions. *J. Psychiatry Neurosci.* 34, 60–65.

Schutter DJ, Harmon-Jones E (2013). The corpus callosum: A commissural road to anger and aggression. *Neurosci. Biobehav. Rev.* 37, 2481–2488.

Schutter DJ, van Honk J (2006). An electrophysiological link between the cerebellum, cognition and emotion: Frontal theta EEG activity to single-pulse cerebellar TMS. *NeuroImage* 33, 1227–1231.

Schutter DJ, van Honk J (2009). The cerebellum in emotion regulation: A repetitive transcranial magnetic stimulation study. *Cerebellum* 8, 28–34.

Snider RS, Eldred E (1952). Cerebro-cerebellar relationships in the monkey. *J Neurophysiol.* 15, 27–40.

Stoodley CJ, Schmahmann JD (2018). Functional topography of the human cerebellum. *Handb. Clin. Neurol.* 154, 59–70.

Styliadis C, Ioannides AA, Bamidis PD, Papadelis C (2015). Distinct cerebellar lobules process arousal, valence and their interaction in parallel following a temporal hierarchy. *NeuroImage* 110, 149–161.

Tang Y, Jiang W, Liao J, Wang W, Luo A (2013). Identifying individuals with antisocial personality disorder using resting-state fMRI. *PLoS One* 8, e60652.

Terburg D, Morgan B, van Honk J (2009). The testosterone-cortisol ratio: A hormonal marker for proneness to social aggression. *Int. J. Law Psychiatry* 32, 216–223.

Valera EM, Faraone SV, Murray KE, Seidman LJ (2007). Meta-analysis of structural imaging findings in attention-deficit/ hyperactivity disorder. *Biol. Psychiatry* 61, 1361–1369.

van Honk J, Harmon-Jones E, Morgan BE, Schutter DJ (2010). Socially explosive minds: the triple imbalance hypothesis of reactive aggression. *J. Pers.* 78, 67–94.

van Honk J, Schutter DJ (2006). Unmasking feigned sanity: A neurobiological model of emotion processing in primary psychopathy. *Cogn. Neuropsychiatry* 11, 285–306.

Van Overwalle F, Van de Steen F, Mariën P (2019). Dynamic causal modeling of the effective connectivity between the cerebrum and cerebellum in social mentalizing across five studies. *Cogn. Affect. Behav. Neurosci.* 19, 211–223.

Viau V (2002). Functional cross-talk between the hypothalamic-pituitary-gonadal and -adrenal axes. *J. Neuroendocrinol.* 14, 506–513.

Viau V, Meaney MJ (1996). The inhibitory effect of testosterone on hypothalamic-pituitary-adrenal responses to stress is mediated by the medial preoptic area. *J. Neurosci.* 16, 1866–1876. Yarim M, Kabakci N (2004). Neurosteroidogenesis in oligodendrocytes and Purkinje neurones of cerebellar cortex of dogs. *Anat. Histol. Embryol.* 33, 151–154.

Zanchetti A, Zoccolini A (1954). Autonomic hypothalamic outbursts elicited by cerebellar stimulation. *J. Neurophysiol.* 17, 475–483.

Zhu JN, Yung WH, Kwok-Chong ChowB, ChanYS, WangJJ (2006). The cerebellarhypothalamic circuits: Potential pathways underlying cerebellar involvement in somatic–visceral integration. *Brain Res. Rev.* 52, 93–106.

Chapter 8

Epilogue

Despite its modest size, high neural density, homologous cellular architecture, and wide infrastructure of connections that spans the entire brain, the cerebellum should no longer be considered a region whose sole function is in the motor domain. The functional expansion of the cerebellum to non-motor related domains is further substantiated by the observation that a significant portion of the cerebellum is linked to subcortical limbic areas and associative non-motor related regions of the cerebral cortex.

Importantly, the division between motor-related functions and operations dedicated to cognition and emotion is not as strict as the literature sometimes suggests. Conceptually, cognitive processes can be considered as higher mental representations of complex motor movements that are manifested not in actual muscle movements but, for instance, in thoughts and reasoning. Terms like motivation and emotion obviously refer to motion and/or intentions to move and capture the intrinsic link between affective processes and the motor system. On the neural level, important motivation- and emotion-dedicated structures are embedded in brain circuits, like the basal ganglia, known to be directly responsible for movement initiation and control. Given the conceptual, functional, and neural overlap between the motor and non-motor related processes, the view that the cerebellum is implicated in emotions and psychopathology sounds almost trivial.

With this book, I have attempted to sketch a theoretical and empirical framework to illustrate the importance of the cerebellum in understanding the neural basis of human emotions and psychopathology. While cerebellum research in the field of affective and clinical neuroscience is still in its initial phase, the empirical studies covered in this book already offer a wealth of knowledge and ideas. Typical of any young scientific discipline, empirical research provides exciting, but at the same time heterogenous, findings on the various levels the cerebellum is being studied. Figure E.1 illustrates the study of the cerebellum at different levels of neural organization.

Deciphering the associations between the cerebellum and affective processes is the first necessary step towards actual mechanistic explanations. This may in part be attributable to the inaccessibility of the human cerebellum when it

Epilogue 149

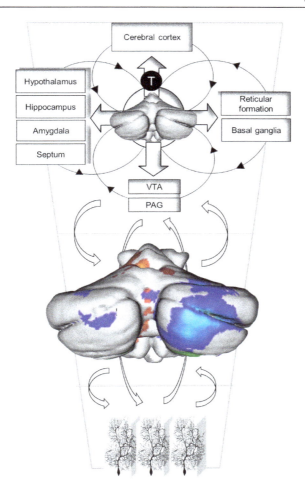

Figure E.1. Different levels of organization that define the operational architectonics of the cerebellum

comes to examining its cellular and neuro-anatomic components. Most of our current knowledge is based on work with the non-human mammalian cerebellum. Even though humans and other animals of the mammalian species share substantial parts of the evolutionary ancient subcortical emotion circuits, the animal brain is a model for the human brain. The latter point is supported by the marked differences in the evolutionary trajectory between the non-primate and primate mammalian brain discussed in Chapter 1. It goes without saying that experimental brain research is fundamental and provides scientists with invaluable insights into the neurobiology of the cerebellum. But when it comes to studying human emotions and psychopathology, there are marked differences in the complexity of these mental states and associated neural processes between animals and humans.

Biological phenomena associated with increasing brain complexity, such as emergence, which is the event of observing a feature with properties its parts do not have on their own, further complicates the prevailing Newtonian functional decomposition approach in science. This is functional decomposition defined as understanding functions based on studying to its constituent parts in such a way that the original function can be reconstructed. So, differences in variation and complexity across the mammalian species make the translation of empirical knowledge from animals to humans not undeniably straightforward in the field of affective and clinical neuroscience. As such, while animal research can provide invaluable insights into the cerebellar mechanics, the neurophysiological plausible models for understanding behavior still await to be formally confirmed in humans. On the other hand, animal research provides truly unique insights into cerebellar working that for technical and ethical reasons is inaccessible to human research.

The differences put aside, there is a remarkable similarity between the animal and human cerebellum relating to the homogenous trilaminar layering of the cerebellar cortex. In fact, the mostly invariant architecture of the cerebellar cortex sharply contrasts with the heterogeneity of cerebellar connections with extracerebellar structures (Schmahmann et al., 2019). The observation that the cellular composition of the cerebellar cortex is strikingly homogenous throughout the entire structure inspired the idea of a 'cerebellar algorithm' with a general signal-transforming capability (Dean et al., 2010).

Closely related to this idea is Schmahmann's concept of the universal cerebellar transform (UCT), which says that the cerebellum integrates internal representations (e.g., low sugar level causing feelings of hunger) with external stimuli (e.g., food availability) and appropriate responses (e.g., food consumption). The general purpose of the UCT is to promote bodily homeostasis, and its underlying processes typically occur automatically and without conscious awareness. Similar to the way the cerebellum is implicated in somatosensory integration and in the monitoring and regulation of coordinated movements by incorporating neural signals related to speed, force, timing, and rhythms, so may the cerebellum orchestrate affective and cognitive processes (Schmahmann, 1991).

In the field of engineering control theory, the workings of the cerebellum have been compared to an adaptive filter (Dean et al., 2010). The general idea behind this specific type of filter is that the cerebellum processes and compares signals across different modalities and provides a differential estimate of the current and desired end-state. At the parallel fiber (pf)-Purkinje cell synapse, the differential estimation is used as a 'teaching' signal that is analogous to the so-called covariance learning rule (Sejnowki, 1977) and can modulate output to the deep cerebellar nuclei and extra-cerebellar regions.

An example of such an adaptive filter is the Kalman filter that keeps track of the estimated state of the system and the variance or uncertainty of the estimate based on a series of measurements taken over time. The workings are comparable to the least-squares method in regression analyses, whereby the best fitting line is calculated on the basis of data points. Each data point represents the relationship between a known independent variable (input) and an unknown dependent variable (output). The Kalman filter can be viewed as a cerebellar heuristic that uses limited information to maximize predictability and minimize uncertainty (**Figure E.2**).

In contrast to the uniform cerebellar cortical architecture, the afferent and efferent connections of the cerebellum with the spinal cord, brainstem, and cerebral hemispheres are more heterogeneous and seem to have a topographical arrangement. So, while the molecular organization is similar across most of the cerebellar cortex, the intrinsic connections between different cerebellar areas, like Crus II, and extracerebellar regions, such as the prefrontal cortex, reveal a degree of functional specialization on the system's level. In support, damage to particular regions of the cerebellum give rise to problems in certain functional domains, like disturbances in the experience of emotion following damage to the vermis, problems in the regulation of anger, and impulsivity following posterolateral damage.

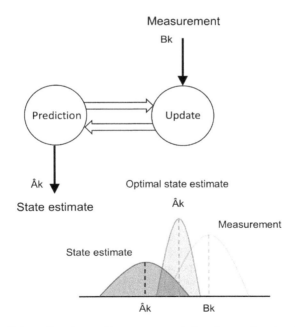

Figure E.2. The Kalman filter is a cyclic process consisting of a predicted and updated phase to determine the optimum state of a system as a function of minimizing uncertainty/prediction error over time

How the basic cellular architecture exactly relates to the functional topography on the regional level remains a topic for future investigation. Perhaps, the general concept of the cerebellar microcircuit as an adaptive filter is used throughout and applied to functionally segregated zones in the cerebellum. An example is the medial regions linked to emotional experience in terms of detecting discrepancies of interoceptive and exteroceptive input, and the posterior regions with the monitoring and regulation of emotions and behavior to restore internal bodily homeostasis.

Problems in internal bodily homeostatic functioning that could well involve the vermis could make an organism vulnerable to the development of stress-related disorders like anxiety and depression. Abnormalities in the somatosensory body maps in the anterior lobe of the cerebellum may cause discrepancies in the perceived and experienced self and may contribute to complex metal disorders, like anorexia nervosa. Lateral cerebellum-related problems in segregating internally generated signals from external sensory input may trigger hallucinations and delusions.

As to whether different emotions and psychopathological conditions can be treated and studied as separate entities associated with distinct neurobiological correlates remains an open question. In fact, when it comes to understanding emotion-related disorders, the search for shared processes (e.g., cerebellar dysregulation) underlying several psychopathologies may be an interesting alternative to finding emotion- and disorder-specific correlates. This so-called transdiagnostic approach aims to surpass the limitations of the established specific diagnostic categories of emotion-related disorders (Krueger & Eaton, 2015).

For example, in a large comparative study, high-resolution structural MRI and diffusion tensor imaging (DTI) were used to examine neural commonalities among schizophrenia (SC), major depressive (MDD), and bipolar disorder (BP) (Chang et al., 2018). Gray matter volumes and white matter integrity were assessed in 485 individuals (135 with SC, 108 with MDD, 96 with BP, and 156 healthy volunteers). Results demonstrated significant common reductions of callosal, thalamocortical, and cerebellar white matter tracts in individuals with SC and BP, but not in MDD, as compared to healthy volunteers (Change et al., 2018).

Speculatively, results may also indicate global white-matter connectivity issues that may be associated with cognitive dysmetria associated with SC and BP. In the advent, the white abnormalities are linked to cognitive dysmetria, then similar white matter abnormalities can be expected in MDD with psychotic features. However, transdiagnostic models have difficulties in simultaneously explaining how a shared neurobiological abnormality contributes to multiple disorders (i.e., multifinality) and how this abnormality is expressed differently across individuals (i.e., divergent trajectories) (Nolen-Hoeksema & Watkins, 2011). This leaves open the possibility for disorder-specific contributions for explaining the link between shared abnormalities and the different expression of a disorder.

Finally, the anatomic and functional features of the cerebellum together with its involvement in many emotional disorders certainly are indicative for a potential shared neuro-anatomic cerebellar abnormality across various psychopathological conditions. While the exact cerebellar working mechanisms remain unknown, these knowledge gaps offer a wide range of new and exciting research opportunities. The sharp rise in scientific publications related to non-motor related functions in the last decade exemplifies the importance of the little brain in operations that complement our traditional view of the cerebellum.

I hope this book has offered an inspiring introduction of the cerebellum in the social, affective, and clinical neurosciences, and has provided the reader with an empirical foundation for the idea that the cerebellum plays an intrinsic role in emotions and psychopathological conditions. The time is ripe to revise our conventional ideas about the function of the cerebellum, and in particular, the contemporary cortico-limbic centered views on emotions and psychopathology.

References

Chang M, Womer FY, Edmiston EK, et al. (2018). Neurobiological commonalities and distinctions among three major psychiatric diagnostic categories: A structural MRI study. *Schizophr. Bull.* 44, 65–74.

Dean P, Porrill J, Ekerot CF, Jörntell H (2010). The cerebellar microcircuit as an adaptive filter: Experimental and computational evidence. *Nat. Rev. Neurosci.* 11, 30–43.

Krueger RF, Eaton NR (2015). Transdiagnostic factors of mental disorders. *World Psychiatry 14*, 27–29.

Nolen-Hoeksema S, Watkins ER (2011). A heuristic for developing transdiagnostic models of psychopathology: Explaining multifinality and divergent trajectories. *Perspect. Psychol. Sci. 6*, 589–609.

Schmahmann JD (1991). An emerging concept: The cerebellar contribution to higher function. *Arch. Neurol.* 48, 1178–1187.

Schmahmann JD, Guell X, Stoodley CJ, Halko MA (2019). The theory and neuroscience of cerebellar cognition. *Annu. Rev. Neurosci.* 42, 337–364.

Sejnowski TJ (1977). Storing covariance with nonlinearly interacting neurons. *J. Math. Biol.* 4, 303–321.

Index

addiction, 92, 140–142
affective dysmetria, 87
aggression, 32, 125–140, 141–142
amygdala, 1, 15, 22–23, 25–26, 28, 32, 39–40, 42, 46, 48, 54–55, 59–60, 66, 74, 79, 91–92, 100, 109, 117–118, 127–128, 131, 136, 138, 142
anger, 3, 20, 23, 25, 27, 31, 111, 126–130, 132–133, 135–139, 141–142, 151
anterior cingulate cortex, 42, 47, 97, 141–142
anterior cerebellar lobe, 8, 10, 11, 40, 45, 101, 129, 130, 152
antisocial, 125–126, 130, 136, 139, 142
anxiety, 23, 25, 32, 38, 39–43, 46–49, 53, 57, 59–60, 64–65, 74, 87, 98, 111, 116, 126, 136, 138, 140, 152
appraisal, 29, 39, 50, 54, 71, 133, 137
association areas, 1, 3–4, 131
associative learning, 22, 51, 53, 56–58, 59–60, 97, 140–141
ataxia, 29, 30, 67, 91, 99
attention-deficit hyperactivity disorder (ADHD), 129–130
autism spectrum disorder (ASD), 92, 106–116, 118-121
autonomic nervous system, 15, 21, 115, 117, 120, 138

basal ganglia, 15–16, 34, 42–43, 68, 97, 100, 142, 148
basket cells, 6–8, 67, 108
biological preparedness, 55
biorhythms, 65, 76, 98
bipolar disorder, 64–71, 73–74, 76, 92, 152
bodily homeostasis, 28, 65, 117, 134, 150, 152

callous-unemotional, 126, 140
care, 23, 116, 137
cerebellar cognitive affective syndrome (CCAS), 29
cerebellar pacemaker, 99
cerebellar peduncles, 12–13
cerebrocerebellum, 9, 10, 12
classical conditioning, 51–52, 54
climbing fibers, 7–8, 47, 51–53, 57, 80, 97, 109, 120
cognitive dysmetria, 88–89, 98, 152
conduct disorder, 125–126, 137
cortico-striatal-thalamo-cortical (CSTC) circuit, 42
cortisol, 38, 41, 45, 77–81, 134–136
Crus I, 13, 26–28, 30, 33, 45, 48–50, 54, 56, 58, 72, 95–96, 108, 113–115, 119, 129, 132–133, 137, 139, 141
Crus II, 13, 27–28, 56, 58, 70, 94–95, 115, 131, 133, 151

deep cerebellar nuclei (DCN), 3, 12, 16, 47, 51–52, 78–79, 90, 97, 101, 120, 141
default attention network, 94
default mode network, 49, 74, 94, 114
dentate nucleus, 3, 11–13, 16, 32, 34, 49, 59, 66, 78, 90
depressive disorder, 16, 64–65, 68, 71–73, 77–78, 80, 93, 142
diffusion tensor imaging (DTI), 14–15, 72–73, 89, 152
disgust, 16, 20, 25, 27, 130
disruptive behavioral disorders (DBD), 125, 126, 128, 130
dream intrusion, 87, 100

electric stimulation, 3, 15, 20, 32, 33, 78, 93, 99, 119–120, 126, 128, 130, 133–134

Index 155

emotion, 2, 15–16, 20–28, 31–35, 38, 40, 42–43, 47, 50, 55, 70–71, 76, 88, 93, 98–99, 101, 112, 115, 118, 130, 132–133, 148–149, 151–152

evolution, 1–4, 14, 16, 20–21, 24–25, 31, 38–39, 55, 64, 115–117, 149

exteroception, 47

extinction, 45, 57–59, 101

extreme male brain hypothesis, 110

eye-blink conditioning, 51, 54, 55, 59

facial expressions, 20, 25, 31, 33, 49, 55, 107, 116–117

fastigial nucleus, 3, 11, 14–15, 32, 34, 54, 78, 91, 101, 120, 131, 133–134

fear, 3, 20-23, 25, 27, 31, 38–41, 45, 47–48, 53–59, 79, 101, 128, 130, 136, 138, 139–140

fear conditioning, 22, 45, 47, 50, 53–57, 59, 128, 138–139

fight, 2, 20–22, 31, 34, 39–40, 43, 47, 55, 78, 117, 127, 133–136, 138

flight, 2, 20–22, 31, 34, 39–40, 43, 47, 55, 78, 117, 128, 133–136, 138

flocculonodular lobe, 8–9, 11, 30

freeze, 21–22

functional resonance magnetic resonance imaging (fMRI), 24, 26–27, 32, 40, 42–43, 46, 49, 56, 71, 76, 80, 89, 93, 95, 114, 119, 129, 132, 137, 139

gamma-aminobutyric acid (GABA), 6–8, 59, 66–67, 75, 91

glomerulus, 7

granular cells, 5–6, 47, 101, 108, 142

grief, 23

happiness, 20, 25, 27, 31, 33

hindbrain, 5

hippocampus, 1, 15, 22, 25, 32, 45–46, 48, 54, 60, 79, 80, 91–92, 100, 109, 118, 138, 142

hypothalamic-pituitary-adrenal (HPA) axis, 45, 66, 76–81, 134–138

hypothalamus, 15, 22–23, 25, 39, 42, 54, 66, 74, 76–81, 92, 98, 100–111, 117–118, 127–128, 133–135, 138, 141

hypothalamus-pituitary-gonadal (HPG) axis, 134–138

inferior olive, 7, 10–11, 47, 51, 57

insula, 1, 25–26, 40, 45, 47–48, 50, 95, 118, 139, 142

interoception, 47

interposed nuclei, 11, 12, 51–54, 57, 59, 90, 134, 141

James–Lange theory, 21

Kalman filter, 151

limbic system, 2–3, 15–16, 22, 27, 34, 42, 57, 66, 73–74, 76, 93, 99, 119, 132–133

lobule IV, 46, 50, 57, 130, 137

lobule V, 28, 41, 53, 71, 130, 131

lobule VI, 26–28, 50, 54, 57, 98, 108, 129–130, 137, 139, 141

lobule VII, 26, 131

lobule VIII, 13, 27, 30, 50, 56, 69, 96, 113, 129, 132

lobule IX, 27, 30, 57, 58, 95–96, 113, 115, 119, 129

lobule X, 30, 69, 96, 115, 129

long-term depression (LTD), 52–54, 80, 108–109

long-term potentiation (LTP), 53–54

Lugaro cells, 6

lust, 23

magnetoencephalography (MEG), 28, 132

magnetic resoance spectropscopy (MRS), 66, 68, 91, 109–110

mania, 64–65

memory trace, 40, 52, 57

midbrain, 12, 14–15, 26, 34, 40, 42, 47, 91, 127, 135

misconnection syndrome, 87

molecular layer, 6–7, 53, 67

mood disorders, 64, 66–68, 71, 73–74, 76–77, 81, 93, 98, 109, 137

mossy fibers, 7–9, 51–52, 80, 101, 109

motivation, 1, 2, 15–16, 20, 24, 31, 33, 68, 78, 93, 98–99, 112, 126, 128–129, 132, 135–136, 148

motor cortex, 3, 12, 42, 48, 90–91, 111

N-acetyl aspartate (NAA), 68, 109, 110

neocerebellum, 3

nucleus of the solitary tract, 117

obsessive compulsive disorder (OCD), 41–43, 46

156 Index

oppositional defiant disorder (ODD), 125, 129–130
oxytocin, 111, 137–138

periaqueductal gray (PAG), 14–15, 22–23, 28, 39–40, 47, 54, 127
pain, 14, 15, 40, 56, 65, 107, 114, 139
panic, 25, 40, 43, 46–47, 138
Papez's circuit, 15, 22, 25, 33
parallel fibers, 7–8, 47, 51–54, 67, 80, 109, 150
paravermis, 9–11, 14, 27, 32, 76
positron emission tomography (PET), 24–27, 43, 48, 55, 118, 141–142
phobias, 47-50
play, 16, 23, 107, 111
Pleistocene, 4
pontine nuclei, 10–12, 25, 51
posterior cerebellar lobe, 8–11, 27, 29, 40, 56, 72, 113, 129
post-traumatic stress syndrome (PTSS), 43–46
prefrontal cortex, 1, 3, 13, 23, 31, 33, 39–40, 42–46, 48–49, 60, 70–72, 76, 80, 93–94, 97, 114, 126, 128, 151
proprioceptive, 10
psychopathy, 126, 130, 136, 138
psychosis, 65–66, 87, 96, 100, 101
punishment, 22, 32, 64, 76, 97, 101, 116, 128, 139, 140, 141
Purkinje cells, 6–8, 11, 13, 47, 51–54, 56, 67, 79–80, 90–92, 99–100, 108–109, 111, 120, 131, 134, 141–142, 150

rage, 23, 126–128, 131, 133, 135, 138
red nucleus, 12, 14
respiratory sinus arrhythmia (RSA), 118
reticular formation, 10–11, 14, 28, 117, 134
reward, 21, 32, 57, 64, 68, 73, 75, 97, 101, 116, 127–128, 131, 139–141

sadness, 20, 25, 27, 64–65, 111, 130
schizophrenia, 65–66, 87–102
Schmahmann's syndrome, 29–30, 88
seeking, 23, 68, 112, 125, 127, 131–132, 139–140, 142
servo-controller, 28, 97

social learning, 20–21
social phobia, 47–50
somatosensory, 10–11, 14, 25, 32, 46, 50, 88, 119–120, 129, 150, 152
spinocerebellum, 3, 9–10, 12, 15
stellate cells, 7–8
stress, 21, 38–46, 48, 57, 64, 66, 73–74, 76–81, 101, 111, 116, 118, 134, 136, 138, 152
substantia nigra, 12, 16
suprachiasmatic nucleus, 100–101
surprise, 20, 48, 65
survival, 2, 38, 40, 43, 47, 55, 58, 137

testosterone, 111, 134–136
thalamus, 11–14, 16, 22–23, 48, 50, 88, 90–92, 99, 109, 117–118, 131
theory of mind, 30, 114–116, 130, 139
threat, 20, 38–40, 43, 46, 50, 55, 58–59, 79, 127, 136–137
transcranial direct current stimulation (tDCS), 55–56
transcranial magnetic stimulation (TMS), 33, 90–91, 93
traumatic experience, 44–45
triune brain framework, 2–3, 21

unipolar disorder, 64, 66–67, 73–74
universal cerebellar transform (UCT), 98–99, 150

vagus nerve, 117–119, 138
vasopressin, 111, 137
ventral tegmental area (VTA) 14, 140–141
vermis, 3, 9–11, 14–15, 25, 27–30, 32, 34, 40, 43–44, 46–47, 50, 54, 57, 58, 68–69, 75–76, 91–93, 95–96, 99, 101, 108, 110, 112, 115, 119–120, 125, 129, 131, 139, 141, 151–152
vestibular nuclei, 2, 10–11
vestibulocerebellum, 3, 9–10
violent offenders, 130–132, 141
visceral, 2–3, 21, 34, 74, 78, 117–118, 129, 133–134, 138

Lightning Source UK Ltd.
Milton Keynes UK
UKHW051359220522
403164UK00025B/177

This groundbreaking volume examines the complex role of the cerebellum in emotional regulation and disorders that are insufficiently understood, subverting the widely held belief that the cerebellum is solely involved in balance and motor functions.

Beginning with the evolution of the cerebellum toward a structure dedicated to homeostatic regulation and socio-emotional behavior, the book examines the growing body of evidence supporting the importance of the cerebellum in emotions, cognition, and psychopathology. Going on to discuss the implications of cerebellar abnormalities, Schutter analyzes groundbreaking research and explores how cerebellar abnormalities are associated with disruption in associative learning in anxiety, the pathophysiology of depression and cognitive regulation, the synchronization of information processing in schizophrenia, the aberrant connectivity patterns in autism spectrum disorders, and explosive forms of aggressive behavior.

Collating pioneering research on the multifaceted role of the cerebellum, this book will be essential reading for students and researchers of neurology and psychopathology.

Dennis J.L.G. Schutter is an associate professor of experimental psychology at Utrecht University, the Netherlands. He is an award-winning researcher on the role of the cerebellum in motivation and emotion, and expert in non-invasive brain stimulation.

EMOTION

Cover image: © Getty Images

www.routledge.com

ISBN 978-1-138-50280-2

Routledge titles are available as eBook editions in a range of digital formats